A DAY
IN THE LIFE

STUDYING DAILY LIFE
THROUGH HISTORY

EDITED BY
PETER N. STEARNS

GREENWOOD PRESS
Westport, Connecticut • London

Library of Congress Cataloging-in-Publication Data

A day in the life : studying daily life through history / edited by Peter N. Stearns.
    p. cm.
  Includes bibliographical references and index.
  ISBN 0–313–33233–9
  1. Manners and customs—History. I. Stearns, Peter N.
GT76.D39 2006
390—dc22   2005020068

British Library Cataloguing in Publication Data is available.

Library of Congress Catalog Card Number: 2005020068
ISBN: 0–313–33233–9

First published in 2006

Greenwood Press, 88 Post Road West, Westport, CT 06881
An imprint of Greenwood Publishing Group, Inc.
www.greenwood.com

Printed in the United States of America

The paper used in this book complies with the
Permanent Paper Standard issued by the National
Information Standards Organization (Z39.48–1984).

10 9 8 7 6 5 4 3 2 1

Contents

Preface

Daily life has a history—that is, it has changed and varied significantly in the past. In fact, arguably, studying daily life is one of the best ways to get a sense of history and an appreciation for historical analysis, because it forces us to think about some of our own daily habits and patterns and realize that people "back then" or elsewhere used to do the same things—things we often take for granted—rather differently. Studying the history of daily life is vital to understand what historians sometimes call the "pastness" of the past—how different things could be (without, however, forgetting important continuities from then to now and important commonalities in the human experience). It is also vital to grasp how current features of daily life have emerged, how they can be explained and given real meaning.

Up until 1800, in western Europe and the United States, bathing with water used to be regarded as dangerous to the health, to be safely indulged in only once or twice a year. Not surprisingly, people used to think about body smells differently from the ways most of us do now; they did not find them offensive, to be covered up as fully as possible. When bathing did begin to find favor, initially experts urged only very cold water: bathing was for hygiene, not for pleasure. Now, in a modern American home, there are often more bathrooms than people. Things have changed a lot in behaviors and in values applied to the body and hygiene. Another example that I've always liked though it's a bit gross: in the late seventeenth century, people in places like the Netherlands used to brush their teeth with human urine, and a few of them wrote about how well this worked. A century later urine was beginning to become disgusting, an attitude most of us still maintain. In the seventeenth century, half of the bites English people were treated for came from humans, and biting was a common part of kissing; a century later, the idea of kisses being soft and increasingly private came into fashion in Western society. Again, things have changed a lot in the daily habits most of us take for granted.

Daily life history is, in fact, one of the real discovery fields of modern historical research. We know far more about it, including intimate matters like emotions or sex, than we did before. We know more about how daily life in the past relates to other historical phenomena like politics or even imperialism. We no longer treat daily life in the past as insignificant or merely a museum case of antiquarian facts—interesting but not really very important. Some historians are even using the history of daily life to explain patterns of behavior today, arguing that only by understanding historical changes and continuities can we get a sense of why people act and think as they do in our own time.

Daily life history is not easy to do. Sources are not as obvious or well organized as those available for the biographies of famous people or the courses of past wars. So daily life history often requires a particular combination of stubbornly hard work and imagination, but for many historians the challenge is part of the attraction. Because everybody has experience with daily life, the field is open to historical inquiries from all sorts of angles—amateurs, along with professionals, can enjoy the field and contribute to it. But even here it helps to know not only what we have already discovered, but also common types of sources and common patterns of analysis.

The greatest interest in history in the United States involves the history of one's own family. (Part of American daily life history might involve analysis as to why this is so—why we're so preoccupied with this kind of historical identity, for the interest goes deep into popular American culture.) But there are more- and less-fruitful ways to explore this interest. Some people merely want to put leaves and roots on the family tree, and more power to them. But others, and obviously I think this is the wiser group, will want to know how family ancestors fit or did not fit common patterns of daily life—how they worked, played, and indeed what kind of family relationships they maintained. Here, family history links directly to the wider history of daily life and, intelligently done, can contribute to it in turn. Some of the best daily life history branches out from a study of particular individuals or families in the past, like Laurel Thatcher Ulrich's prizewinning book, *Midwife's Tale*, based on the diaries of Martha Ballard.

Daily life history, in other words, is a rich, informative, and challenging field. It has greatly added to historical knowledge more generally. Furthermore, it is now being used to understand the present as well—from excessive fears about kidnapping to the emergence of an unusual kind of nostalgia that helps explain why current Americans (when they can afford it) like big homes and traditional furnishings; and from socially supported diseases like anorexia nervosa to why the United States has more serial killers than most other societies. It relates to some of the deepest historical interests many Americans have, though with some admitted tensions between what professional historians look for and what many family tree-ites may value. There are all sorts of reasons and ways to pursue this vital use of the past.

This book is intended to illustrate and guide daily life history. It covers what seem to be the key topics: family patterns and related issues of emotions, manners, and the senses; the body, health, and medicine (this last topic is seen not in terms of great doctors so much as ordinary medical practice and expectations);

politics as part of daily life, and also challenges to order such as crime; popular culture, focused heavily on the real nature of religious and scientific beliefs as manifested by ordinary people rather than simply the preachers and intellectuals who wanted to tell people what to think; material life, the trappings of ordinary existence; work and economic life; and leisure.

The chapters also invite connections between one key aspect of daily life and the others. What happened not only to children, but to family life more generally, when they were pushed to replace work with schooling? How has emotional life changed as service work, often involving efforts to please customers, superseded work in factories and on farms? How has television affected not only leisure habits but daily political life as well? Studying daily life requires grounding in key subfields, like popular culture or health habits, and exploration of the inter-relationships among these subfields as well.

Not one of the chapters is intended to survey its topics in a textbook sense. Some deal mainly with the United States and modern times; others range more widely. Each seeks to achieve several key goals: first, to illustrate how this aspect of the history of daily life has been successfully handled, and what kinds of sources and interpretive challenges have been involved; second, to give some sense of particularly interesting or representative findings, usually across several places and/or time periods; third—and this is vital in daily life history—to mention some of the common distinctions among social classes, racial and ethnic groups, and the two genders, lest we oversimplify daily life or mistakenly end up with only the patterns of the high and mighty; and fourth, to suggest some of the many areas that still invite further work.

Daily life history is a living field, with lots still to do, in American history and the histories of other societies alike. Hopefully, most readers will look at these essays in several ways. They'll be seeking guidance and models of how daily life history can be done. They'll be looking for some "aha" experiences—I didn't know that about the past, and it's very interesting; I wonder how we got from that pattern to the patterns we live with today. They'll also be looking for gaps and opportunities—what aspects of daily life behavior haven't been handled particularly well. As a professional historian, I am most excited by the kind of history that includes some aspects of daily life opened to historical inquiry for the first time, like the history of smell and disgust (mentioned earlier), which first gained historical attention only a few years ago. I am also intrigued by the history of posture, which I worked on myself because I wondered why, in the United States, we had dropped our earlier insistence that kids sit and stand up straight (I think I found out why, but the subject is far richer than I realized, and it is still being worked on). Another historian is just now trying to figure out, by studying earlier precedents but also recent changes in daily life, why so many young Americans, particularly females, like to pierce their bodies, in contrast to the more limited outlets of the past.

There is still a lot to do to understand the past and to use the past to understand ourselves.

1

Introduction: The History of Daily Life: Whys and Hows

Peter N. Stearns

Sometime between the 1770s and the 1830s, many respectable French people changed their approach to smell. They decided that some things that used to be regarded as neutral or even pleasant, like human urine, smelled disgusting. (Many Europeans had brushed their teeth with urine just a century before.) Increasingly, these people began to rely less on their sense of smell, regarding it mainly as a source of disgust (though they did use increasing amounts of perfume, the goal was more to mask the smell than to appeal to it). Reliance on vision increased. This change, which spread widely in the Western world though perhaps a bit less decisively (the French are still rated unusually high in their esteem for light and vision), had all sorts of consequences, even aside from the perfume business. When they could afford it, many people moved away from the smellier parts of cities; changes in the balance of the senses played a role in suburbanization. Interest in more frequent bathing increased, which gradually led to alterations in home construction to allow for running water. We still live with many of these consequences—including a reduced capacity to use our sense of smell, compared to our ancestors.

Historians now write frequently on the history of the senses, developing examples dealing with hearing as well as smell and sight. Twenty years ago, projects of this sort would have been regarded as almost impossible and perhaps not very interesting. But the definition of useful, even compelling history has dramatically changed during the past generation, and the history of daily life—including daily experiences such as those provided by the senses or by emotions—has played a fundamental role in this revolution.

Several developments prompted the growing interest in the history of daily life. First, historians of various sorts became convinced that a better understanding of the conditions and behaviors of ordinary people in the past would provide a fuller sense of the past itself and a better appreciation of ordinary people themselves. During the 1930s in France, and then in the 1950s and 1960s in Britain, the United States, and elsewhere, social historians began to trumpet their concern for giving the masses a history of their own. Sometimes the focus was on points at which ordinary people clearly affected the larger course of history—for example, during revolutions. But increasingly, the interest in ordinary people led to an interest in the way they lived their daily lives—how they worked, what their families were like, and what kinds of recreation they valued.

Shading off from this commitment to ordinary people was a sense that conventional history—centered on the doings of presidents and kings, generals and philosophers—had been studied so much that it was becoming a bit jaded. New topics would spark an interest in the past, and many aspects of daily life clearly fit the bill. On the other hand, some historians of daily life, though fascinated by new materials and new insights, argued that their topics improved the understanding of standard historical topics. Thus a historian of colonial America, in a pathbreaking book on the relations between fathers and sons in daily life, argued that changes in these relations ultimately help explain the outbreak of the American Revolution. His argument was that sons became concerned that their opportunities to inherit land or positions from their fathers were being narrowed, and that this personal or family worry turned them to wider political issues in which they sought new opportunities for themselves.

Once the movement toward the history of daily life gained momentum, many historians and social scientists realized that we get a better understanding of why people behave as they do in today's society if we look at how ordinary behaviors emerged from the past. Why, for example, have Americans on average gained more weight than Europeans during the past 20 years? There are several ways to approach this question, but one involves looking at the history of daily eating, child discipline, and dieting, to see why and how patterns in the United States took on their current shape.

Different motivations for studying the history of daily life can overlap, but they also lead to various ways to choose daily life topics. People interested in the history of immigrants in the United States might easily be led into special investigations of the development of neighborhoods or housing, which play such a vital role in the immigrant experience. Here, in other words, a daily life topic emerges from engagement with groupings of ordinary people. Historians studying the Meiji reforms in Japan—from 1868 onward, an inescapable mainstream topic in modern Japanese history—might turn to the experiences of ordinary people in the new primary schools that the government set up after 1872, or to their situation as workers in the pioneering factories of the period, as part of a fuller understanding of conventional history. Similarly, other specialists might wonder how changes in the work lives of Russian factory hands help explain the willingness to participate in revolutions in 1905 and 1917. Here, daily life topics stem from efforts to explore or explain standard historical topics more fully.

Increasingly, however, the history of daily life emerges from daily life itself, or from social scientific study of daily life. From social science studies, leading anthropologists have helped us understand the social and symbolic roles of certain kinds of entertainments, such as cockfights in parts of Indonesia. This encourages historians to look at the symbolic aspect of games or events from the past; one scholar, for example, explored the meaning of an unusual massacre of cats in Paris in the early eighteenth century. (Interactions between people and animals in the past, including the development of formal pets, play a role in the broader history of daily life.) Some sociologists used to argue that urban life inevitably bred increases in the crime rate. This encouraged historians to look at actual crime rates over time (where they found that the old sociological picture was wrong). Social scientists of various sorts, in other words, study daily life, and they have stimulated historians to want to add a past dimension or to test theories that have historical implications.

And then there's daily life itself. A historian muses about what happened during the twentieth century to concerns about posture in the United States, because he remembers that his father used to fuss about posture and realizes that he, as a parent, paid no attention to it at all. When did correct posture become an issue in American society, and when and why did it stop being an issue? Once the topic is raised, it turns out, first, that posture can be historically investigated, and second, that the rise and fall of American posture says a lot about the relationship between manners and health experts, on the one hand, and ordinary parents and children in homes and schools on the other. Score one for improved understanding of the history of daily life from an unexpected angle. Another historian wonders about the uses of history in understanding relationships among siblings. Modern American parents worry considerably about sibling tensions (though the worry was greater when the idea of sibling rivalry was first introduced in the 1920s), but the topic had not been explicitly discussed in the nineteenth century. What had changed in ideas about siblings and actual relationships among them? There is still more work to be done on sibling history (for example, interactions between brothers and sisters in the past), but we already know that history contributes directly to a grasp of the distinctive nature of some current concerns. Score another for using daily life to organize historical research, which moves us back to daily life with better understanding.

Excitement with this approach as a focus for historians led to a school of German historians in the 1970s who called their approach *Alltagsgeschichte,* which is German for "the history of daily life." These historians summed up many of the basic arguments for studying daily life in the past: it provides an opportunity to give ordinary people serious historical attention by examining what they normally did and thought about. It also allows a new look at conventional topics. Some of the *Alltagsgeschichte* group were particularly interested in a better understanding of what Nazism meant in German society, and they argued that looking at how people lived their daily lives under Hitler would explain Nazism and its role better than most of the conventional political approaches.

Daily life has become a vital part of historical inquiry. There are several reasons for this, and several ways to explore what the history of daily life contributes. And there's an abundance of exciting work and opportunities for more.

The history of daily life has an almost limitless array of possible topics, because daily life itself has so many facets. There are few, if any, components of daily life that don't have a significant historical dimension, from material features like toys or clothes to family relationships and sexuality to work and leisure. Even sleep, which might be regarded as impossible or unproductive as a historical topic, has now received attention as an experience that responds to particular historical contexts and, in turn, might explain other aspects of the past. For example, put an inquiry into sleep into the same hopper as a history of lighting and a history of caffeine, and you have some immediate possibilities about how sleep can change or vary in different past periods or from past to present.

The history of daily life did not, however, emerge without conflict, and some of this must also be understood before we go back to the reasons to pursue the history, and the methods and pitfalls in doing so. Two kinds of objections emerged, and though they're related, they come from slightly different sources and require somewhat different responses.

Objection number one, somewhat ironically, came from many pioneering social historians who in the 1950s and 1960s were opening up the study of ordinary people. Concerned with justifying their innovations, these social historians often identified the history of daily life as antiquarian—what they liked to call "pots-and-pans" history. What they were referring to was an older kind of social history, focused on how people lived in the past, with purely descriptive portrayals of clothing, toys, or food habits (the emphasis tended to be on the material aspects of daily life). The purpose often seemed nothing more than showing how quaint the past was. A number of these pots-and-pans histories existed in the United States, often written by people who were not professional historians; and while they won some popular readership, they did not score well in academic circles. The so-called new social historians, bent on dealing with workers, slaves, or other elements of the masses, wanted to make it clear that their subjects were a serious part of history, not primarily to be captured by looking at what kinds of kitchen utensils they used. The new social historians focused instead on somewhat different kinds of behavior, such as social protest or mobility. These topics seemed more important than pots and pans; protest, for example, evoked the fighting spirit of ordinary folk and could also spill over into political change. The topics were also open to distinctive methods beyond purely descriptive coverage; mobility called on sophisticated quantitative techniques to tally changes and continuities between fathers and sons. Even family history, which has become a staple in the examination of the history of daily life, was initially studied through counting family or household size rather than looking at some of the more routine aspects of family life.

The attack on pots-and-pans history has largely vanished, and this is one of the preconditions for not only the success but also the nature of the more recent inquiries into the history of daily life. Before turning to how this happened, we need to record the second, and somewhat more durable, objection to this history.

Many conventional historians, trained in traditions that privileged formal political, military, or intellectual life, have long thought, and sometimes continue to think, that a history of daily life is simply too trivial to pass muster. They are often joined by conservative educators who believe that the purpose of history is to inspire young people with the deeds of exceptional, heroic individuals and to instill a focus on the nation-state as part of appropriate political socialization. Ordinary people and ordinary behaviors need not apply.

A young social historian, for example, gets a job at a good university in Texas, where she wants to offer a course in her research specialty: the history of consumer behavior (along with teaching conventional survey courses in Western civilization or world history). She's told that consumerism is not a worthy subject, because consumer behavior is superficial and venal; she'd be better off focusing on, say, the Spanish Civil War. Another young historian has studied the work lives and relations with employers of the first generations of modern factory labor in France. His rationale emphasized how early work experiences could color the formation of a new social class culture and would later influence the nature of labor protest in France. He has completed a book on the subject, but his university press readers insist that it can't be accepted unless it's turned into an explanation of the French Revolution of 1848, a recognizable, conventional staple in researching and teaching French history. And countless historians interested in the history of leisure have been told that their courses or books are not worthy of serious consideration, because leisure is, after all, a trivial pursuit, not to be mentioned in the same breath as the presidency of Grover Cleveland or the War of Jenkin's Ear. Or finally, another historian eager to justify the new range of historical research ventures the cute comment that historians should be as interested in studying the history of menarche as of monarchy, and a conservative critic of the more novel kinds of history blasts him for frivolity, because obviously (in her mind) the doings of kings are much more significant than the experiences of older women.

This second set of concerns has not been as easy to address as the first. Conventional habits die hard, and the rise of conservative commentary in the United States has added strength to some of the objections to too much emphasis on the study of daily life. Take a look at conventional history textbooks, particularly at the high school level. Daily life may figure in at a few points, mainly as asides designed to spark student interest; they rarely receive extended comment in books that continue to treat the political experience as central historical subject matter. Yet, despite constraints, historical understanding of daily life has moved forward, which means that these objections, too, have gradually lost some of their force. The historian who wanted to teach consumerism finally got her course approved; the book on French factory work was ultimately published, without irrelevant reference to 1848; the history of leisure and recreation has become a large and fruitful subfield; and we do pay at least some attention to the past experiences of older women. The field is moving forward, and here, too, as with the initial attack on pots-and-pans history, the progress can be explained and, in the process, the subject itself more fully understood.

REMOVING THE POTS-AND-PANS LABEL

Accusations that the history of daily life is antiquarian, a matter of meaningless pots and pans, had ceased by the 1980s. As we have seen, the social history commitment to studying ordinary people was one of the fruitful sources of daily life history, and what had been an antagonism yielded to ardent courtship. There were two reasons for the change.

First, historians interested in the common person could simply not avoid the realization that daily life figures hugely in the topic. It's fine to deal with protest, but protest often stemmed from a housewife's realization that bread prices had risen so high that the family budget was jeopardized, or from a worker's frustration that his pace of work is driving him to nervous distraction. It's fine to chart birthrates with the most sophisticated quantitative techniques, but ultimately, if one wants to know why birthrates change, one needs to know something about daily life sexuality and about expectations and roles for children. It no longer seems prosaic to look at children's toys, for example, if they reveal something about what parents want from children and through this the basis for family strategies for raising children or even assessing economic success. When ordinary people began to include women, as was true in historians' accounts by the 1960s, even pots and pans themselves could gain meaning as part of explaining what women's lives were all about.

The second reason the label of antiquarianism disappeared was that historians of daily life found ways to introduce serious analysis into their accounts of material culture, leisure, and emotion. Descriptions of "how things were" back then might begin an inquiry into daily life, but they did not end it. Various analytical devices have entered the daily life field. Comparison is one: the ways Americans treated jealousy in the past can be compared to patterns in France, and in the process the historian can try to explain any significant differences. The whole subject can gain greater meaning through comparison. Connections are another possibility: the kinds of dolls used in one period often connect to expectations about the roles children should play in the family or should anticipate in adulthood. (What does it mean, for example, that dolls for American girls in the 1870s and 1880s often came complete with caskets and mourning clothes?) The foods immigrants emphasize connect to larger attitudes to their identity and their relationship with a new society. Some immigrants quickly pick up a new diet, which is a sign of unusual openness to adaptation; others insist on the old country's fare. But most common is an effort at combination of old and new, like the Arab-Americans who combine Thanksgiving turkey with a beef and rice dish from the Middle East. Another set of connections is just being developed: an imaginative historian is looking at the evolution of American homesickness and nostalgia and linking this to patterns of consumerism in housing and home furnishings. Shading off from connections is the effort to deal with causation. In early modern France, when men accused of a crime sometimes referred to their legitimate anger, but women never did (instead, sometimes invoking their jealousy), the patterns cry out for explanation: why could men feel that it was acceptable to be angry but women could not, and at the same time, why did women find jealousy more appropriate? Explaining key features of daily life can give great insight into power relationships and other fundamental features of a past society. They move the historian into deeper and more demanding territory than the mere description of daily life can hope to do.

The subject of change, however, is the analytical angle that has most clearly stripped the antiquarian label from the study of daily life. If you just describe the parlors of respectable nineteenth-century American families, you may not be saying much of great interest. But if you can chart the transformation of parlors into living rooms and can explain what this change meant in terms of the dynamics of family life and the relationship of family to the larger society, you may touch on some profound shifts in function and meaning. (Continuity amid change does the same work: why, for example, did Italian Americans pre-serve the parlor idea longer than most Americans did?) Another change is the transformation of American movie audiences from loud and boisterous to silent (save for a few subcultures). Here's a very simple shift, but explaining why it happens and what it means says a lot about the role of movies in leisure, the rise of individual-passive and the decline of spontaneous-communitarian audience forms, and sheer power relationships in leisure (with middle-class respectability winning over working-class impulses). The big step away from antiquarianism in the history of daily life involved the realization that fundamental features of the way people live change, and that the historian can seek causes for this change and can try to assign meaning to it. In the process, daily life moves away from being a sterile backdrop and enters the mainstream of historical thinking.

THE ISSUE OF TRIVIALITY

Refuting the charge of lack of seriousness has not proved as easy as shedding the old pots-and-pans image. There are historians still who think that civiliza-tions, and therefore a meaningful human past, are defined solely in terms of the institutions and ideas shaped by an elite, and who are not even interested in the daily lives these same elites experienced. There are certainly conservative com-mentators who continue to bemoan the expansion of historical inquiry, arguing that historians should stick to staples like the great thinkers of ancient Athens, the American Constitution, or the heroes and battles of the American Civil War. Not only standard textbooks, but also the kinds of tests many states now impose on their students reflect little of the exploration of daily life. The argument con-tinues, and once in a while, it still even turns nasty.

But in practice, among historical researchers and many consumers of history, the interest in daily life has steadily expanded, so that charges of triviality are effectively bypassed. Several factors are involved in this reorientation. First, larger redefinitions of what history should cover, though not initially designed to justify the study of daily life, have turned out to serve that purpose. Take, for example, the Protestant Reformation, which has been a standard historical topic for centu-ries. It used to be studied primarily through the doctrines of the Reformers and their interactions with governments of the time, and these approaches remain valid. But, with the rise of social history, attention has steadily shifted toward the involvement of ordinary people with the Reformation and within the Catholic response—how did they get involved, and how were they affected? This has led to serious inquiry into family life (the Reformation gave new support to family life and to a more companionable marriage, and Catholic regions ultimately par-ticipated in these changes as well) and, of course, into popular religious belief (the impact of the Reformation on traditional reliance on magic turned out to be very significant), but as part of a recognizable interest in a standard historical subject. The Reformation, in other words, influenced, and was influenced by, a number of key features in daily life; in turn, studying relevant features of daily life improves the understanding of this religious change, and vice versa. Another example is the industrial revolution, which has long been an inescapable historical topic, particularly in west European and U.S. history. But it was once handled mainly in terms of major inventions and relevant legislation to fit into a standard events-based historical approach. Yet the real meaning of the industrial revolution lies in its consequences for human life, including daily life: the removal of work from family settings, the changes in work pace, the redefinition of childhood toward more emphasis on education, and so on. With social history, the importance of the industrial revolution as a topic escalated, and this in turn soon encouraged new explorations of changes in daily life. As both of these examples illustrate, discussion of certain aspects of the history of daily life became increasingly imperative simply as part of a standard historical agenda.

It is also true that the exploration of daily life in the past tests some classic generalizations that initially emerged from conventional history or social science. The impact of Puritanism is often referenced in standard discussions of American character to explain an unusual prudishness about sex. But actual inquiry into Puritan daily life shows a considerable interest in sex (admittedly, just within marriage) and also great pleasure in drink. So some features of American character have either been misstated or (more likely) arose somewhat later, and for different reasons than Puritanism itself. Here, too, we gain a better understanding of some widely discussed staples if we actually investigate the daily life in which they were involved.

Supplementing this rethinking of conventional topics are even more specific connections. A study of toy soldiers and their increasing ubiquity in western Europe in the later nineteenth century makes a convincing case for their role in helping shape the attitudes of adult males toward war by 1914. Playthings and a staple historical topic, the origins of World War I, have a legitimate relationship. Social Security legislation in the American New Deal led (not surprisingly) to major reductions in the reliance of old people on family support by the 1940s, another significant shift in daily life related to a standard subject in national political history. Even if one's principal definition of history remains conventionally tied to politics and high culture, attention to changes in daily life improves understanding of the factors and outcomes involved.

A second element that has reduced charges of triviality is the unmistakable interest of a wider public in presentations concerning the history of daily life. Historical museums are not a recent invention, but their number has expanded, their attendance has exploded, and their focus has shifted during the past two decades. Millions of Americans are interested in presentations that convey how ordinary people used to live, whether the museum is a new federal project in a former textile factory in Lowell, Massachusetts, centered on showing factory and housing conditions in early industrialization, or an expansion of colonial Williamsburg to include artisan shops and slave quarters, designed (along with more luxurious buildings like the Governor's Palace) to give people a feel for the texture of daily life. It is hard to dismiss the doubling of visits to historical museums during the 1980s in terms of a public addiction to mere superficiality. In this sense, too, daily life has meaning.

Third, as already suggested, the growing production of serious, analytical studies of features of daily life impressed social scientists long interested in similar topics. By the 1990s, social science discussions of key aspects of human behavior routinely included historical research projects, not simply as backdrops to serious study but as direct components of that study. Examples include the need to deal with historical changes in drinking as an ingredient of inquiries into patterns and problems of alcoholism; or an awareness of the origins, causes, and evolution of modern anorexia nervosa as a part, along with more purely medical considerations, of understanding this important contemporary issue. The history of crime, including periods in which serious crime declines despite growing urbanization, not only tests and refutes some earlier social science theory, it also contributes directly to criminological research today. Social psychologists prove interested in historians' findings about changes in emotional patterns, such as the efforts to reduce guilt as an emotional disciplinary tool in the United States from the 1920s onward; and they have to pay attention to research on shifts in the roles and expectations of women as part of psychological understanding of gender. The point is clear: various social sciences have long studied key aspects of daily life. History now contributes to this research, providing better information about trends and factors in a host of ordinary activities, from murder to mental illness to romantic love. And so social scientists routinely use findings in the history of daily life (sometimes contributing their own research directly), and this enhances both the utility and the prestige of this kind of historical work.

Finally, and arching above the first three factors, there is the importance of daily life itself and the interest it inevitably inspires. Sigmund Freud once argued that people evaluate their own lives in terms of work, play, and love (or sex). As it becomes clear that history helps us get a better handle on variations and changes over time in work and leisure, family emotion, and sexuality, there is really no way to dispute the legitimacy of this kind of inquiry.

When, for example, did the first modern sexual revolution occur? Many historians argue pretty persuasively that, in the Western world, it was during the later eighteenth century, when rates of premarital sex (and illegitimate births) began to rise steeply. Why this happened and what it meant can't help but interest a variety of people, even if their main historical concerns focus on the American Revolution or the history of science.

Has the quality of play deteriorated with modern life, as one Dutch historian persuasively argued? Studies of daily leisure help us answer this question, which helps us understand ourselves better. (Did the rise of the amusement park in late-nineteenth-century America show a new capacity for enjoyment or a need to depend on commercial fare and professional entertainment in a society increasingly starved of spontaneous play? Where does TV watching fit in a larger history of play and leisure?) One point is certain: the arrival of modern, industrial societies typically worsened leisure, at least for a time. Attacks on the tradition of popular festivals, which were not compensated for in the emergence of more modern holidays, introduced serious complexity in the evaluation of the nature and quality of leisure over long stretches of time, from premodern to modern.

The issues involved in areas like sexuality and leisure are often tough, requiring debate; but it's hard not to recognize their importance. The history of daily life flourishes, despite some continued carping, mainly because it sheds light on the ways we think about ourselves and the societies around us.

The history of daily life benefits from some earlier work, even though much of it was outside the mainstream of professional history, and from a real explosion of research over the past 30 years. A host of topics flourish, some with challenging conceptual frameworks. The history of childhood arrived, for instance, with a persuasive claim that traditional Europeans did not recognize children as children (partly because after infancy, they saw them as workers) but that a differentiation increasingly emerged with modern times. This framework has been disputed by people who find well-defined childhoods in earlier times, but the whole debate has stimulated a vigorous subfield in childhood history.

Another theory argues, again for the Western world, for a progressive tightening of manners and etiquette so that human impulses came under greater control. It does seem true that certain kinds of violence have declined from the Middle Ages to the present and that more prosaic habits like spitting have been disciplined. Manners drew increasing attention as a window into how individuals and social expectations interact.

A number of historians continue to explore another generalization applicable to daily life on the more political side: the idea that at some point in modern times, community life declined in favor of more attention to separate families and to individualism (and outright loneliness). Here again, this is a debate rather than a conclusive finding; as one authority notes, there's a danger of finding declining communities in every generation in American history since the late eighteenth century. But there's a concern involved here that organizes a real aspect of daily life analysis, of interest to a variety of users of history. A related interest in exploring the origins of modern ideas about personal privacy—for kissing, as an example—stimulates important research about individuals and community.

Besides some of the larger concepts, sometimes generating them, come a parade of pathbreaking individual discoveries. Thirty years ago historians who paid any attention whatsoever to consumerism assumed that it emerged in the later nineteenth century as a result of industrialization and growing wealth. Now, thanks to fundamental research findings, we know that modern consumerism originated in places like Britain in the seventeenth and eighteenth centuries, before industrialization; and so it requires a different set of explanations and gains new meaning in the process of analysis. Even more recently we've learned that modern ideas of comfort, such as home heating or lighting or carrying an umbrella when it rains, also emerged in the eighteenth century in societies that had long scorned comforts in the name of other values. (Even in the eighteenth century, when umbrellas from France began to spread throughout England, some people argued that English virtue was being compromised by this artificial avoidance of nature's weather.) Why did this change emerge, and what results has it produced?

Regarding friendship, we now know that in the nineteenth century, young, middle-class men in America were often passionately in love with each other, touching each other and writing outpourings of emotion, yet they were not what we would call homosexual. What did this kind of friendship mean, and why, with what results, did it stop?

Fundamental discoveries about the past and its connections to daily life in the present keep tumbling out, and there's no real sign of stagnation. Some of the most interesting ones help us ask questions about what is natural in being human, and what is the product of particular historical experiences. Do mothers (on average) naturally love children or, as some have argued in looking at this aspect of the history of daily life, was this in part a modern invention? How much anger do people naturally have, and how much can it be reduced or channeled by particular historical cultures (like the one that emerged in the eighteenth and nineteenth centuries that argued that respectable women should not even feel anger).

The history of daily life produces fascinating vignettes. It provokes debate. It provides a key means of exploring the constraints and opportunities people lived with in the past and those they live with today.

Doing the history of daily life is not easy, though clearly increasing numbers of historians are showing that it's possible. There are four issues to note here.

First, and most fundamental, is the issue of data. Many projects on daily life struggle to find necessary source materials. On the whole, the more remote past is more challenging than the quite recent, but there is some variety even here. There are topics that simply can't be explored as fully as one would like. Some aspects of sexual behavior, to take an obvious example, leave no record. Getting an adequate sense of the frequency of certain behaviors is often difficult; there are scattered examples, perhaps a few comments by outsiders, but establishing patterns can be elusive. Take early industrial work, for instance. We know that some workers really liked factory jobs—they commented on the joys of manipulating powerful equipment. We also know that some workers hated such jobs. Social inquiries caught them in anguish, saying that their work created such nervous tension that they could barely stay alive. We know that some workers didn't particularly like their jobs but found ways not to become overwhelmingly upset. But what was the distribution among these three types (not to mention what caused the differences)? It's not easy to pin down.

This said, historians of daily life have become increasingly resourceful about data, and complaints about absolute informational voids have virtually disappeared. Some aspects of daily life can be teased out from quite conventional sources—for example, travelers' accounts. The use of diaries and autobiographies for recent centuries is extremely fruitful, and there is some lower-class involvement here. Diaries in Japan and autobiographies as a new form in nineteenth-century India, as well as more familiar opportunities in the Western world, are fertile repositories. Court records prove to be another terrific source, not only for crime but for records of emotions, insults, standards for the care of children, and so on. Material artifacts have gained increasing prominence, which is not surprising given their importance in daily life. Popular music has probably been underutilized, but its role also gains increasing recognition.

In general, it is important to note that gaps in sources sometimes remain troubling; most daily life historians have to think hard about where to get information. But with imagination and, often, hard work, materials can usually be found to address significant questions about daily life. The pioneering scholarship, of the past two decades has made it clear that it was the failure to identify good topics and research problems, more than a lack of materials, that was holding back our historical understanding of daily life.

A specific second issue springs from the questions about data: it is often easier to find out what people said about how daily life should operate than how it actually operated. Societies generate a vast amount of what is called prescriptive literature, materials telling people how to behave. In traditional Western society, sermons did a good bit of this work, and they allowed comments about sexuality, drinking, gambling, treatment of family, appropriate and unrespectable leisure, and so on. In more modern societies, manuals about marriage and childrearing, rule books concerning job behavior or how to conduct oneself in an interview, laws designed to regulate leisure activities, and many other sources say pretty clearly what people in authority thought the standards of daily life should be.

Prescriptive materials play a direct role in the history of daily life. An idea put forward as a code of conduct may affect the way social institutions run. For example, new concern about children's jealousy and guilt began to develop in the United States during the 1920s. By the 1970s these concerns generated new rules that prevented college professors from posting grades publicly (lest emotions be bruised). The idea that anger has no place in family life lies behind the emergence of no-fault divorce laws in the United States.

At the same time, however, prescriptions are not behaviors, and historians who use prescriptive materials have to be careful about assigning impact. American family manuals in the 1820s began urging parents not to express anger in punishing children, but this does not mean that many parents listened. (In this case, over time, there was some impact on behaviors: by the 1920s, manuals stopped emphasizing the prescription because it could be assumed most middle-class parents knew better.) Historians of daily life often struggle to get evidence about behaviors that goes beyond prescriptions, and this becomes part of the complex quest for adequate sources.

Social class, race, and gender offer a third complexity in dealing with the history of daily life, often related to issues of data and prescription. Different social groups and races, the two genders, and different age categories have varied patterns of daily life. All research on daily life has to keep this in mind, and some projects may emphasize comparisons among key groups. Variations result from gaps in wealth and income, and also from diverse standards of behavior, though the degrees of variation themselves vary in specific times and places. Not surprisingly, it is easiest to get at the daily life and relevant standards of middle- and upper-class groups that leave more abundant records (like letters and diaries or formal works of art) and often preach to the rest of society about how daily life should be conducted. Some daily life studies confuse ease of access with the possibility of generalization, and talk as if the experiences of the middle class apply to the whole of society; this overgeneralization, or neglect of diverse lower-class patterns, was one of the problems of the unanalytical pots-and-pans history. And there are sources for the daily life of key lower-class groups; they are simply more difficult to find. But there is, unquestionably, a problem about doing balanced histories of daily life that manage to take all groups into account or specify what groups they are in fact talking about. Here too, however, the problems involved are manageable, with a combination of awareness of social differentiation and imagination in source materials; the advances in the understanding of the daily life of women in the past show how concerted effort pays off in expanded knowledge. It is even possible to explore the ways some lower-class groups in the past learned to imitate aspects of middle-class daily life patterns, to avoid conflict or gain a sense of advancement, while preserving separate standards and private behaviors, in fact.

One final issue about doing daily life history, rather different from the key questions of sources, prescriptions, and social categories, involves geography, and particularly the treatment of daily life history in societies outside the United States and western Europe. The surge of historical interest in daily life first developed in, and about, the United States, western Europe, Canada, and Australia. This is where social history initially took deepest root. This is also where political issues, of the sort for example associated with attacks on colonialism, declined in salience, leaving more room for historical research on novel topics outside the conventional political sphere. Historical attention in places like Africa or south Asia (both in the regions themselves and on the part of Western historians dealing with the regions) understandably focused more heavily on reactions to imperialism, peasant resistance, and the emergence of new nations. This did not preclude attention to some aspects of daily life, particularly associated with power relationships, but it did tend to limit the range of coverage. In some cases, distinctive data issues long constrained attention to daily life. Indian historians note, for example, that whereas in the West there is a long tradition of autobiographical writing, this emerged in India only in reaction to Western contacts from the later nineteenth century onward.

The geographical disparities in the history of daily life are beginning to yield. Russian historians, for example, no longer focus their social history simply on explaining the 1917 revolution and its consequences; instead, they are generating important work on sexuality, orphanages, and disabilities—the kind of concerns typical of a maturing interest in the history of daily life. Significant studies in the history of childhood emanate from Latin America. African historians deal with historical patterns of reactions to death, sexuality, and youth. In the process, issues of sources are being handled with the kind of imagination and careful combination previously developed for Western topics, though the specific sources may differ.

It is important to remember, then, that even as some of the more novel topics seem to have a distinctively Western purchase, the history of daily life is potentially and increasingly a world history, and that regions outside the West are hosting important studies and generating some striking findings about diversity and change in daily life patterns. This injunction is all the more significant given the influence of Western standards and popular culture in the world at large over the past two centuries or more. The impact of Western consumer habits on daily life for many people in Africa, Asia, and Latin America, from toys to personal appearance to sports, is a compelling aspect of the global history of contemporary daily life. Here too, however, there is no need to be carried away with excessive "Westernism." First, many places specifically resist Western intrusions on daily life. There is more disagreement, for example, between Middle Easterners and Americans over gender issues or the proper approach to homosexuality than over political systems. Many people, without completely resisting Western-style daily life, blend important regional features with seeming foreign forms. Mexican comic books were copied from the United States from the 1930s onward, but they quickly developed distinctive national characteristics as they played a growing role in popular entertainment. The same holds for Japanese versions of American television game shows, where the shaming of unsuccessful contestants reflects a traditional emotional culture quite different from that which has developed in the West. Other correctives include the realization that, again in recent decades, Western daily life has itself been influenced by global forces. Japan, for example, using a combination of traditional art forms and a keen awareness of shifts in Western consumer culture (including a commitment to cuteness in children), gained a leadership role in key children's fads, such as the Hello Kitty product line and the Pokémon dolls. More generally, Japanese animation won world leadership in providing key types of television entertainment; at one point in the 1990s Iranian women rated a Japanese animated heroine as one of their most admired role models. By 2003, in fact, popular culture exports—animation, fashion, comic books, and music—topped Japan's export list, as the nation provided international leadership in "cool" styles. Finally, and most important, global influences on daily life are not recent phenomena alone. Food historians have done important work on the spread of food products and cooking styles in earlier stages of human history, with places like Italy, for instance, the beneficiaries of foodways initially developed in the Middle East and North Africa.

The history of daily life is frequently highly regional, dependent on local resources and traditions. But it often has a larger framework, and looking for more extensive global patterns and influences should be built into the inquiry. Comparison can also highlight what aspects of daily life are truly distinctive within a region and why, in contrast to features that are more widely shared. A purely Western focus, or an assumption that the West increasingly defines the world, is off the mark, despite some imbalances in historical work to date.

FACETS OF DAILY LIFE

The chapters in this book divide daily life into several major components. The divisions are somewhat arbitrary: work life, for example, obviously relates closely to leisure, and both, in turn, relate to family and even to personal emotions. Still, the divisions allow consideration of major findings in the history of daily life and specific guidance on how to set up particular kinds of studies— how to frame questions and how, on more focused topics, to deal with issues such as sources, class differences, and global versus more local relationships.

We begin with family and personal life, one of the obvious cross-sections. Family history took shape several decades ago, with many American historians taking a lead (perhaps because American families often seemed particularly troubled, the need for historical perspective on this aspect of daily life history stood out in bold relief). The more personal aspects, like emotions and the senses, are more recent products, some of them stemming from issues first encountered in dealing with families (such as emotional relationships between parents and children).

Health and the body constitute a vital part of actual daily life, and increasingly a revealing part of its history as well. The study of health in history has steadily moved away from the more traditional history of medicine, with its reliance on great doctors and their discoveries. What interests historians now is how people actually defined disease and wellness, and what they actually did about health problems (including their interactions with doctors, but not confined to these). The body relates to health, of course, but also to changing definitions of gender and a larger imagery that can deeply influence other activities, such as how children are raised. Important facets of this general topic include mental health and also experiences and attitudes relating to death.

Popular culture, including popular religion, is an aspect of daily life that bears a complex relationship with more conventional historical studies of ideas and beliefs. It is also an area in which research has rapidly advanced during the past two decades, when attention to cultural issues accelerated. An understanding of popular religious ideas and practices, including witchcraft and magic, forms part of the topic, and it can extend to the revival of religion in many parts of the world in recent decades. But popular understandings of science must also play a role. Education and literacy have received growing attention from historians of daily life, again linking to more formal institutional histories but with great interest in how children experienced education and what actual school lessons and discipline were like. The impact of consumerism on popular culture—indeed, a definition of what consumer culture itself means in different places—plays a role in this focus on the historical evolution of daily beliefs and rituals.

Material life is central to the history of daily life, and it's in this area that particular advances in data and concepts moved the whole topic away from pots-and-pans antiquarianism to a more challenging analytical status. The study of food in the past, including changes that resulted from trade and cultural contacts, has gained great vigor in recent years. The history of clothing has moved from catalogues of what people once wore to examination of how different types of dress expressed different kinds of group identity and personal meaning; men, as well as women, are definitely appropriate subjects by this point. Housing and artifacts have their own rich history, again in close relationship to other aspects of family life.

Further, daily life includes participation in communities, often including a formal state. Political history, when approached from the standpoint of daily life, emphasizes local organizations (villages, guilds, and the like), but also points at which more organized central states affect ordinary people. The social history of the military, focusing on ordinary soldiers and sailors and how their daily lives were organized at war and at peace, has gained increasing attention as part of a larger definition of how to do meaningful political history. In some systems, of course, formal political participation through voting and other activities is a reasonable part of daily life studies. We have seen that a prime motive for the German *Alltagsgeschichte* involved exploring how daily life functioned under Nazism, as a means of understanding what this political system actually meant. Daily life and politics also involve a discussion of deviance, particularly crime, in which people intentionally or unintentionally defy community norms. Changes in the definition of crime and shifts in the nature of punishment have generated exciting findings not only about deviant people themselves but about others for whom normal community behavior was indirectly defined by notions of deviance.

The next section, on economic life, focuses particularly on work. This calls for discussion of changing relationships between people and technologies and raises key questions about improvement or deterioration with the advent of more modern, industrial conditions. Historians have often focused more on work-based protests, like strikes, than on work itself, but by this point an understanding of historical evolution in daily work patterns is well advanced. The topic has extended into some of the less formal types of work, such as housewives' labor and even children's chores. For the elderly, the cessation of work, through retirement, is a special twist on economic life, looming large in modern times but under renewed debate as the percentage of the old-age population soars in many countries. Social divisions, not only slavery but also indentured servitude and other arrangements, set key frameworks where work and economic life are concerned; indeed, along with culture, work roles often define social class. And economic life also leads to considerations of living standards that go beyond work itself, moving into the roles people play in daily consumer life.

Finally, leisure and recreation have been one of the growth industries in the history of daily life, moving up from marginal status in professional historical research. Sports has been a particular focus, and there is also exciting work on the roles of music and dance and, of course, in modern times, the spread of professional entertainments of various sorts, from vaudeville and British music hall onward. Other historians have dealt with roles of drinking and recreational drugs in the history of leisure; this is another category in which social class, gender, and age groupings play a vital role.

All people participate, at any time or in any place, in all seven of these daily life categories. What they do in one affects what they do in others—popular religious beliefs color family life, which, in turn, is affected by material conditions, and on down the list. Larger generalizations must normally be assessed against each of the categories. For example, a number of historians and sociologists have explored the idea that life has become more informal in Western society in recent decades. This obviously needs to be tested against family hierarchies, sexual contacts, friendships, and personal manners. It also relates to appropriate behavior in economic life (when and why in the United States did strangers begin to call each other by first names when trying to sell products?). It relates closely to recreational behavior and to clothing styles. It affects political styles as well, as candidates seek to project a more folksy image. The body may be restructured to seem less formal, and certainly death practices—the decline of formal mourning—pick up on the modern mood. It's useful to break daily life down into its major categories, but then the challenge is to put it back together again, to deal with larger questions about what daily life is all about, and to determine how key aspects change or persist.

The history of daily life is a work in process. The findings, and often the excitement, have been impressive. We really do know more about how people function, about the variety of human experience, and also about how current daily life patterns can be explained by their emergence from the past, as a result of this genuine flowering of innovative historical research. Barriers that once seemed to preclude many kinds of daily life histories have, for the most part, been transformed into issues and challenges. Increasingly, not only historians but also other scholars see history as a laboratory in which many questions about ordinary behavior can be posed and answered.

Problems remain, of course. There is the question of audience. Histories of daily life have won considerable public attention in museum presentations. They have not been as successful in other media or in book form, though there have been a few exceptions, mainly in the area of past family life. Figuring out how to win more consistent attention from a public that can really benefit from historical understanding remains a challenge. There is also the question, possibly related, of the role of daily life history in school history. Many practitioners believe that introducing students to serious debates about findings in the history of daily life, or about appropriate data and methods, would greatly advance an understanding of what historical analysis is all about. And there are splendid individual examples of teachers accomplishing precisely this. But the textbooks don't help much, and the government-mandated social studies testing programs positively discourage the approach as they focus on standard political data. Here again is a task for the future, which logically argues for a blending of textbook history with focused analysis of at least one daily life topic in any history survey course.

Historians themselves often worry about the fragmentation of the history of daily life. We have terrific studies of anger, sound, crime, and the rise of car racing—the list is, in fact, huge. But what links some of these specific topics? Are there key points where major changes occur, thanks to world religions, industrialization, or globalization, so that we can do better than just talking about one facet after another? Some historians contend that we should be working harder to identify basic points of change—key historical periods—for the history of daily life, and recognize that these periods may not be the same as those used for standard political or military history. Many historians argue for some sweeping differences in a wide range of aspects of daily life, between modern and premodern, but this may beg the question about when "modern" begins (lots of debate here on specific topics); it also sounds excessively Western, as if patterns in modernizing Europe or the United States then set up fundamental categories for the rest of the world. Some practitioners also worry about too much emphasis on the purely modern, urging that there is benefit as well in probing more remote periods, where past daily life is both interesting and revealing, rather than rushing toward explaining the recent trends.

And, of course, there are many aspects of daily life still relatively unstudied. What about the historical experience of left-handers? to take an example of interest to some of us. What about studying changes and comparisons in the way people apologize, or fail to apologize, as part of the emotional and interpersonal experience of living daily life. Loneliness has been referred to but not really studied as a historical variable in daily experience. There is lots still to be done. But this, of course, is where the excitement continues to lie. We have learned a great deal about fundamental changes and contrasts in basic, daily human existence. We will learn a great deal more as new generations of historians and history students take up the charge. There are few, if any, more satisfying or revealing ways of exploring what makes up the experience of being human.

FURTHER READING

For the history of the senses, Alain Corbin, *The Foul and the Fragrant: Odor and the French Social Imagination* (Cambridge, MA, 1986) and Mark Smith, "Making Sense of Social History," *Journal of Social History* 37 (2003): 165–86. On issues like siblings and posture, Peter N. Stearns, *Anxious Parents: A History of Modern Childrearing in America* (New York, 2003). On family and political repercussions,

Philip Greven, *Four Generations: Population, Land, and Family in Colonial Andover* (Ithaca, NY, 1970). For an early statement of the "new" history of daily life, James Gardner and G.R. Adams, eds., *Ordinary People and Everyday Life: Perspectives on the New Social History* (Nashville, TN, 1983), includes comments on the older pots-and-pans approaches. On *Alltagsgeschichte*, Alf Luedtke, *History of Everyday Life*, trans. W. Templer (Princeton, NJ, 1995). For the critique of the new history, Gertrude Himmelfarb, *The New History and the Old* (Cambridge, MA, 1983). On connecting daily life history to daily life today, Peter N. Stearns, ed., *American Behavioral History* (New York, 2005).

On sleep, Roger Ekrich, "The Sleep We Have Lost: Preindustrial Slumber in the British Isles," *American Historical Review* 106 (2001): 874–913. On material culture, Thomas Schlereth, *Cultural History and Material Culture: Everyday Life, Landscapes, and Museums* (Charlottesville, VA, 1992) and Katherine Grier, *Culture and Comfort: People, Parlors and Upholstery, 1850–1930* (Washington DC, 1997). On comfort, John E. Crowley, *Comfort: Sensibilities and Design in Early Modern Britain and Early America* (Baltimore, 2001). Other striking works include Ruth Cowan, *More Work for Mother: The Ironies of Household Technology from the Open Hearth to the Microwave* (New York, 1983); Philippe Ariès, *Centuries of Childhood*, trans. R. Baldick (New York, 1965); Norbert Elias, *The Civilizing Process*, trans. E. Jephcott (New York, 1978); Joan Jacobs Brumberg, *Fasting Girls: The Emergence of Anorexia Nervosa as a Modern Disease* (Cambridge, MA, 1988); Peter N. Stearns, *Fat History: Bodies and Beauty in the Modern West*, rev. ed. (New York, 2002); Roy Rosenzweig, *Eight Hours for What We Will: Workers and Leisure in an Industrial City* (Cambridge, MA, 1985), a classic on leisure, change, and social class; John D'Emilio and Estelle Freedman, *Intimate Matters: A History of Sexuality in America* (New York, 1988); Beth Bailey, *Sex in the Heartland* (Cambridge, MA, 1999); Peter Schollers, ed., *Food, Drink and Identity* (New York, 2001), with other references to recent work in food history; Pieter Spierenburg, "Faces of Violence: Homicide Trends and Cultural Meanings, Amsterdam, 1431–1816," *Journal of Social History* 27 (1994): 701–16; Neil McKendrick, Colin Brewer, and J.H. Plumb, *The Birth of a Consumer Society* (Bloomington, IN, 1982).

2

Writing the History of Private Life

Steven Mintz

Traditionally, history was the story of public affairs: diplomacy, government, politics, revolutions, and war. In recent years, however, historians have turned their attention toward the private side of life: the way that ordinary people lived, along with their emotions, beliefs, and mental assumptions. By tapping new sources of evidence—census registers, wills, family papers, domestic architecture, etiquette books, cookbooks, and fashion magazines—and using methodologies drawn from such fields as cultural anthropology, demography, econometrics, and folklore, social historians have discovered that family life, childhood, and people's sexual practices have histories at least as fascinating as the battles, the elections, and the political and diplomatic maneuvering that dominated historians' attention in the past.

Each generation must write a history that speaks to the distinctive concerns of its own time. Ours is a time preoccupied with issues involving intimacy and private life. In recent decades, as divorce rates rose across the Western world, unprecedented numbers of mothers entered the workforce, birthrates plummeted, day care for toddlers became increasingly common, and sexual behavior, including same-sex relations, grew increasingly open, scholars sought to recover the history of family life, childhood, and sexuality.

Contemporary society attaches enormous importance to private life. Family ties, parenting, and other intimate relationships provide individuals with their deepest sources of emotional satisfaction. Earlier societies did not attach as much significance to the private realm. In classical antiquity and the Middle Ages, life's meaning was found in the public sphere: politics, military service, religious rituals, and other public activities. During the Reformation and Counter-Reformation of the sixteenth and seventeenth centuries, however, there was a growing affirmation of the value of private life. Among religious thinkers, there was a growing sense that the fullness of a Christian existence was to be found in marriage, family life, and one's earthly calling. During the eighteenth century, an emphasis on personal privacy and individual choice grew. An increasing number of novelists and moralists took the position that selection of a marriage partner should be a private decision, free from outside meddling; that marriage should be based on sympathy, affection, and friendship; and that reason and parental example were more effective than coercion in governing children. Meanwhile, houses began to be constructed with hallways, to enhance personal privacy. Armchairs, too, became more common, as did separate beds for children—symbols of a heightened emphasis on the individual. An understanding of social history is essential if we are to understand how private life, personal privacy, and individual choice became central to people's sense of themselves.

The realization that significant changes have occurred in family and sexual life, along with the importance contemporaries attach to these topics, has promoted a real outpouring of vigorous research. Attention has also tended to shift from the more purely structural features of family life—how many people lived in ordinary households, including non-kin, or what the birthrates were—to the more subjective subjects. Changes in the emphasis and, possibly, the nature of love, or new efforts to reduce anger within families, along with the attention to sexuality, highlight topics now central to family history. Family topics also form the leading source of interest in history on the part of most Americans, though here the focus is their own family and its genealogy. Linking these interests with the more formal analysis of family history constitutes one of the challenges in this aspect of the study of daily life. Furthermore, despite the amount of work available, a host of topics remain open to research—the histories of sibling relations and of grandparenting are, for example, just beginning to be sketched.

Work on the history of family life, including emotional qualities, almost always involves some tension between social expectations—prescriptions by religious figures, legal authorities, psychologists, or other experts—and actual patterns of behavior. This is particularly true for the lower classes and the minority groups, but it applies even to wealthy families. Finding materials that allow discussion of actual practices, including the influence of common prescriptions, is a final challenge of this important historical field. Again, considerable progress has allowed exciting conclusions about changes and continuities in family history, but additional opportunities remain.

THE FAMILY IN HISTORICAL PERSPECTIVE

The family is the basic unit of social organization in all human societies. Since prehistoric times, the family has been the primary institution responsible for raising children, providing people with food and shelter, and satisfying their emotional needs. This does not mean, however, that the family has been a static and unchanging institution. Its size and composition, its roles and functions, and its emotional and power dynamics have dramatically shifted over time.

Over the centuries, families have undergone far-reaching changes in their functions, roles, sizes, structures, and emotional and power dynamics. Courtesy of the Library of Congress.

Before the industrial revolution, the family's roles were far broader than they are today. The contemporary family is primarily an emotional unit where people relax, enjoy themselves, and devote their energies to raising children. In the past, the family was also a workplace where parents and children engaged in a variety of productive tasks. Families also served various educational, religious, insurance, and welfare functions. Parents taught their children basic literacy as well as craft skills. Families were also responsible for caring for the sick and the elderly. Since the industrial revolution, many of the family's traditional responsibilities have shifted to public and private institutions such as schools, hospitals, insurance companies, and nursing homes. Today, the family specializes in two functions. It is responsible for caring for the young and for providing love and emotional support for its members.

Most ancient societies had no term that exactly corresponds to the modern word for family. This was because ancient families varied widely in their size and structure depending on social class. The wealthiest households were very large units containing dozens of kinsfolk, servants, and slaves. At the same time, slaves and poor free people had no opportunity to establish independent households. Marriages in most ancient societies were arranged by the heads of families. Women were often married at very young ages, around or even before puberty. In ancient Greece and Rome, the average marriage age of women was between 12 and 15, while men married much later, usually in their mid- or late twenties. The result was a very substantial age gap between husbands and wives, which resulted in families that were very hierarchical. In the Roman family, the household head, known as the paterfamilias, was endowed with absolute authority. Under Roman law, he could sell his children, abandon them, or even put them to death.

The ancient world permitted a variety of family practices that Christianity (and also other religions such as Islam) would later condemn. One such practice was exposure. Parents would leave a newborn child out of doors, allowing handicapped or sickly infants to die. Many ancient societies also permitted marriages that the Christian Church would regard as incestuous. In ancient Egypt, men were allowed to marry their sisters. In addition to permitting easy access to divorce, many ancient societies practiced polygyny and concubinage (allowing a husband to cohabitate with a woman who was not his legal wife). The purpose of polygyny and concubinage was to provide children when a wealthy or powerful man's first wife failed to produce an heir.

In the early Christian era, family patterns in western Europe began to diverge from those in the non-Western world. As early as the fourth century A.D., a growing number of women in western Europe never married or bore children. In some parts of western Europe, more than 20 percent of adults remained unmarried. Those women who did marry were at a relatively late age, usually in their late teens and twenties, when they took husbands. Western European families were also distinctive in the emphasis placed on the bond between husband and wife, as opposed to broader kinship relationships.

Christianity played a critical role in the emergence of new family patterns. The church encouraged many young men and women to remain celibate and enter religious orders. It also condemned the exposure of infants and opposed concubinage, polygyny, arranged marriages, marriages with close kin, and divorce. The church's insistence on the indissolubility of marriage helped make the nuclear family more important than in the past.

Households during the Middle Ages varied widely in size. The household of a noble might contain 40 or more people, including many non-relatives such as pages (sons from wealthy families) and servants. But the average medieval household was much smaller, usually containing only four or five members. Because of a late age of marriage and a short life expectancy, most European women bore only four or fewer children.

In northwestern Europe, most households consisted of nuclear families, although some families took in an in-law or an elderly parent. In eastern and southern Europe, nuclear families were less common, though they usually made up at least half of all families. One kind of family frequently found in southern France, Germany, and Austria was the stem family, in which a son (usually the eldest or youngest) and his wife and children lived with his parents. Another family form found in Italy, southern France, and eastern Europe was the joint family. In a joint family, brothers and their wives and children lived under the same roof.

In medieval and early modern Europe, most houses were cramped and lacked privacy. Relatives often shared beds, and the same rooms were used for working, entertaining, cooking, eating, storage, and sleeping. Separate bedrooms and dining rooms did not become common until the late seventeenth or eighteenth century. During the Middle Ages, there was no sharp separation between the home and the workplace. Medieval households were productive units. Wives preserved food, made textiles and clothing, tended gardens, and brewed beer. In addition to farming, many husbands engaged in crafts such as carpentry, iron working, and barrel making.

Family life in medieval Europe was highly unstable. As many as half of all children died by the age of five. Economic pressures forced many parents to send their children away from home at very young ages, often before the age of eight. Because of the high death rate, remarriages were common. A quarter of all marriages involved partners who had been married before. Consequently, many medieval families contained stepparents, stepchildren, orphans, and half orphans.

During the Middle Ages, conflict arose between the Christian Church and wealthy families eager to preserve their land holdings and form alliances with other powerful families. The Christian Church opposed marriages between relatives and prohibited divorce and remarriage. Many wealthy families opposed church rules that allowed children to marry without parental consent and barred marriages between kin. To prevent the fragmentation of family estates, many wealthy families in England adopted a custom known as primogeniture, in which parents left their estate to their eldest son. This practice discouraged younger sons from marrying. Instead, many joined the church or the military. In central France and northern Italy, it was common for all children to inherit their parents' property jointly. This required them to live together after their parents' death. In eastern Europe, where stem families were common, parents customarily passed property to one child, usually the eldest or youngest son. He was responsible for caring for his parents in their old age as well as for any unmarried brothers and sisters.

In colonial America, as in Europe, the family was the basic unit of society. It educated children, cared for the elderly and the infirm, taught occupational skills to the young, and functioned as the economic center of production. All family members participated in the family's support. Wives gardened, milked cows, brewed beer, harvested fruit, kept chickens, and preserved food. They also cooked, laundered, spun yarn, wove cloth, and made clothing. Children assumed work responsibilities before the age of seven. In colonial New England, every person was required to live in a family. Bachelors and single women paid special taxes and were forced to live as boarders or servants. Married couples who lived apart from each other were fined.

Seventeenth-century Americans conceived of the family as a hierarchical unit in which the father was endowed with patriarchal authority. He sat in a chair, while others sat on benches, chests, or stools. Child-rearing manuals were addressed to him. He had to give his legal consent before his children could marry. His control over inheritance kept his grown sons and daughters dependent on him for years while they waited for his permission to marry and to establish a separate household.

Families in colonial America were very diverse. During the seventeenth century, enslaved Africans had few opportunities to establish a stable, independent family life. Most lived on farms or on plantations with fewer than 10 slaves. These units were so small and widely dispersed, and the number of women was so low, that it was very difficult to find a spouse. A high death rate meant that most of the enslaved did not live long enough to marry or, if they did, that their marriages were brief. By the early eighteenth century, it became easier to establish families, as the number of Africans forcibly imported into the colonies increased, the size of plantations grew, and life expectancy rose.

Seventeenth-century white colonists in Maryland, Virginia, and the Carolinas also suffered from a high death rate and a skewed sex ratio. In Virginia, death broke half of all marriages before the seventh wedding anniversary. Two-thirds of all children lost a parent before their eighteenth birthday, and a third lost both. As a result, many seventeenth-century southern households consisted of step-parents and stepchildren.

During the mid-eighteenth century, family life in colonial America underwent far-reaching changes. Family life in the southern colonies grew more stable. Across the colonies, love and affection were increasingly viewed as the only proper reasons for marriage. At the same time, parents became more interested in their children's development. Instead of viewing children as miniature adults, parents regarded children as creatures with special needs and began to buy them children's books, games, and toys. Young people also acquired greater leeway in selecting a spouse.

It was during the early nineteenth century that a new division of domestic roles appeared, with the husband as breadwinner and the wife as full-time homemaker and mother. More middle-class parents kept their children home into their late teens instead of sending them out as servants and apprentices. By the middle of the nineteenth century, the family vacation had appeared as well as such new family-oriented celebrations as the birthday party and decoration of the Christmas tree.

During the nineteenth century, middle-class family patterns were confined to a small minority of the population. For many immigrant and working-class families, low wages and a lack of year-round employment meant that all family members had to work. While middle-class families could rely on a single bread-winner, working-class families had a cooperative family economy in which all members contributed to the family's support. Wives did piecework in the home, took in laundry, or rented rooms to boarders. Children under the age of 15 earned as much as 20 percent of an urban working-class family's income.

No families lived under greater strain than those of enslaved African Americans. Under slavery, African American families lacked legal protection. Between 1790 and 1860, a million slaves were sold from the Upper South to the Lower South, and another two million slaves were sold within states. As a result, about a third of all slave marriages were broken by sale and, during their teen years, about half of all slave children were taken from their parents and sold. Even in instances in which marriages were not broken by sale, slave spouses often resided on separate plantations. On large plantations, one slave father in three had a different owner than his wife and could visit his wife and family only with his master's permission.

Despite the frequent breakup of families by sale, enslaved African Americans forged strong family and kin ties. In spite of the refusal of the law to recognize the legality of slave marriages, most slaves married and lived with the same spouse until death. To sustain a sense of family identity, slaves named their children after parents, grandparents, and other kin. Enslaved African Americans also passed down family names to their children, usually the name of an ancestor's owner rather than the current owner's. Ties to an immediate family stretched outward to an involved network of extended kin. Whenever children were sold to neighboring plantations, grandparents, aunts, uncles, and cousins took on the functions of parents. When blood relatives were not present, strangers cared for and protected the children.

At the end of the nineteenth century, many Americans were anxious about the family's future. The divorce rate in the United States was the highest in the Western world. Infant and child death rates were also very high, with as many as a third of children dying by the age of 15. Meanwhile, nearly 20 percent of American women never married, and the birthrate of women had sharply fallen during the nineteenth century. Instead of bearing seven or more children as the typical middle-class woman had in 1800, she gave birth to only three.

At the beginning of the twentieth century, Progressive Era reformers instituted a variety of measures to improve the well-being of families and children. Reformers promoted pasteurized milk, fought to end child labor, and lobbied for special pensions to allow widows to raise their children at home, instead of sending them to orphanages. To combat the rising divorce rate, a new family ideal emerged by the 1920s. Called the companionate family, it held that husbands and wives should be "friends and lovers" and that parents and their children should be "pals."

During the Great Depression of the 1930s, unemployment, lower wages, and the demands of needy relatives tore at the fabric of family life. Many people were forced to share living quarters with relatives, delay marriage, and put off having children. The divorce rate fell, since fewer people could afford one, but desertions soared. By 1940, 1.5 million married couples were living apart. Families sought to cope by planting gardens, canning food, and making clothing. Children took part-time jobs, and wives supplemented the family income by taking in sewing or laundry, selling groceries from their parlor, or housing lodgers.

World War II also subjected families to severe strain. During the war, families faced a severe shortage of housing, a lack of schools and child-care facilities, and prolonged separation from loved ones. Five million "war widows" ran their homes and cared for their children alone, while millions of women went to work in war industries. The stresses of wartime contributed to an upsurge in the divorce rate. Tens of thousands of young people became unsupervised latchkey children, and rates of juvenile delinquency and truancy rose.

The late 1940s and 1950s witnessed a sharp reaction to the stresses of the Depression and the war. The divorce rate slowed, and couples married earlier than their parents had. Women bore more children at younger ages and closer together than in the past. The result was a baby boom.

Since the 1960s, families in all industrialized countries have undergone far-reaching changes. Birthrates have dropped, divorce rates have risen, mothers have entered the labor force in record numbers, and a growing proportion of children were born to unmarried mothers. In the United States, between the mid-1960s and the early 1980s, the proportion of working mothers doubled, the number of divorces tripled, and the percentage of couples living together outside of marriage quadrupled.

As recently as 1960, 70 percent of the households in the United States consisted of a breadwinner father, a homemaker mother, and two or more kids. Today, the

male-breadwinner–female-homemaker family makes up only a small proportion of American households. Among the common family arrangements are
two-earner families, where both the husband and the wife work; single-parent
families, usually headed by a mother; childless families; reconstituted families,
formed after a divorce; and empty-nest families, created after the children have
left home.

Since the early 1980s, the pace of familial change has slowed, but public anxiety about the family has remained high. Many factors contribute to public concern, including high rates of teenage pregnancy, out-of-wedlock births, juvenile
crime, and children growing up in poverty. In the twenty-first century, families
face many challenges, one of the most important being the need to balance the
demands of work and family life. Working parents must care not only for their
young children but, because of increasing life spans, their aging parents as
well.

Although scholars have charted the general outlines of familial change in
Europe and North America, many subjects remain to be studied. We have much
more to learn about class, ethnicity, and regional diversity, as well as about the
impact of major historical events and processes such as industrialization, immigration, and war on family life. A growing area of interest involves the history of
public policy toward the family, including such subjects as the history of adoption, domestic violence, family law, illegitimacy, and welfare. Work on family
emotional life—changing definitions of and emphasis on love and grief within
the family—has yielded some important findings, but there is more to be done in
a vital but inherently different area. In addition, an enormous amount remains to
be discovered about family history in Africa, Asia, and Latin America.

MARRIAGE AND DIVORCE IN HISTORICAL PERSPECTIVE

Although many people think of marriage as a timeless and unchanging institution, it is as enmeshed in the historical process as any other social arrangement.
The motives for marriage, the average length of a marriage, access to marriage,
and the likelihood of divorce have all radically changed over the centuries,
reflecting shifts in the family's functions, in gender roles, and in emotional
expectations. Many of the rituals commonly associated with marriage, such as
the shower, the white bridal gown, and the honeymoon, are surprisingly recent
innovations, dating only to the eighteenth and nineteenth centuries. The elements
that contemporary society most closely associates with marriage—romance and
companionship—were rarely connected with marriage until recent times.

In contemporary Western societies, a successful marriage is regarded as a
key to personal happiness and individual fulfillment. The high expectations
invested in marriage contrast sharply with earlier views. The early Christian
Church regarded marriage as an unfortunate necessity to accommodate human
weakness. The best St. Paul could say for marriage is, "It is better to marry than
to burn."

Among economic and political elites, marriage was a way of forging economic
and political alliances. For landed families, marriage was a private contract
designed to ensure that property remained within a particular lineage. For
poorer families, marriage was, first and foremost, a productive arrangement

to which each spouse was expected to bring skills and resources. In many Western societies, a bride and groom were expected to bring financial resources, known as a dowry and brideswealth, to a marriage.

During the Protestant Reformation and the Catholic Counter-Reformation, many earlier ideas about marriage came under attack. Sixteenth-century Protestant reformers criticized the Catholic Church for allowing young people to marry without parental consent, forbidding clergy to marry, and prohibiting divorce and remarriage when marriages

11434, The Wedding March.

The wedding ceremony that we think of as traditional is less than two centuries old. Courtesy of the Library of Congress.

broke down. Many Protestant societies, including those founded in Puritan New England, required parental consent to make a marriage valid and instituted laws against wife beating and adultery. In addition to abolishing monasteries and convents, many Protestant countries recognized a right to divorce in cases of abandonment, adultery, and extreme physical cruelty.

It was not until the Reformation and the Counter-Reformation that the emotional bond between husband and wife began to be viewed as central to marriage. Yet even as late as the seventeenth and early eighteenth centuries, love was not considered a prerequisite for marriage and it was assumed that love would follow marriage. Indeed, romantic love was considered a form of madness. Protestant ministers frequently advised individuals to select a spouse on practical and pragmatic grounds. In Puritan New England, parents had a legal right to consent to their children's marriages and were expected to play an active role in negotiating marriage settlements. Not surprisingly, relations between spouses tended to be highly formal. Husbands commonly referred to their wives as "dear child," and wives addressed their husbands as "sir" or "mister." By the late eighteenth century, in contrast, marriage was increasingly viewed as an emotional bond involving love and affection. Spouses displayed affection more openly, calling each other "honey" or "dear."

Over time, government involvement in marriage has increased. Prior to the late nineteenth century, many American marriages were informally contracted since clergy were scarce and formal weddings were expensive. At the end of the nineteenth century, legal regulation of marriage expanded with enactment of laws prohibiting polygyny, marriages between close relatives, and racial intermarriage. In 1967, when the U.S. Supreme Court finally declared antimiscegenation statutes unconstitutional, 16 states still had laws barring interracial marriages.

A gradual expansion of married women's rights is one of the most striking developments of the past two centuries. During the colonial and early national periods, Anglo-American family law presumed that the husband was the head of the household. Upon marriage, he acquired all of his wife's personal and real property, and it remained his even if he committed adultery, abandoned her, or went to jail. He also exercised control over any wages that she earned and had custody of their children in the event of a separation or divorce. During the nineteenth century, American courts and legislatures gradually abandoned the doctrine of coverture, the notion that a woman's legal identity was subsumed in her husband's. Beginning with Mississippi in 1839, the states enacted married women's property acts, which permitted women to control their own wages, to own real and personal property, to enter into contracts, and to sue or be sued. Courts also adopted the tender-year rule, the legal presumption that mothers should have custody of young children in cases of divorce or separation. It was not until the 1970s and 1980s, however, that the states fully embraced the notion that marriage is an equal partnership based on mutual consent. Today, all of the states have repudiated the notion that men have a right to intercourse with their wives or that they are immune from suits brought by their spouses. Nor is it assumed that only a wife may receive alimony or that a wife's legal residence is automatically her husband's abode.

Although marriage is often thought of as a solemn or sacred institution, it also carries many economic and legal rights. According to some estimates, American marriage legally confers over 600 benefits involving custody and parental rights, wills and inheritances, and medical care. In recent years, many European countries have allowed cohabiting couples, including same-sex couples, to register in civil partnerships (or, in France, civil solidarity pacts) that give them inheritance and pension benefits, and next-of-kin rights in hospitals. In 2000, Vermont became the first American state to recognize civil unions, and in 2004, Massachusetts became the first to legalize same-sex marriages.

Despite the recent increase in divorce and nonmarital cohabitation, marriage is not a dying institution. About 90 percent of Americans marry and have children, and most who divorce eventually remarry. In certain respects, marriage today is actually stronger than it was in the past. Not only do couples invest higher expectations for sexual and personal fulfillment in marriage, but declining death rates mean that many couples are more likely to grow into old age together than in the past. At the same time, however, a narrowing of the family's functions has meant that the bonds holding families together have weakened. Today, the adhesive that unites couples is primarily emotional rather than economic, and these emotional bonds often prove to be fleeting.

As marriage came to be viewed as an emotional partnership, legal access to divorce expanded and the number of divorces shot up. Divorce, however, is not a modern phenomenon. Most ancient and many non-Western societies permitted easy divorce. The early Christian Church was unique in embracing the doctrine of marital indissolubility. During the early modern era, however, many Catholic and especially Protestant reformers favored divorce as a way to punish moral wrongdoing such as adultery. During the Reformation, most Protestant countries, with the notable exception of England, liberalized access to divorce. The goal of much early divorce legislation was punitive; in most instances neither spouse was allowed to remarry.

In the late eighteenth century, access to divorce with a right to remarry increased. The French Revolution witnessed the first experiments in no-fault divorce. The American Revolution not only provided ideological justification for divorce from patriarchal tyranny, it also encouraged the substitution of judicial for legislative divorce. In the 1830s, a number of states allowed judges to grant divorces on any grounds deemed appropriate. The federal system meant that divorce statutes varied widely; it also encouraged liberalization of divorce laws, as some states, including Indiana and later Nevada, competed to attract divorcing couples. In the late nineteenth century, recognition that the United States had the Western world's highest divorce rates led reformers to restrict the grounds for divorce. Nevertheless, divorce rates steadily mounted, as jurists interpreted statutes allowing divorce on grounds of physical cruelty to encompass mental cruelty. By the 1920s, 200,000 divorces were taking place in the United States each year.

Divorce remained disreputable well into the twentieth century, even in the United States, and most Europeans were unable to obtain divorces until after World War II. A surge in divorces followed the war, but a steep rise only began in the 1960s, which encouraged enactment of no-fault divorce laws to reduce divorce's stigma, produce less adversarial proceedings, and eliminate the connivance that frequently accompanied divorce suits. In 1969, California adopted the United States' first no-fault divorce law.

A low divorce rate does not necessarily mean that marriages were happier in the past. Marriage was an economic necessity and mutual love was not considered an essential element. Families were interdependent economic units, and almost all unmarried women lived in extreme poverty, forcing many to foster out their children. The threat of physical violence or witchcraft prosecutions and a lack of economic and residential options forced women to tolerate unhappy marriages. Increased opportunities for wage labor, longer life spans, and an emphasis on the individual as opposed to the family as a corporate unit were essential elements in the spread of divorce.

It is essential to distinguish divorce, a legal process that only became common in Western societies in the nineteenth century, from marital breakdown, which occurs in all societies. Although marriage partners in the past probably had lower expectations of marital happiness, there also existed escape hatches from miserable marriages, including desertion, separation, concubinage, and bigamy. In early modern England, the complexities of the marriage process under ecclesiastical and civil law (including rules about parental consent) allowed some partners to terminate marriages. One of the most striking folk customs was "wife sale," described in Thomas Hardy's novel *The Mayor of Casterbridge*. A woman, wearing a halter, was led to a marketplace where she was "sold" for a small, symbolic sum to another man.

Historically, divorce has been a woman's weapon; today, the overwhelming majority of petitioners for divorce are female. Therefore, legislative efforts to reduce the incidence of divorce have tended to restrict women's ability to exit unhappy marriages. Still, divorce and women's interests are not identical, and divorce usually results in an immediate drop in women's income. Partly, this is due to inadequate child support awards and men's failure to pay, as well as women's willingness to bargain child support for child custody.

Today's high divorce rates do not necessarily signal, as some fear, a declining commitment to marriage. Precisely because contemporaries attach a higher valuation to emotional and sexual fulfillment than their predecessors, they are less likely to tolerate loveless or abusive marriages. Even as alternatives to marriage have grown more prevalent, marriage rates remain high in most countries, and marriage serves as the paradigm for other intimate relationships, including many same-sex unions.

Many topics related to marriage and divorce offer fruitful subjects for study. How did individuals in the past deal with unhappy or abusive marriages? How did unmarried adult men and women manage in the past? Why do rates of marriage, divorce, and remarriage vary so widely across various social groups and societies? Further, how can we explain the recent "deinstitutionalization" of marriage across the Western world as formal, opposite-sex marriages began to increasingly coexist with other relationships, including unmarried cohabitation and same-sex unions?

CHILDHOOD IN HISTORICAL PERSPECTIVE

Children preoccupy contemporary Western societies. Childhood is regarded as a special period of life that deserves all the attention parents can give it. Biographies emphasize individuals' early years as the key to understanding their personalities and intelligence. Many movies and television shows dwell on the joys and agonies of growing up. Contemporary politics emphasizes children's issues such as education, teenage smoking and drinking, youth crime, and children's access to health care. Thus it comes as a shock to discover that our predecessors in antiquity, the Middle Ages, and the early modern era never expressed nostalgia for childhood, nor did they find it intrinsically interesting.

This is not to say that earlier societies lacked a conception of childhood or to suggest that parents in the past did not love their children, regard them as a source of pleasure and amusement, or mourn their deaths. They did. But it does remind us that childhood is not an unchanging stage of life. Every aspect of childhood, including children's relationships with their parents and peers, their proportion of the population, and their paths through childhood to adulthood, has dramatically changed over the past four centuries. Methods of child rearing, the duration of schooling, the nature of children's play, young people's participation in work, and the points of demarcation between childhood, adolescence, and adulthood are products of culture, class, and historical era. Just two centuries ago, there was far less age segregation than there is today and much less concern with organizing experience by chronological age. There was also far less sentimentalizing of children as special beings who were more innocent and vulnerable than adults.

How, then, has childhood changed over the past centuries? Four broad transformations have taken place. The first involves shifts in the timing, sequence,

The experience of childhood has widely varied by class, ethnicity, gender, geographical location, and historical era. Courtesy of the Library of Congress.

and stages of growing up. Over the past four centuries, the stages of childhood have grown much more precise, uniform, and prescriptive as formal schooling has become the major pathway to a successful adulthood. Demography has been another force for change. A sharp reduction in the birthrate has more rigidly divided families into distinct generations and allowed parents to lavish more time, attention, and resources on each child. A third major shift involves the separation of children from work, the equation of childhood with schooling, and the increasing integration of the young into a consumer society. The fourth transformation is attitudinal, as adult conceptions of childhood shifted profoundly over time. The seventeenth-century Puritan image of the child as a depraved being who needed to be restrained was supplanted by the enlightened notion of children as blank slates that could be shaped by environmental influences; the Romantic conception of children as asexual creatures with innocent souls and redeemable, docile wills; the Darwinian emphasis on highly differentiated stages of children's cognitive, physiological, and emotional development; the Freudian conception of children as seething cauldrons of instinctual drives; and contemporary notions that emphasize children's competence and capacity for early learning.

There has been a tendency to conceive of the history of childhood as a story of progress, with gentleness replacing rigorous discipline and scientific knowledge superseding superstition. Contributing to this narrative of progressive improvement is the fact that child-rearing practices before the eighteenth century differed radically from those today. Well-to-do parents often dispatched their newborns to wet nurses, who sometimes had depleted milk supplies and abused or neglected their charges. Infants in many European cultures were tightly wrapped in swaddling clothes, seemingly depriving them of physical and emotional stimulation. Children as young as seven or eight toiled as servants or apprentices in other people's households. Especially troubling is the high rate of infant and child mortality, often resulting from easily preventable causes such as suffocation in bed, burns from fireplaces, and falls down wells or from rooftops. Since many families gave later-born children the same name as deceased siblings, it seems easy to conclude that parents in the preindustrial world did not regard young children as unique, but rather as interchangeable and easily replaceable beings.

It would be a mistake, however, to assume that parents in the past were indifferent toward their children. Wet-nursing reflected parental priorities different from our own, especially women's need to devote their time and energy to productive labor. In many instances, wet-nursing was prompted by a mother's difficulty in breast-feeding or an insufficient milk supply. Mothers took great pains in selecting nurses, who usually lived either within the mother's household or nearby, allowing the baby's biological mother to maintain close contact with her child. Children often developed extremely strong emotional bonds with their nurses.

Swaddling also served many positive functions: It kept the babies warm and prevented infants from scratching themselves, crawling into open fires, or placing dangerous objects in their mouths. It had the added advantage of keeping infants passive, since the practice has been shown to depress the heartbeat and reduce crying. Swaddling was also believed, mistakenly, to prevent rickets and ensure that the baby's limbs grew straight.

The practice of "fostering out" children to other households was not as heartless as it might seem. Typically, young people in early modern Europe did not enter into service or apprenticeship for protracted periods of time until their mid- or late teens. Even then, many children maintained close ties with their parents, who generally lived nearby. It was common for parents to closely monitor their child's apprenticeship or term of service and complain when they felt their child was being abused or failed to receive the training that had been promised. While young people in medieval and early modern Europe certainly entered the world of work earlier and spent more time in the company of adults than children and youth do today, they also had large amounts of time to socialize with peers.

Nor did children in the preindustrial world die as frequently as previously assumed. Although there were periods of plague and epidemic disease when infant and child death rates soared to extremely high levels, in general, mortality was much lower. In early modern England, about 85 percent of all newborns reached the age of 5, and nearly three-quarters reached the age of 10.

Rather than assuming that parents in the preindustrial world were less caring than their contemporary counterparts, it is more useful to recognize that our predecessors approached childhood with a very different set of cultural assumptions and priorities. For example, whereas modern societies treat childbirth as a medical process, in medieval and early modern Europe, each phase of the birth process—from a woman's first recognition that she was pregnant to baptism and the rituals of thanksgiving and purification a month after the child's birth—was surrounded by religious and secular ceremonies as well as by customs intended to ensure a safe birth and a healthy infant. It was widely believed that if a mother looked upon a "horrible spectre" or was startled by a loud noise, her child would be disfigured, and that if a hare jumped in front of her, her child was in danger of suffering a harelip.

In many European societies, children were baptized a few days after birth, to give relatives time to assemble. At this ceremony, the child's godparents typically announced the child's name, pledged the child to the church, and immersed the infant in the baptismal font. Parents chose godparents with great care, since godparenthood established or reinforced links of kinship, friendship, and interest. During the seventeenth century, the practice of godparenthood declined in many Protestant countries, as the Protestant clergy argued that godparenthood had no scriptural sanction, and rejected the idea that godparents could issue a declaration of faith on the child's behalf.

Traditionally, godparents had the privilege of naming the child, often naming newborns after themselves. Sometimes, children received a saint's name, especially the name of the saint on whose day they were born. The custom of allowing godparents to bestow their own name on a child sometimes led to more than one sibling bearing the same name. Communities differentiated among children with the same names by assigning "pet" names. Thus English boys named William might be known as Wilcock, Wilkin, Willin, or Wilmot. Gradually, many of these pet names evolved into surnames. During the sixteenth and seventeenth centuries, some Protestant clergy rejected these traditional customs and argued that children's names should be chosen from the Bible or, especially for girls, signify a particular virtue such as Patience or Mercy.

Between the sixteenth and late eighteenth centuries, an intense debate about the advantages and disadvantages of wet-nursing and maternal nursing raged in Europe. Many theologians insisted that nursing was a mother's Christian responsibility, and that like the Virgin Mary, she should suckle her own child. A growing number of physicians argued that children were more likely to survive if they were nursed by their own mothers. At the same time, many prominent women and men, particularly among the gentry, not only continued to practice wet-nursing but openly defended the custom.

By looking at the past, we can appreciate the distinctiveness of our current child-rearing practices. Contemporary society is unusual in the stress it places on the formative influence of early childhood and the extreme emphasis it attaches to individuation. The United States, in particular, encourages much more physical isolation of infants than has been typical throughout human history. Not only do infants sleep in their own cribs, usually in their own rooms, but the bulk of infant's play is done in isolation from others.

Weaning was considered a significant milestone in a child's life. It was an event of particular significance when it coincided with the baby's separation from a wet nurse. Weaning was a source of great anxiety because a child's immunity to diseases declined drastically after nursing ended. Generally, European children were weaned during the second year of life—two or more years earlier than children in many African or Native American societies, who typically were weaned around the age of four.

Another major milestone occurred around the age of five or six. In most cultures children around the age of six are assigned new roles and face distinctly different expectations than younger children. In the preindustrial world, the years of middle childhood marked a child's entry into the world of formal education or increased involvement in work routines. In Elizabethan and Stuart England, the transition to boyhood and girlhood was symbolically signaled by a change in clothing. Boys around the age of six went through a formal ceremony when they began to wear breeches. Although girls did not undergo a ceremony comparable to breeching, they, too, began to wear clothing distinctive of a shift in status.

Until the eighteenth century, the prevailing attitude toward human development, with roots going back to Aristotle, was that people only gradually acquired the attributes of full humanity, including rationality and maturity. People passed from a near-animal state of childhood through the passions and follies of youth and only slowly acquired the wisdom and restraint of age. This assumption shaped the prevailing forms of child rearing. Early modern society expressed a great deal of anxiety about children's animal-like qualities. To discourage infants from crawling like beasts and to encourage them to stand upright as quickly as possible, they were placed in walking chairs somewhat similar to modern-day walkers. Leading strings—called "reins"—were also attached to children's clothes. Lacking our extreme sentimentalization of childhood, parents sometimes took young children to hangings and funerals and told them scary tales as a way to discipline them, toughen them, and prepare them for the possibility of early death.

There was a tendency to compare the rearing of a child to the taming of a horse and to assume that corporal punishment was necessary to discipline children. Medieval and early modern Europeans largely rejected the modern notion that young children need to be treated with gentleness and indulgence. They considered young children to be soft and weak creatures that should not be treated too tenderly, lest they be susceptible to sickness and vice. Corporal punishment was an integral part of child rearing, education, and apprenticeship. The view that he who spares the rod spoils the child was a basic assumption of educational theory. Sixteenth- and early-seventeenth-century moralists regarded physical punishment as a useful and even desirable form of discipline, necessary in teaching children deference, breaking sinful wills, and preparing the young for the disappointments of the adult world. One authority claimed that human beings had been given buttocks so that they could receive correction without serious injury to the rest of their bodies.

It would be a mistake, however, to exaggerate the prevalence of corporal punishment. Extant diaries and memoirs suggest that most parents typically used physical punishment only as a last resort. Rather than relying exclusively on force, parents enlisted a variety of disciplinary practices, as evidenced in surviving personal papers. While some parents boxed children's ears and whipped their buttocks, others indulged their offspring, prayed for them, or scolded them. Most parents apparently wanted their offspring to be subject to some discipline and control at school, but desired moderate as opposed to brutal punishments. Some parents would not tolerate any brutality toward their children.

It is hard to evaluate the psychological meaning of physical discipline in a society where it was not restricted exclusively to the young. In contrast to contemporary Western societies, corporal punishment in the preindustrial world was not confined solely to children. Servants and others in a servile condition were whipped; sailors and criminals were flogged; and heretics and political prisoners were tortured. Strict physical punishment was regarded as an appropriate way to prepare children to function in a hierarchical society that demanded deference in all aspects of life. From an early age, young people were expected to make elaborate displays of deference toward their parents. Today, in stark contrast, we live in a much more fluid and mobile society that requires adults to be independent and self-assertive. The disciplinary techniques that child-rearing experts recommend today, such as time-outs, are intended to allow parents to instill self-discipline and sensitivity to the needs and feelings of others within children without reliance on physical force.

Our society considers play to be children's work, an activity essential to children's cognitive, physical, and social development. Early modern society, in contrast, viewed play much more negatively. From Aristotle came the idea of play and games as a mere simulation of reality. Play was regarded as "childish" in a pejorative sense: trivial, unserious, and insignificant. Unlike children's play in our time, there were few games or toys that were explicitly educational. Nevertheless, children played many games, like marbles and blindman's buff, and with a variety of toys still familiar today: tops, blindfolds, yo-yos, soap bubbles, ropes, stilts, hoops, rattles, balls, and trumpets. Dolls, known as "babies," were also popular, though before the late nineteenth century they were modeled after adults rather than after babies or children, signifying the assumption that children should strive to leave the state of childish dependency as rapidly as possible.

One of the chief functions of toys in modern societies is to encourage children to entertain themselves. Television and video games encourage solitary behavior, while many soft toys, such as teddy bears, serve as substitutes for human companions. Toys and games in early modern Europe, in contrast, tended to emphasize social interactions. Children's play also served a wide range of developmental functions. Some of these games—those involving cooking, baptismal or marriage ceremonies, keeping house, hunting and war—imitated adult activities. Other activities such as swimming, spinning, rolling downhill, standing on one foot, or holding one's breath allowed children to test their physical dexterity, become aware of their bodies, test their limits of endurance, and break free of conventions of normal posture and movement. Particularly popular were games that allowed children to confront fears of supernatural beings such as elves, ghosts, hobgoblins, and bogeymen. Struggles for power or superiority were an important feature of play in the early modern era. Many games were competitive, involving running, hiding, chasing, catching, or fighting. Also popular was play involving chases and escapes or attack and defense. Hazing and initiation rituals, sometimes involving dunking children's heads in water, were also common. Cruelty, especially toward animals, was apparently widespread. It was widely agreed that children took special delight in tormenting animals—for example, torturing birds or stealing their eggs.

Children in the preindustrial era were likely to experience considerable disruption and dislocation while growing up. In early modern England, between half and two-thirds of young women lost a father before they had married, and perhaps a third of all young people lost a father before an apprenticeship began; but the prospect of losing both parents was not very high. In many instances, a parent's death or remarriage resulted in a child joining another family's household. About 30 percent of marriages in sixteenth- and seventeenth-century England were remarriages, and older children might be sent away to reduce friction with stepparents or other siblings. Even in intact families, however, it was common for children to live temporarily with another family. While most children did not enter into service or apprenticeship before their mid-teens, many young children did leave home for periods of several weeks, months, or a year or longer. The reasons for leaving home were diverse. Some children were sent away to relieve overcrowding, to protect them from plague or infectious disease, or to provide them with an education or training.

Early modern society was characterized by familial tensions very different from those found today. The prevalence of remarriage after a parent's death was one source of tension. Tensions between children and stepparents, and stepbrothers and stepsisters were apparently commonplace. The principle of primogeniture, which refers to the right of the eldest son to inherit family property, created a set of tensions and anxieties that found expression not only in the plays and poetry of the period, but in diaries and court records as well. Many sources, especially among landowning families, reveal older sons waiting uneasily for their fathers to die, and younger sons begrudging their older siblings. Meanwhile, parent-child conflict centered on different issues than it does today. Especially among the well-to-do, parents took a much more active role in influencing children's decisions over marriage and employment. Parents also seem to have been more willing to threaten to disinherit a child or to ask the child to leave home. Nevertheless, high rates of parental death meant that many children escaped such pressures.

Child labor was a basic fact of life in preindustrial societies. Today, much of the work that young children are asked to do is symbolic. Making one's bed, cleaning up one's room, putting away one's toys, and washing dishes are more a test of a child's moral character than a genuine contribution to the family economy. In earlier societies, rural children were drawn into the workforce early in their lives. Yet unlike the kinds of child labor that arose with industrialization, young children's work tended to be irregular and accompanied by a great deal of leisure. A gender division of labor also began early. By the age of four or five, girls were assigned to babysit and fetch water. They also began to learn such tasks as cooking, brewing, milking, washing, mending, spinning, and knitting. Rural boys gathered wood, went on errands, herded and pastured livestock, watered horses, and spread dung to manure the soil.

Access to schooling was related to gender and social rank. In early modern Europe, education began at home, and scholars were expected to have mastered basic literacy before enrolling in school. In England, the sixteenth and seventeenth centuries witnessed a substantial increase in the number of schools for elementary and higher education. In part, the expansion in the number of schools reflected a heightened recognition of education's economic value. But there was also a strong concern to get children off the streets, to accustom them to obedience and discipline, and to inculcate religion, good behavior, and civility. While attending grammar school, scholars often lived under a master's watchful eyes and wore uniforms outside of school to facilitate surveillance.

Contemporary Western societies are obsessed with dividing childhood into stages and giving each one a precise label. We regard childhood development as discontinuous and believe children go through a series of distinct developmental phases, carefully distinguishing among toddlers, preschoolers, preadolescents, and early adolescents. Earlier societies, in contrast, tended to see childhood development as more continuous. The ancient, medieval, and early modern worlds did identify several stages of youthful development, such as infantia, pueritia, adolescentia, and juventus. But there was little agreement about the number or duration of these stages. In various formulations, infancy stretched from 1 to 4, 5, 6, or 7; pueritia from 7 to as old as 12 for girls and 7 to 14 for boys. Compared with earlier societies, ours is much more rigidly age-graded. Schools confine children to narrow age groupings, and young people's interactions with adults tend to be limited primarily to parents and professional providers of services to youth, such as teachers and pediatricians. In contrast, in the Middle Ages and the early modern era, the mixing of ages took place in public spaces, work sites, and schools. Many amusements that we consider children's games were played by people of all ages.

Of the stages of childhood development, adolescence is the one that currently attracts the most public scrutiny and concern. Although the word *adolescence* entered the English language in the fourteenth century, it only took on widespread use in the twentieth century. Before then, the term used to describe the teenage years and early twenties was *youth*—a much more amorphous category than adolescence. Not only were the youth stage's chronological boundaries vaguer, but the term was not as closely linked to sexual, social, and emotional maturation. Nevertheless, early modern societies did regard the youth stage as an important period of transition, involving profound changes in social behavior and work patterns. It was during this life stage that most young people left home and began to work as servants or apprentices.

In much the same way that our society associates adolescence with such characteristics as moodiness and rebelliousness, sixteenth- and seventeenth-century England associated youth with certain distinctive traits. Youth was wild, headstrong, frivolous, arrogant, rebellious, and licentious. The young, it was said, were rowdy, steeped in carnal lusts, and absorbed in rioting, swearing, and sensual gratifications. Yet despite the charge that young people preferred dancing, clowning, and play to the word of God, by modern standards, the youth stage in sixteenth- and early-seventeenth-century England was primarily a period of self-denial and celibacy. Youth inhabited a sharply sex-segregated world, with little opportunity to establish intimate relations with members of the other sex. Many of the popular activities that involved mixed-sex socializing—such as round dances, in which partners were frequently traded—discouraged young people from pairing off. Young people also spent large parts of their teen years away from their families and their immediate neighborhoods. Unlike modern adolescence, which is a period of prolonged dependency spent living in their parents' homes and attending school, the teen years in Shakespeare's England involved a much greater degree of mobility apart from one's family, as a servant or apprentice.

Today, a sharp line separates the music, jargon, and clothing styles of adolescents and adults. The line between youth and adults was much more permeable in the sixteenth or seventeenth century. Adults played many games that now belong exclusively to children. Nevertheless, like young children, youth in their teens and early twenties occupied distinctive subcultures of their own. Although youth in sixteenth- and seventeenth-century England and continental Europe spent much more of their time with adults than young people do today, they spent their evenings, holidays, and slack periods in peer-group activities. They participated in organized gangs, entertainments, dress, dancing, singing, and games.

Today, we often think of youth culture as an oppositional or adversarial culture that stands in stark contrast to adult society. In Elizabethan and Stuart England, youth were frequently condemned as rowdy, disrespectful, and anarchic. But unlike youth today, they did not seek self-consciously to prolong youth or glorify a distinctive set of youth values. In fact, youth played a critically important role in reinforcing communal values such as a belief in the need for church marriage and the immorality of adultery and illegitimate childbearing.

Unlike France and other continental societies, sixteenth- and seventeenth-century England did not establish hierarchically organized youth groups (known in France as "youth abbeys" or "youth kingdoms") that persisted over long periods of time. The closest thing to modern youth culture was to be found in London, where apprentices numbered between 10,000 and 20,000 by the seventeenth century, or about 15 percent of the population. In the capital, apprentices formed a distinctive subculture with a strong sense of fraternity and a tradition of violent collective action. Publishers of chapbooks produced a large amount of escapist literature as well as religious literature targeted at this subculture.

Since the late nineteenth century, a myth has taken root that modern society delays adulthood until an unusually late age, and that in the past the transition to adulthood was smoother and briefer. This myth is incorrect. Not only was the transition to full adulthood as long in early modern England as it is today, but it also posed many hardships, demands, and challenges. Young people had to switch between various skills, masters, and working environments. Furthermore, early modern society did not have a clearly defined border between youth and adulthood. Instead, the boundary was ragged. Although the age at which the young attained full adulthood varied, it usually was not until their late twenties that young men married, set up an independent household, practiced a craft, or ran a farm. Young women typically married in their mid- or late twenties.

Like present-day adolescents, youth in early modern England felt frustrated by the delayed transition to full adult status. But unlike our society, early modern England sanctioned a variety of rituals that provided safety valves for the release of tensions. During certain holiday festivities, such as Twelfth Night, Plough Monday, St. Valentine's Day, Shrove Tuesday, May Day, and Halloween, the social order was inverted and forbidden forms of behavior were permitted. Known as "rituals of misrule," these festivals allowed young people to mock their elders, release their resentments, and express their antagonisms ritually and symbolically. These carnival-like rituals of derision and social mockery also reminded adults of the limits of their authority. One of the best-known rituals was barring out. Schoolboys locked their master out of the school and refused to readmit him until he agreed to a set of demands, including amnesty for the boys' misbehavior and a list of holidays and play days.

Youth in early modern England played a pivotal role in enforcing communal norms. Groups of young people, known as "charivaris," engaged in ritualistic forms of hazing and ridicule. To the sound of rough music made with pots, pans, bells, guns, and fireworks, charivaris derided and tormented cuckolds, wife beaters, domineering wives, and squabbling couples. Charivaris hanged in effigy figures of those who offended communal norms. Through ritualized practices such as mock trials, charivaris gave expression to shared communal values, such as the need for marriage in church, belief in the immorality of adultery and bastard bearing, and a commitment to marital harmony under the patriarchal authority of the husband.

The essential point is that compared with youth today, young people in the early modern era played a more integral and influential role in their society than do their contemporary counterparts. From a long-term historical perspective, the most distinctive feature of childhood today is the lack of roles for today's young people and the shrinking avenues available for young people to express their increasing maturity and semiadult status. In sharp contrast, early modern England not only assigned young people a variety of productive roles, but also established various rituals to help the young navigate the process of growing up and to express their inevitable frustrations and resentments.

During the late sixteenth and early seventeenth centuries, adults in Europe became increasingly preoccupied with childhood and youth. This heightened awareness of the young can be seen in a proliferation of books on pediatric medicine, guides on child rearing, and a marked expansion of grammar schools. It was also apparent in the construction of foundling hospitals to care for abandoned children. Child abandonment was widespread in scale in the ancient, medieval, and early modern eras. In a society in which contraception was regarded as a mortal sin, and abortion-inducing drugs were condemned by the church, there were few means, apart from abstinence, to reduce births. Recognizing that many impoverished parents were unable to feed or clothe all of their children, Christian theologians were surprisingly tolerant of the practice. Beginning in the sixteenth century, and greatly accelerating in the seventeenth and eighteenth centuries, foundling hospitals were established across Europe. Unfortunately, gross overcrowding, poor sanitation, and inadequate or careless breast-feeding produced mortality rates of up to 90 percent in these hospitals.

The sixteenth and seventeenth centuries also witnessed an intensifying cultural debate over children's nature and the proper ways to rear them, along with the enactment of statutes and the establishment of public institutions to address the problems of youthful delinquency and vagrancy. For the first time, diarists discussed how they felt about rearing children and provided specific details about how they brought up their children. During this period, a growing number of humanist educators and religious reformers seized on childhood and youth to discuss issues of human nature, authority, legitimacy, and discipline. It was out of this cultural ferment that recognizably modern ideologies of childhood emerged. Both the modern seriousness about childhood and the intensified effort to shape children's character through child-rearing techniques and schooling were products of the early modern era.

Radically differing images of childhood proliferated. One view, which stressed children's natural innocence and purity, offered a precursor to both the environmentalist ideas of John Locke and the sentimental image of childhood championed by the romantic poets. "A child is," the humanist John Earle observed in 1628, "…the best copy of Adam before he tasted of Eve or the Apple.… His soule is yet a white paper unscribled with observations of the world, wherewith at length it becomes a blurr'd Notebooke. He is purely happy, because he knowes no evil."[1] An opposing viewpoint, expressed by the Protestant Separatist John Robinson in the same year, emphasized children's inherent willfulness and depravity. In a frequently quoted phrase, he observed, "Surely there is in all children, though not alike, a stubbornness, and stoutness of mind arising from natural pride, which must, in the first place be broken and beaten down."[2] By the seventeenth century, childhood had assumed a heightened cultural significance. It had become recognized at once as a social problem, a key to social reformation, and a symbolic link to a supposedly more stable and orderly past.

A mounting source of concern was youthful vagrancy, which prompted authorities to hatch ambitious plans to cope with the problem of undisciplined youth. In England, public actions included incarcerating idle children in workhouses, conscripting disorderly youth into military service, and transporting youthful vagrants overseas. A parliamentary act of 1576 provided for the establishment houses of correction where "youth may be accustomed and brought up in labour and work, and then not like[ly] to grow to be idle rogues."[3] In the seventeenth and eighteenth centuries, overseas colonies were used as dumping grounds for vagabond pauper children and rebellious indentured servants.

Puritan reformers were less concerned with youthful vagrancy and crime than with instilling piety and promoting spiritual conversion. In New England, the Puritans were eager to suppress England's traditional youthful culture of maypole dancing, frolicking, and apprentice riots. They aggressively proselytized among the young, pressed for an expansion of schooling, and sought to strengthen paternal authority and suppress sinful customs and rituals. The Puritans published many of the earliest works on child rearing and pedagogy and dominated the field of children's literature until the end of the seventeenth century. They were among the first to condemn wet-nursing and to move beyond literary conceptions that depicted children solely in terms of innocent simplicity or youth precocity. They also were the first group to publicly state that entire communities were responsible for children's moral development and the first people to criminalize the physical abuse of children.

During the eighteenth century, a new world of childhood emerged. In growing numbers, parents gave their offspring unique names, including middle names in recognition of each child's individuality. Well-to-do mothers suckled their own newborns instead of sending them off to wet nurses and stopped confining infants in tight swaddling clothes. Mortality declined as children began to receive inoculations against diseases such as smallpox, and nutrition improved as children began drinking larger amounts of cow's milk. Meanwhile, parents began to spend larger sums of money on their children's dress, education, entertainment, and amusement. Distinctive children's fashions, coloring books, literature, toyshops, and portraits of children sitting on their mothers' laps all spread rapidly.

The eighteenth century produced two new conceptions of childhood and youth with vast repercussions for the future. From the Enlightenment came a conception of the child as a highly plastic creature whose character could be shaped for good or ill. From the Romantic movement came a conception of the child as a symbol of organic wholeness and spiritual vision, a creature purer and more sensitive and intuitive than any adult. The nineteenth-century urban middle class would simplify and popularize these notions, depicting the child in terms of asexual innocence, sinless purity, vulnerability, and malleability. This attitude could be seen in the practice of dressing young girls and boys in identical asexual smocks or gowns and leaving young boys with long curls. It was also evident in a proliferation of children's furniture painted in pastel colors and featuring pictures of animals, and in mounting efforts to shelter young people from the contamination of the adult world.

The nineteenth-century urban middle class embraced a somewhat contradictory set of values. If childhood was to be a carefree period of play, it was also to serve as training ground for adulthood, a time when such character traits as punctuality, self-discipline, and personal responsibility were to be instilled. Unable to transmit their status directly to their children, middle-class parents adopted a variety of new strategies to promote their children's future success. They reduced birthrates in order to devote more attention and resources to each child's upbringing. Meanwhile, industrialization and urbanization took the urban middle class father from the home, leaving the mother in charge; this situation led to new child-rearing techniques. There was a greater emphasis on the maternal role in shaping children's moral character through the manipulation of guilt and withdrawal of affection, rather than reliance on physical coercion. At the same time, young people's residence in the parental home became more prolonged and continuous, usually lasting until their late teens or early twenties. Perhaps the most important development was the emergence of new systems of public schooling emphasizing age-graded classes, longer school terms, and a uniform curriculum.

It is a pointed historical irony that the very years that saw the invention of the modern middle-class childhood combining intensive maternal child rearing, play, and prolonged and systematic schooling also greatly increased the value of the labor of working-class children on farms, and in domestic industries, mines, and mills, and on city streets. Children had always worked, but child labor became more intensive, regimented, and profitable with the expansion of a market economy. In the late eighteenth century, many children toiled in household industries, spinning thread, weaving cloth, making shoes, and manufacturing hats and other consumer products. Their labor helped their families pay debts, purchase consumer goods, and send sons to school.

After 1820, the household industries that had employed thousands of children began to decline and were replaced by manufacturing in city shops and factories. For an inexpensive and reliable labor force, many factory owners turned to child labor. During the early phases of industrialization, textile mills and factories producing agricultural tools, metal goods, nails, and rubber had a ravenous appetite for cheap teenage laborers. In many mechanized industries, from a quarter to over half of the workforce was made up of young men or women under the age of 20. Children also worked in increasing numbers in mines and in outwork (manufacturing performed in individual homes). In the nineteenth-century United States, working children under the age of 15 contributed about 20 percent of their family's income. Meanwhile, in growing cities, thousands of impoverished young street urchins slept in alleyways and supported themselves by scavenging, theft, and prostitution. In the eighteenth century, destitute and delinquent children had been absorbed into rural and urban households as servants, farm laborers, or apprentices. But with the decline of household industries, the demise of the apprenticeship system, and the growth of factory enterprise, these households were no longer able to absorb sufficient numbers.

As early as the 1790s, reformers in Europe and the United States were shocked by the sight of gangs of youth prowling urban streets, young girls selling match-books on street corners, and teenage prostitutes plying their trade in front of hotels or alongside city docks. To care for indigent and delinquent children, philanthropists established charity schools, Sunday schools, orphan asylums, houses of refuge, and reformatories. As an alternative to institutionalization, charity workers in England and the United States also experimented with plac-ing-out systems, sending tens of thousands of street children to farm families in Canada and the American Midwest.

In the late nineteenth century, a heightened concern with child protection was apparent in the enactment of laws to suppress obscene materials that might be viewed by the young, and of statutes raising the age of consent to sexual intercourse from as young as 7 to 16 or 18. "Child-savers" also combated child abuse through the formation of societies for the prevention of cruelty to children, attacked child mortality by establishing pure milk stations, and sought to remove children from the streets by constructing playgrounds. In the early twentieth century, a profound demographic shift took place, sharply reducing the proportion of the population under the age of 15. During this time, western European and North American societies made significant strides toward univer-salizing the middle-class ideal of childhood by effectively restricting child labor, instituting compulsory school attendance laws, expanding secondary education, and providing pensions to single mothers, allowing them to keep dependent children at home.

Around the turn of the twentieth century, age grading became an increasingly significant aspect of children's experiences. Contributing to age grading were a lengthening of schooling, the rise of new scientific and medical theories about child development, the proliferation of adult-led youth organizations, and the expansion of a consumer culture targeting young people by age. Age grading had an ironic side effect: inside age-graded schools, young people would create their own distinctive cultures, revolving around sports, dating, and the peer group.

Schools were among the first rigidly age-graded institutions. In the early nine-teenth century, a one-room schoolhouse might contain children as young as 2 or 3 and as old as 20. The founders of publicly funded school systems in Prussia, the Netherlands, and the northeastern United States concluded that it was easier to discipline schoolchildren and devise a uniform curriculum if the pupils were classified by age. At first, schools were largely confined to children between the ages of 7 and 12 or 13. But after the turn of the twentieth century, high school education greatly expanded to meet the demand for growing numbers of white-collar employees.

New medical and scientific ideas reinforced age consciousness. In the mid-nineteenth century, pediatrics emerged as a distinct medical specialty, and the first children's hospitals were established. Charles Darwin's theory of evolution helped inspire the first systematic studies of children's physical, cognitive, and emotional stages of development. In the 1880s and 1890s, the study of child development was institutionalized, as educators, physicians, and psychologists—led by G. Stanley Hall, Harvard's first Ph.D. in psychology—gathered empirical information about children's physical growth, psychological development, and sexual maturation. Hall became best known for identifying adolescence as a distinct turbulent period between puberty and physical maturity, brought on by rapid physical, mental, and emotional growth; sexual maturation; and an impulse to separate from parents. Contributing to the acceptance of the idea of adolescence was concern about working-class youth exposed prematurely to adult vices and languishing in dead-end jobs, and middle-class youngsters rendered soft and effeminate by the comforts of urban life and excessive feminine supervision. The architects of modern adolescence argued that the best way to promote a healthy adjustment to adulthood was to give adolescents time to mature in carefully controlled, adult-monitored environments, such as the high school, and adult-directed extracurricular activities.

An expanding consumer culture reinforced age consciousness. New consumer products, targeted at children by age, proliferated at the dawn of the twentieth century. There were stuffed animals for infants, who had begun to sleep in cribs in their own rooms. There were crayons and coloring books for younger children; Erector sets, Tinker Toys, and Lincoln Logs for older boys; and tea sets, dollhouses, and dolls for older girls. There were also new book series, featuring such characters as the Bobbsey Twins, Tom Swift, the Hardy Boys, and Nancy Drew, calibrated for children by age. Beginning in the second decade of the twentieth century, high school students developed the custom of dating, in which boys took girls out to a form of commercial entertainment, such as a movie. By the early 1940s, when the word *teenager* was coined, a distinctive youth culture with its own music, clothing and hairstyles, jargon, and demeanor had come into being.

After a global economic depression and a second world war, it seemed, at midpoint of the twentieth century, that the middle-class ideal of childhood as a privileged period devoted to play and schooling was on the verge of being universalized. Yet social changes that would fundamentally alter children's experiences were under way. These included a declining birthrate, which allowed parents and grandparents to lavish much more money on children than in the past; and an unprecedented influx of mothers into the wage labor force, which has led to a marked increase in the institutionalization of preschoolers in day-care centers and nursery schools. Meanwhile, rapidly rising rates of divorce and unmarried cohabitation produced less stable and more complex kinship arrangements. An information revolution gave young children increasing access to information about adult realities. Through television, movies, advertising, video games, and the Internet, they are exposed to sexual innuendo and graphic violence earlier and more intensively than in the past. Other significant developments include the intensive targeting of young people as independent consumers by marketers; expanded roles for teens as service workers; and increasing diversity among the young, produced by global migration and differential birthrates among ethnic groups.

One of the most noticeable developments has been the elaboration of the notion of children's rights. Prior to the 1960s, the concept typically involved enumerating children's needs, such as a right to an education, a right to play, and a right to be loved and cared for. Proponents of children's rights during the 1960s and 1970s had a different goal in mind. They wanted to award minors most of the same legal rights of adults, including the right to make medical or educational decisions on their own, and a right to have their voices heard in decisions over adoption, custody, divorce, termination of parental rights, or child abuse. In a series of landmark decisions, the U.S. Supreme Court in 1967 granted young people certain procedural rights in juvenile court proceedings (*in re Gault*), and in 1969 guaranteed students the right to free speech and expression (*Tinker v. Des Moines*). In 1977, the court invalidated state laws prohibiting the sale of condoms to minors (*Carey v. Population Services International*), subsequently struck down state laws requiring parental notice or consent if their children sought contraceptives, and extended access to abortion to juveniles. Legislation and judicial rulings prohibited sex discrimination in any educational program or activity and guaranteed all children with disabilities access to a free and appropriate public education.

Another prominent development involved the "discovery of risk," particularly the risk of injury from dangerous and faulty products and from physical and sexual abuse. Beginning in the 1970s, parents began to self-consciously baby-proof their homes, install safety seats for children in cars, and require children to wear bicycle helmets. At playgrounds, metal jungle gyms and swings were replaced with safer, if less enjoyable, substitutes. As birthrates fell and more mothers worked outside the home, parental guilt and anxiety over children's well-being soared.

Reinforcing parental anxiety were panics over teenage pregnancy, stranger abductions, youth gangs, and declining scores on achievement and aptitude tests. Panics about children's well-being were nothing new. During World War II, there was an obsession with latchkey children and fears about a purported explosion in juvenile delinquency. After the war, there were panics over youth gangs, radioactivity in the milk supply, and, most remarkably, the supposedly deleterious effects of comic books. But there seems little doubt that the panics since 1970 have been more widely publicized and have had a greater impact on public perception and policy. One outcome was that younger middle-class children had fewer opportunities for free, unstructured play outside adults' watchful eyes.

Another conspicuous development was a trend toward hyperparenting, as ambitious parents sought to promote their children's achievements much more aggressively than in the past. Upper-middle-class parents had long provided children with piano lessons, ballet classes, and swimming lessons, but their efforts became more high-pressured and goal-directed than in the past. Some overbearing parents sought to transform their children into sports stars, while others sought to promote their academic performance to help them gain admission to prestigious colleges and universities.

We live in a time of profound uncertainty about what constitutes a child. Physiologically, young people mature more quickly than in the past. Even young children frequently dress in fashions associated with the teen years or early adulthood. The young also engage in sex at an earlier age. Young people speak knowingly about matters previously associated with adulthood, such as sexual orientation and substance abuse, and the popular media treat them not as naifs but as grownups in miniature. There is no longer a consensus about the proper dividing line between childhood, adolescence, and adulthood. There is great division within contemporary societies about when a young person is old enough to have sex, to smoke or drink, to do paid work, or to take full responsibility for criminal behavior.

In the United States, there have been repeated efforts through public policy to preserve childhood as a time of innocence. Such policies as random drug tests for students in extracurricular activities, abstinence-only sex education programs, and more stringent enforcement of statutory rape laws represent attempts to counteract the impact of permissive culture on young people's lives. By installing V-chips in television sets, imposing curfews and school dress codes, and using restrictions on driver's licenses to enforce prohibitions on teen smoking and drinking, adult society has sought to empower parents and reassert childhood as a protected state. Yet it seems clear that none of these policy initiatives has significantly slowed the transformations taking place in young people's lives. Two pivotal ideas that shaped childhood for the past two centuries appear to be breaking down: that childhood is an especially vulnerable stage of life that must be separated from the adult world, and that childhood dependence must be prolonged to properly prepare children for adult roles.

Much of the history of childhood is actually about adults: their attitudes toward children, their parenting practices, and the ways that they represented children in art and other media. Many of the topics that have absorbed the attention of historians of childhood, such as age consciousness, child abandonment, adoption, juvenile delinquency, and orphanhood, have focused on law or institutions (like orphanages or reform schools) rather than on children's voices and experiences. In the future, the history of childhood will certainly adopt a more child-centered focus and seek to recover children's experiences of work, schooling, and camping; their changing forms of play; and their rituals, like dating, sock-hops, and proms. It will also look more closely at the way children of diverse social classes and ethnic backgrounds have navigated the difficult paths to adulthood. And finally, the history of childhood will become a truly global history that will explore the experiences of children outside of Europe and North America.

THE HISTORY OF SEXUALITY

The history of sexuality is often conceived as the story of its liberation from repression and superstition. There is some truth in this perspective. Scientific and medical knowledge of sexual physiology has greatly increased. Public

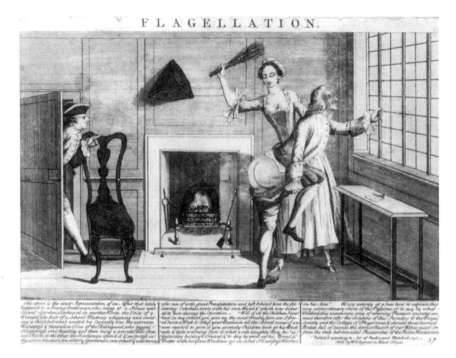

An example of eighteenth-century British pornography. Courtesy of the Library of Congress.

discussion of sexual matters has grown more open, and sexual imagery on television and in film and advertising has proliferated. Women and men wear more-revealing clothing than in the past and have greater access to contraception and abortion. Yet the history of sexuality is much more complicated than a story of increasing openness. Rather than conceiving of the history of sexuality as a story of increasing freedom and enlightenment, it is more productive to focus on a series of specific developments: the emergence of modern conceptions of sexual orientation, the shifting role of government in regulating sexual behavior, and the evolution of commerce involving sex.

The study of the history of sex is no easy task. The historical evidence is difficult to find. Religious and moral prescriptions tell us little about actual sexual practices. The biggest problem is that at any point in time, diverse sexual ideas and customs have coexisted. Yet despite these challenges, historians have uncovered a great deal of information about sexuality in the past. Perhaps the most significant finding is that there has been substantial variation in human sexual behavior and ideas over time. Some societies have condemned masturbation as sinful and wicked, while some have ignored the practice and others have condoned it. Similarly, infant sexuality and premarital sexual intercourse have sometimes been overlooked and sometimes harshly suppressed. Up until the late eighteenth century, many societies believed that women had stronger sexual passions than men. During the nineteenth century, in contrast, many British and American medical and moral authorities claimed that women lacked sexual feelings.

Attitudes toward homosexuality have also widely varied. Greek societies in the fourth and fifth centuries B.C.E. idealized sexual relations involving older men and prepubescent male youth as the purest form of love, and classical Rome considered bisexuality to be normal. According to the historian Edward Gibbon, during the first two centuries of the Roman empire, only one emperor (Claudius) was not bisexual or homosexual.[4] In contrast, toward the end of the twelfth century the Roman Church declared homosexual acts to be sins against nature. At a time when western Europeans grew increasingly alarmed by heretics, Jews, and witches, homosexuality became a capital offense. Yet even at times when societies deemed homosexuality a serious crime, homosexual behavior was often tolerated among a social elite, for example, in Elizabethan and Stuart England. During the nineteenth century, homosexuality began to be defined increasingly as a pathological medical or psychological condition. Not until 1974 did the American Psychological Association remove homosexuality from its list of pathological illnesses.

Another key historical finding is that all societies, including our own, surround sexuality with taboos, moral injunctions, and religious prescriptions. The reason is straightforward: unrestrained sexuality is considered a threat to the stability of the family and the community, to the orderly transmission of property, and to established gender roles. Contemporary Western societies are especially sensitive to nonconsensual forms of sex. They have repudiated the notion that husbands have a right to their wives' sexual services and have grown more aggressive in punishing rape. Modern societies are especially sensitive to the sexual abuse of children. Earlier societies surrounded sexuality with other admonitions and rules. The New England Puritans, for example, forbade sexual intercourse on the Sabbath.

A third major historical conclusion is that in Western societies, sexuality has frequently served as a cultural battleground in which a cacophony of conflicting customs and ideas contended. While one code of sexual morality may have predominated at a particular time, its dominance was often contested. Thus, during its first 1,200 years, the Christian Church repeatedly debated whether clergy should be allowed to marry.

The contemporary United States is distinctive in its contradictory attitude toward sex. American popular culture is preoccupied with sex. Many popular novels and films take adultery, infidelity, extramarital sex, and teenage sexuality as their dominant theme. Television shows bombard viewers with sexual images and references, while providing little information about birth control or sexually transmitted diseases. As advertisers have long known, the most effective way to sell a product is to associate it with sex appeal.

Yet the explicitness in popular culture is combined with reticence in many other aspects of life. Almost all parents strive to hide sexual relations from their children. They feel very uncomfortable discussing sexuality with their children, who learn about sex mainly from peers, popular culture, or experience. Sex education in schools is very incomplete, with many schools adopting an abstinence-only curriculum that provides no instruction in contraception. Meanwhile, public discussion of certain aspects of sexuality—menstruation, masturbation, and infantile sexuality—makes Americans feel uneasy. To discourage early

sexual experience, American society separates boys and girls in many preadoles-
cent and early-adolescent leisure activities.

To understand this mixture of sexual obsessiveness and reticence, it is helpful
to examine the history of sexual ideas and behavior over a period of two millen-
nia. Around the second century c.e., a new sensibility about sex arose inside and
outside the Christian Church, as Stoics, Neoplatonists, and influential church
fathers upheld an ethic of sexual asceticism. Over time, the Christian Church
increasingly took the position that chastity was superior to marriage, that the
only natural purpose of sexual intercourse was procreation, and that non-pro-
creative sexual practices (including masturbation, anal intercourse, and homosexuality) should be punished as sins. Yet despite the high valuation attached
to virginity and the association of sexuality with sin, it was not until the twelfth
century that the Roman Church finally established that priests could not marry.
This was about the same time that the church declared homosexuality a crime
against nature.

Anxieties about adultery, bigamy, concubinage, fornication, illegitimacy,
incest, and sodomy intensified during the sixteenth and early seventeenth centuries, the era of the Reformation and Counter-Reformation. As religious conflict
increased, population growth accelerated, and poverty deepened, deviant sexual
behavior became an increasing source of concern. In one English county, Essex,
with a population of 40,000 adults, some 15,000 people were summoned to court
for sex offenses over the 45 years from 1558 to 1603.

Like their counterparts in England, the colonists who settled British North
America in the seventeenth century made premarital and extramarital sex illegal. But novel circumstances, including slavery, made it difficult to enforce these
laws. Interracial sex among servants and slaves in the Chesapeake colonies
was not uncommon during the seventeenth century. In one Maryland county, a
third of the children born to unmarried white servant women were fathered by
African or African American men. As slavery expanded in scale in the early eighteenth century, the sexual exploitation of slave women intensified. Despite enactment of statutes prohibiting miscegenation, many slave owners in the southern
colonies had sexual relations with their slaves. Thomas Jefferson's father-in-law,
for example, had six children by one of his slaves.

In contrast to the Caribbean and, to a lesser extent, South Carolina, where such
liaisons were sometimes openly acknowledged, in the Chesapeake colonies of
Maryland and Virginia, these relations were usually the source of discomfort.
Meanwhile, in the backcountry, many couples married or divorced informally.
Even in the more settled parts of the colonies, many colonists began to cohabit
following espousals, a binding commitment to marry, which often took place
months prior to marriage.

Although the New England Puritans are often assumed to have been "puritani-
cal" in matters relating to sex, in actuality they considered sexual gratification an
essential element of a healthy marriage. Puritan churches excommunicated those
who denied conjugal fellowship to their spouses, and permitted divorce in cases
of impotence. The Puritans did consider sexual relations outside of marriage a
moral offense and punished unwed mothers and fathers with fines, whipping,
and public humiliation. In general, however, punishments for fornication were
light, and convictions for adultery, bestiality, and sodomy were rare.

In the seventeenth century, illegitimacy and rates of premarital pregnancy remained very low, reflecting the ability of family patriarchs and local communities to monitor and control the sexual behavior of the young. By the end of the colonial era, however, parents' ability to control youthful sexuality had declined. By the 1770s, as many as 30 to 40 percent of brides may have been pregnant on their wedding day. To provide parents with some oversight over their children's sexual behavior, a curious practice known as "bundling" emerged. Parents permitted their daughter and her suitor to share a bed. Bundling provided a way to avoid guesswork in determining the paternity of a child that an unmarried daughter might bear.

By the early nineteenth century, bundling was distinctly out of fashion. Victorian prudery was a defining characteristic of respectable middle-class culture. Foreign observers scoffed at middle-class Americans for calling a chicken breast a bosom and covering piano and table legs with cloths. But far from simply being a period when discussion of sexuality was repressed, the nineteenth century was an era in which sexual attitudes were hotly contested. In Victorian America, a variety of sexual subcultures coexisted. There was a vigorous urban commerce in sex, evident in the growth of commercial erotica such as "French postcards" and police gazettes, which flaunted obscene images. Many cities had red-light districts, and prostitutes openly plied their trade at hotels, saloons, gambling dens, opera houses, dance halls, and theaters. In New York City, estimates of the proportion of young women who engaged in prostitution for at least a brief period of time ranged from 5 to 10 percent.

At the same time, a small but vocal band of freethinkers, including such reformers as Robert Dale Owen, Frances Wright, and the utopian socialist John Humphrey Noyes, attempted to disseminate information about birth control. The most radical freethinkers, such as Ezra Heywood and Victoria Woodhull, advocated sexual fulfillment for women and free love outside the bonds of marriage. Meanwhile, a variety of health reformers sought to distribute information about sexual physiology, much of which was only partially accurate. Some of the health reformers, such as Sylvester Graham and John Harvey Kellogg, spread bizarre theories about the dangerous effects of masturbation.

Challenging the commercial sexual subculture and various freethinkers and health reformers were popular novelists like Susanna Rowson, whose *Charlotte Temple* (1794) called on girls to resist the entreaties of male seducers with chaste virtue. Concurrently, Protestant evangelicals and anti-vice crusaders sought to suppress sexual sin by waging reform campaigns against liquor, prostitution, and obscenity in literature and art. Invoking a concern with child protection, these reformers achieved one of their greatest successes in 1873 with passage of the federal Comstock Act, which prohibited the distribution of obscene materials through the mail. This law banned not only obscene literature and art, but also birth control information and devices. Moral purity crusaders also succeeded in raising the age of consent to intercourse from as young as 7 at the end of the Civil War to 16 or 18 by 1900.

Contraception and abortion also became major objects of contention. In 1800, the American birthrate was higher than the birthrate in any European nation. The typical American woman bore an average of seven children. She had her first child around the age of 23 and proceeded to bear children at two-year intervals until her early forties. Had the American birthrate remained at this level, the nation's population would have reached 2 billion by 1990.

Beginning in the late eighteenth century, however, Americans began to have fewer children. Between 1800 and 1900 the birthrate fell 40 percent and even more sharply among the middle and upper classes. Where the typical American mother bore seven children in 1800, the average number of children had fallen to three and a half in 1900. And instead of giving birth to her last child at the age of 40 or later, by 1900 the typical American woman bore her last child at the age of 33. The decline of the birthrate is such an important historical breakthrough that it has its own name: the demographic transition.

The sharp decline in birthrates is a phenomenon easier to describe than to explain. The drop in fertility was not the result of sudden improvements in contraceptive devices. The basic birth control techniques used before the Civil War—coitus interruptus (withdrawal), douching, and condoms—were known in ancient times. Ancient Egyptian papyri and the Old Testament describe cervical caps and spermicides, while ancient Greek physicians were aware of the contraceptive effects of douching. Contraception was not unknown in the past; it was simply used haphazardly and ineffectively. Nor was the imposition of limits on birthrates a result of urbanization. Although fertility fell earliest and most rapidly in the urban Northeast, the decline in fertility occurred in all parts of the country, in rural as well as urban areas and in the South and West as well as the North.

What accounted for the declining birthrate? In part, the reduction in fertility reflected the growing realization among parents that in an increasingly commercial and industrial society, children were no longer economic assets that could be productively employed in household industries or bound out as apprentices or servants. Instead, children required significant investment in the form of education to prepare them for respectable careers and marriages. The emergence of a self-conscious middle class concerned about social mobility and maintaining an acceptable standard of living also encouraged new limits on family size.

The shrinking size of families was not merely a matter of economics, however. It also reflected a growing desire among women to assert control over their lives. Much of the impetus behind birth control came from women who were weary of an unending cycle of pregnancy, birth, and nursing. A letter written by a sister of Harriet Beecher Stowe suggests the desperation felt by many women who were single-handedly responsible for bearing and rearing a family's children. "Harriet," her sister observed, "has one baby put out for the winter, the other at home, and number three will be here the middle of January. Poor thing, she bears up wonderfully well ... She says she shall not have any more children, she knows for certain for one while."[5]

How did Americans limit births? Periodic abstinence, or what is now known as the rhythm method, was the most widely advocated method of birth control. Unfortunately, knowledge about women's ovulation cycles, menstruation, and conception was largely inaccurate, and most advice writers suggested that the "safe period" was the 10 days halfway between menstrual periods, which is in fact the time when a woman is most likely to conceive.

Other principal methods of contraception included coitus interruptus—withdrawal prior to ejaculation—and douches of the vagina after intercourse. Less common was the insertion of a sponge soaked in a spermicidal fluid into the vagina. None of these methods, however, were especially effective in preventing conception, since each of these techniques can still allow small amounts of semen to reach the vagina. Other popular forms of contraception were heavily influenced by superstition. These included ingesting teas concocted out of fruitless plants, having a woman engage in violent movements immediately after intercourse, and having intercourse on an inclined plane in order to prevent the sperm from reaching the egg or to prevent the egg from leaving the ovary.

Charles Goodyear's discovery in 1839 of the vulcanization of rubber permitted the mass production of an inexpensive and effective birth control device: the condom. But during the nineteenth century, condoms were mainly used for protection against venereal disease, not for birth control. Given the ineffectuality of other methods of contraception, it is not surprising to learn that abortion was a major method of population control. By 1860, according to one estimate,

Around the turn of the twentieth century, sexual behavior began to be displayed more openly, marking the beginning of a sexual revolution that has continued to this day. Courtesy of the Library of Congress.

20 percent of pregnancies were terminated by abortion, compared to 30 percent today.[6] Some of the popular practices for inducing abortion included taking hot baths, jumping off tables, performing heavy exercises, having someone jump on a pregnant woman's belly, drinking nauseating concoctions, and poking sharp instruments into the uterus.

Why were abortions so widespread during the Victorian age? In part, it reflected the general ignorance of the reproductive process. It was not until 1827 that the existence of the human egg was established. Before that time it was believed by many scientists that the human sperm constituted a miniature person that grew into a baby in the mother's womb. Thus there was no modern notion of a moment of conception when egg and sperm unite.

Furthermore, for most of the nineteenth century, it was difficult to determine whether a woman was pregnant or simply suffering menstrual irregularity. A mother knew she was pregnant for sure only when she could feel the child stir within her. This occurs around the fourth or fifth month of pregnancy, and in most jurisdictions abortions prior to this time were not considered crimes. It would not be until the late nineteenth century that most jurisdictions in the United States declared abortions to be criminal offenses.

A number of groups agitated for the criminalization of abortion. These included nativists, alarmed by the fact that immigrant birthrates were higher than those of the native-born, and some pioneering feminists, who feared that abortion encouraged male sexual exploitation of women. But abortion's leading opponents were physicians, motivated both by a concern for women's health and by professional competition from abortionists.

The turn of the twentieth century marked the beginning of a sexual revolution that has continued to this day. The clock had struck "sex o'clock," declared a notorious magazine cover in 1913. Even before World War I, growing numbers of young women in Europe and North America had begun to shorten their skirts, roll their stockings below their knees, and take part in "petting and necking" parties. Vice films, with suggestive titles like *Trapeze Disrobing Act* (1901), seemed to symbolize a revolution in morals and manners. In the United States, women who came to maturity after the turn of the century were twice as likely to have sexual relations before marriage than their mothers. Premarital sexual experience among men did not increase, but it occurred less often with prostitutes. Taken together, it appears that fewer women regarded sex as something disgusting and instead had begun to regard it as a normal part of life.

Nevertheless, bitter cultural conflicts over sexuality persisted. Access to contraceptive information was one arena of conflict. In 1913, the U.S. post office refused to deliver an issue of a New York newspaper because it contained an article about syphilis written by Margaret Sanger. The next year she was indicted by an all-male grand jury for writing about birth control in a magazine called the *Woman Rebel*. In 1916, Sanger opened the first American birth control clinic in Brooklyn, New York, with the slogan "Every child a wanted child." Ten days later, police shut down the clinic and arrested Sanger and another woman, but not before nearly 500 women had visited the clinic. Not until 1965 did the U.S. Supreme Court rule in *Griswold v. Connecticut* that state statutes that criminalized birth control intruded upon marital and doctor-patient privacy.

Homosexuality and oral and anal sex were other sources of contention. Between 1900 and 1920, the number of states where one could be prosecuted for male oral sex doubled to 24. In 1935, Oklahoma became the first state to allow prosecution for oral sex on a woman. In 1955, the American Law Institute issued a Model Penal Code calling for decriminalizing sex acts between consenting adults in private. In 1962, Illinois became the first state to accept this advice. During the 1970s, 19 state legislatures repealed their laws governing private consensual sex acts. In 2003, the U.S. Supreme Court struck down state laws that criminalized sodomy among same-sex partners, reversing a 1986 ruling that had upheld a state sodomy law.

In the years ahead, one major area of historical investigation will be to understand how people made sense of their sexual experience before the development of the modern vocabulary of sexual identity. Beginning in the late nineteenth century, an intricate language of sexuality, involving such terms as *heterosexual, homosexual,* and *bisexual,* arose, which presupposed that people have a distinct sexual identity at the core of their personality. How, then, should we understand earlier patterns of behavior that are documented in letters and diaries, including emotionally intense relations among men and among women, which sometimes involved kissing and caressing and sharing beds? By exploring sexual jokes and anecdotes, popular sexual behavior, houses of prostitution, and other underexplored topics, we can explore understandings of sexuality that predate the medically and psychologically informed concepts of the twentieth and twenty-first centuries.

It is easy to assume that the history of private life is a trivial matter, a chronicle of insignificant shifts in custom and fashion. Such a view is grossly mistaken. Many of history's most significant transformations were the cumulative product of the decisions of individuals in their private lives. The emergence of the emotionally intense, inward-turning, child-centered family; the separation between the home and the workplace; an emphasis on childhood as a carefree period of life devoted to play and schooling; and the widespread use of birth control all resulted from the private behavior of ordinary people. Meanwhile, the elaboration of new notions of privacy, individualism, and personal autonomy, and a new emphasis on friendship and child nurture were also the product of the private decisions of countless individuals in their ordinary lives. Private life is as significant a force for historical change as the wars, elections, and revolutions that dominate our attention.

KEY TERMS

Arranged marriage: A marriage negotiated by parents.

Aunt and uncle: An aunt is the sister of a person's mother or father. An uncle is a parent's brother. An uncle's wife is also called aunt, and an aunt's husband is also called uncle.

Bilateral kinship system: In cultures with a bilateral kinship system, such as that of the Inuit (the Eskimos), a couple might join either the husband's father's family or the wife's mother's family, or form an independent household.

Blended family: The family unit formed when a divorced or widowed parent remarries.

Child marriage: A marriage that takes place at or before puberty.

Complex family: A complex family includes kin other than parents and children. Usually, complex families contain several generations of family members (including grandparents, parents, and children), or contain two brothers or sisters and their families.

Concubinage: The practice in which a husband is allowed to cohabitate with a woman who is not his legal wife. The purpose of concubinage was to provide children when a wealthy or powerful man's first wife failed to produce an heir.

Consensual union: A unit in which couples cohabitating outside of marriage have children and live in a nuclear family.

Cousin: A first cousin is the child of a person's aunt or uncle. The child of a first cousin is a person's first cousin once removed. Children of first cousins are second cousins to each other.

Demography: The study of population statistics, including birth, marriage, and death rates.

Empty-nest family: The family unit formed after grown children have left home.

Extended family: The unit of social interaction that includes relatives who share a common ancestry.

Family: A family is usually defined as a group of people related to one another by birth, marriage, or adoption. In contemporary society, the word *family* is often applied to any group of people that feels a sense of kinship, whether or not they are related by marriage, biology, or legal ties.

Family economy: The pattern common in preindustrial families and working-class families during the early stages of the industrial revolution in which all family members were expected to contribute to the family's support.

Family wage: The notion that a single breadwinner should be able to support a family on the basis of his or her wages.

Fictive kin: Non-kin who are treated as if they are family members.

Godparent: A person who sponsors a child at baptism.

Half orphan: A child with one surviving parent.

Half-sibling: A child who shares either the same biological mother or the same biological father as a brother or sister, unlike biological siblings who have the same father and mother.

Household: The kin and non-kin who live under a single roof.

In-law: A relative that a person gains through marriage.

Joint family: A family form found in Italy, southern France, and eastern Europe in which brothers and their wives and children lived under the same roof.

Matrilineal society: In matrilineal societies, like the Navajo and the Pueblo of the American Southwest, a husband joins his wife's mother's household. In matrilineal societies, a mother's older brother was often responsible for disciplining children and offering advice about marriage.

Nuclear family: The family unit that consists of a father, a mother, and their children.

Patrilineal society: Patrilineal societies, including many in pre-twentieth-century Africa and China, are those in which it is common for a husband and wife to reside with the husband's father and his kin after marriage.

Polygyny: A practice in which men are allowed to take more than one wife. In such societies, the taking of more than one wife is usually restricted to a small elite.

Siblings: Children who share the same parents.

Single-parent family: The family unit headed either by a mother or a father.

Stem family: A unit frequently found in southern France, Germany, and Austria in which a son (usually the eldest or youngest) and his wife and children lived with his parents.

Step-siblings: The children from a previous marriage when divorced or widowed parents remarry are considered to be step-siblings.

SOURCES OF INFORMATION

Etiquette books, self-help manuals, and the popular writings of **Advice** experts on child rearing provide a window into shifting cultural **Manuals** values. While it is essential to recognize that prescriptive litera- ture does not describe actual behavior, such works can be useful in helping us to pinpoint changes in public ideals and in cultural anxieties. Etiquette books, for example, help us understand behavioral ideals, expectations of proper man- ners and demeanor, and shifting notions of civility and delicacy. Child-rearing manuals chronicle changes in attitudes toward discipline, the division of labor between mothers and fathers, nursing and weaning, sleeping, thumb sucking, toilet training, maternal affection, and infantile and childhood sexuality. Readers do not respond passively to advice books, and one of the challenges facing social historians is discerning how consumers of this literature understood and applied the advice they received.

Official censuses and also earlier kinds of data such as parish records provide vital information about key family patterns, including size of households, birth- **Census** rates, and also mortality rates. Changes in these areas are impor- **Materials** tant in themselves and also trigger additional research questions, such as why families might decide to change birthrates or how emotional reactions to deaths in the family were subject to change.

Cemeteries provide a great deal of evidence for social historians. Gravestones not only contain information about birth and death dates, life spans, and family relationships, they also shed light on shifting values. Between the seventeenth and the nineteenth centuries, the images on **Gravestones** gravestones in New England underwent a profound change, reflecting deep changes in attitudes toward death. One can trace a shift from a Puritan perspective, which viewed earthly existence with contempt and empha- sized resignation in the face of death, to a Romantic view, which stressed hope for immortality and reunion of families in heaven along with the importance of grieving. The location of graveyards also shifted. Early graveyards were located near the center of communities. Beginning with the construction of Mount Auburn Cemetery in a rural area near Boston in the early nineteenth century, the modern rural "park" cemetery appeared. This was a place where the living could commune with the dead in a parklike setting. Many gravestones carry an epitaph, an inscription in memory of the dead. Sometimes the epitaph offers a warning to the young. Some express resignation in the face of death. In other instances, the epitaph offers a brief description of the deceased.

Legal cases provide a revealing glimpse into the controversies that have sur- rounded private life. Courts have dealt with such socially divisive topics as bans on interracial marriage, polygyny, common-law marriage, the **Legal Cases** legalization of abortion and birth control, and custody rights of divorced mothers and fathers. The law has also been a battleground in which contending parties have struggled over children's rights to freedom of expression, due-process protections, and access to contraception and abortion. Court records and judicial decisions offer a detailed record of the contest between various conceptions of the family, parental roles, and children's rights.

Oral histories preserve memories that are available through no other sources. They can help us understand what people thought and felt, how they lived, and

Oral History

how historical events influenced their lives. They can provide a family's oral traditions. Careful listening is essential to the success of an oral history. Tone and inflection may be as important as the stories that the interviewee relates. Like any historical source, the information gathered in oral histories must be used cautiously. Memories can be faulty. Inaccuracies, distortions, and exaggerations can creep in. Also, later events can reshape memories of the past. To reduce the possibility of inaccuracies or distortions, it is often helpful to provide an interviewee with contemporaneous records, such as photographs, letters, and newspaper stories, and to check oral testimony against independent sources of information.

Images of the family and of children in art provide an index to shifting cultural ideals and attitudes. Through paintings and portraits, we can see an increasing emphasis on domestic life and on the individuality of family

Paintings and Portraits

members. We can witness a shift from formal and hierarchical images of family life to less formal and more companionate ideals. We can also see how children moved from the margins of family life to its center, how children became increasingly identified with innocence and with nature, and how play came to be viewed in a more positive light. In addition, paintings help us glimpse differences in family life and childhood along lines of class, ethnicity, and region.

Pictures, we are often told, are worth a thousand words. This is certainly true about family photographs, whether they are professional photographs or infor-

Photographs

mal snapshots. These images can tell us a great deal about a family's status, about attitudes toward children, and many other topics. In examining a family photograph, the key question one must ask is, what can this picture tell us about the people's lives and attitudes? Pictures of a family home might tell us something about the family's economic condition and the conditions of their everyday lives. Pictures of family events, such as birthdays, vacations, and weddings, might shed light on these activities.

Much more than mere playthings, toys reveal a great deal of information about shifts in children's lives and about parents' values and expecta-

Toys

tions. Stuffed animals, for example, appeared in the early twentieth century at the very time that infants began to sleep in different rooms from their mothers. During the nineteenth and early twentieth centuries, toys often served an educational function. Intended to prepare children for adult roles, toys tended to be heavily gendered, with construction toys and guns for boys, and dolls, dollhouses, and sewing kits for girls. As the twentieth century progressed, fantasy toys grew in popularity.

NOTES

1. John Earle, *The Autograph Manuscript of Microcosmography* (Leeds: Scholar Press, 1966), I. The Child, 1.

2. Robert Ashton, ed., *The Works of John Robinson, Pastor of the Pilgrim Fathers* (Boston: Doctrinal Tract and Book Society, 1851), Vol. I, 246–47.

3. Act for Setting of the Poor on Work, and for the Avoiding of Idleness, 18 Elizabeth 1, C.3.

4. Edward Gibbon, *Decline and Fall of the Roman Empire* (New York: Modern Library, 1932), Vol. 1, 68 n.49.

5. Catharine Beecher to Mary Beecher Perkins, Fall 1837, Beecher-Stowe Collection, Folder 17, Schlesinger Library, Radcliffe Institute for Advanced Study, Harvard University.

6. James C. Mohr, *Abortion in America: The Origins and Evolution of National Policy, 1800–1900* (New York: Oxford University Press, 1978), 50.

FURTHER READING

Reference Resources

Encyclopedias

Clement, Priscilla Ferguson, and Jacqueline S. Reinier, eds. *Boyhood in America: An Encyclopedia.* Santa Barbara, Calif.: ABC-CLIO, 2001.

Fass, Paula S., ed. *Encyclopedia of Children and Childhood: In History and Society.* New York: MacMillan Library Reference, 2003.

Forman-Brunell, Miriam, ed. *Girlhood in America: An Encyclopedia.* Santa Barbara, Calif.: ABC-CLIO, 2001.

Hawes, Joseph M., ed. *The Family in America: An Encyclopedia.* Santa Barbara, Calif.: ABC-CLIO, 2001.

Lerner, Jacqueline V., Richard M. Lerner, and Jordan Finkelstein, eds. *Adolescence in America: An Encyclopedia.* Santa Barbara, Calif.: ABC-CLIO, 2001.

Ponzetti Jr., James J., ed. *International Encyclopedia of Marriage and Family.* 2nd ed. New York: Macmillan Reference USA, 2003.

Handbooks and Research Guides

Hawes, Joseph M., and N. Ray Hiner, eds. *American Childhood: A Research Guide and Historical Handbook.* New York: Greenwood Press, 1985.

———, eds. *Children in Historical and Comparative Perspective: An International Handbook and Research Guide.* New York: Greenwood Press, 1991.

Hawes, Joseph M., and Elizabeth I. Nybakken, eds. *American Families: A Research Guide and Historical Handbook.* New York: Greenwood Press, 1991.

Turner, Jeffrey Scott. *Families in America: A Reference Handbook.* Santa Barbara, Calif.: ABC-CLIO, 2002.

West, Elliott. *Growing Up in Twentieth-Century America: A History and Reference Guide.* New York: Greenwood Press, 1996.

Historiographical Introductions and Overviews

Anderson, Michael. *Approaches to the History of the Western Family, 1500–1914.* New York: Cambridge University Press, 1995.

Heywood, Colin. *A History of Childhood: Children and Childhood in the West from Medieval to Modern Times.* Cambridge, Eng.: Polity, 2001.

Journals

Child Welfare Review (online) http://www.childwelfare.com/kids/news.htm

Family Relations http://www.iog.wayne.edu/FR/homepage.html

History of Education Quarterly http://www.sru.edu/depts/scc/hes/heq2.htm

The History of the Family: An International Quarterly http://www.public.iastate.edu/~quarterly/

International Journal of Law, Policy and the Family http://www3.oup.co.uk/lawfam/

Journal of Divorce & Remarriage http://www.haworthpressinc.com/

Journal of Family History http://www.sagepub.com/

Journal of Family Issues http://www.sagepub.com/

Journal of Marriage and the Family http://www.ume.maine.edu/~JMF/

Journal of Social Welfare and Family Law http://www.tandf.co.uk/journals/titles/09649069.asp

Marriage and Family Review http://www.haworthpressinc.com/

Private Life (General Works)

Ariès, Philippe, and Georges Duby, eds. *A History of Private Life.* 5 vols. Cambridge, Mass.: Belknap Press of Harvard University Press, 1987–1991.

Green, Harvey. *The Uncertainty of Everyday Life, 1915–1945.* New York: HarperCollins Publishers, 1993.

Hawke, David Freeman. *Everyday Life in Early America.* New York: Harper & Row, 1988.

Larkin, Jack. *The Reshaping of Everyday Life, 1790–1840.* New York: Harper & Row, 1988.

Schlereth, Thomas J. *Victorian America: Transformations in Everyday Life, 1876–1915.* New York: Harper & Row, 1991.

Taylor, Charles. *Sources of the Self: The Making of the Modern Identity.* Cambridge, Mass.: Harvard University Press, 1989.

Wolf, Stephanie Grauman. *As Various as Their Land: The Everyday Lives of Eighteenth Century Americans.* New York: HarperCollins Publishers, 1993.

The History of Families and Children

Classical Antiquity

Dixon, Suzanne. *The Roman Family.* Baltimore: Johns Hopkins University Press, 1992.

Golden, Mark. *Children and Childhood in Classical Athens.* Baltimore: Johns Hopkins University Press, 1993.

Pomeroy, Sarah B. *Families in Classical and Hellenistic Greece: Representations and Realities.* New York: Oxford University Press, 1997.

Saller, Richard P. *Patriarchy, Property, and Death in the Roman Family.* Cambridge: Cambridge University Press, 1996.

Middle Ages

Alexandre-Ridon, Daniele, and Didier Lett. *Children in the Middle Ages.* Notre Dame, Ind.: University of Notre Dame Press, 1999.

Ben-Amos, Ilana Krausman. *Adolescence and Youth in Early Modern England.* New Haven, Conn.: Yale University Press, 1994.

Cleverley, John, and Denis C. Philips. *Visions of Children: Influential Models from Locke to Spock.* Rev. ed. New York: Teacher's College Press, 1986.

Gies, Frances. *Marriage and the Family in the Middle Ages.* New York: Harper & Row, 1987.

Gottlieb, Beatrice. *The Family in the Western World from the Black Death to the Industrial Age.* New York: Oxford University Press, 1994.

Herlihy, David. *Medieval Households.* Cambridge, Mass.: Harvard University Press, 1985.

Orme, Nicholas. *Medieval Children.* New Haven, Conn.: Yale University Press, 2001.

Ozment, Steven. *Ancestors: The Loving Family in Old Europe.* Cambridge, Mass.: Harvard University Press, 2001.

Schultz, James A. *The Knowledge of Childhood in the German Middle Ages, 1100–1350.* Philadelphia: University of Pennsylvania Press, 1995.

European Families and Children since the Middle Ages

Davidoff, Leonore, and Catherine Hall. *Family Fortunes: Men and Women of the English Middle Class, 1780–1850.* New York: Routledge, 2002.

Heywood, Colin. *A History of Childhood: Children and Childhood in the West from Medieval to Modern Times.* Cambridge, Eng.: Polity, 2001.

Kertzer, David I., and Marzio Barbagli. *The History of the European Family,* vols. 1–3. New Haven, Conn.: Yale University Press, 2001–2003.

Opie, Iona, and Peter Opie. *Children's Games in Street and Playground.* Oxford: Clarendon Press, 1969.

Pollock, Linda A. *Forgotten Children: Parent-Child Relations from 1500–1900.* New York: Cambridge University Press, 1983.

———. *A Lasting Relationship: Parents and Children over Three Centuries.* London: Fourth Estate, 1987.

Sarti, Raffaella. *Europe at Home: Family and Material Culture, 1500–1800.* New Haven, Conn: Yale University Press, 2002.

Stone, Lawrence. *The Family, Sex, and Marriage in England.* New York: Harper & Row, 1977.

American Families and Children

Overviews and Interpretations

Degler, Carl N. *At Odds: Women and the Family in America from the Revolution to the Present.* New York: Oxford University Press, 1980.

Demos, John. *Past, Present, and Personal: The Family and the Life Course in American History.* New York: Oxford University Press, 1986.

Illick, Joseph E. *American Childhoods.* Philadelphia: University of Pennsylvania Press, 2002.

Mintz, Steven. *Huck's Raft: A History of American Childhood.* Cambridge, Mass.: Belknap Press of Harvard University Press, 2004.

Mintz, Steven, and Susan Kellogg. *Domestic Revolutions: A Social History of American Family Life.* New York: Free Press, 1988.

Demography

Wells, Robert V. *Uncle Sam's Family: Issues in and Perspectives on American Demographic History.* Albany, N.Y.: SUNY, 1985.

Domestic Environment

Calvert, Karen. *Children in the House: The Material Culture of Early Childhood, 1600–1900.* Boston: Northeastern University Press, 1994.

Clark, Clifford Edward. *The American Family Home, 1800–1960.* Chapel Hill: University of North Carolina Press, 1986.

Colonial Family Life

Levy, Barry. *Quakers and the American Family.* New York: Oxford University Press, 1992.

Lewis, Jan. *Pursuit of Happiness: Family and Values in Jefferson's Virginia.* New York: Cambridge University Press, 1983.

Lombard, Anne S. *Making Manhood: Growing Up Male in Colonial New England.* Cambridge, Mass.: Harvard University Press, 2003.

Morgan, Edmund. *The Puritan Family.* New York: Harper & Row, 1990.

Smith, Daniel Blake. *Inside the Great House.* Ithaca, N.Y.: Cornell University Press, 1995.

Wall, Helena M. *Fierce Communion: Family and Community in Early America.* Cambridge, Mass.: Harvard University Press, 1995.

Nineteenth-Century Families

Faragher, John. *Women and Men on the Overland Trail.* New Haven, Conn.: Yale University Press, 1979.

Marten, James Alan. *The Children's Civil War.* Chapel Hill: University of North Carolina Press, 1998.

Ryan, Mary P. *Cradle of the Middle Class.* Cambridge: Cambridge University Press, 1980.

Werner, Emmy E. *Reluctant Witnesses: Children's Voices from the Civil War.* Boulder, Colo.: Westview Press, 1998.

Twentieth-Century Families

Bailey, Beth, and David Farber. *The First Strange Place: Race and Sex in World War II Hawaii.* Baltimore: Johns Hopkins University Press, 1994.

Bane, Mary Jo. *Here to Stay: American Families in the Twentieth Century.* New York: Basic Books, 1976.

Breines, Wini. *Young, White, and Miserable: Growing Up in the Fifties.* Boston: Beacon, 1992.

Clausen, John A., and Glen H. Elder. *American Lives: Looking Back at the Children of the Great Depression.* Berkeley: University of California Press, 1995.

Coontz, Stephanie. *The Way We Never Were: American Families and the Nostalgia Trap.* New York: Basic Books, 1992.

———. *The Way We Really Are: Ending the War over America's Changing Families.* New York: Basic Books, 1998.

Elder, Glen H. *Children of the Great Depression.* Boulder, Colo.: Westview Press, 1998.

Litoff, Judy Barrett, and David Smith, eds. *Since You Went Away: World War II Letters from American Women on the Home Front.* Lawrence: University Press of Kansas, 1995.

May, Elaine Tyler. *Homeward Bound: American Families in the Cold War Era.* New York: Basic Books, 1988.

Stacey, Judith. *Brave New Families: Stories of Domestic Upheaval in Late Twentieth-Century America.* Berkeley: University of California Press, 1998.

Tuttle, William. *"Daddy's Gone to War": The Second World War in the Lives of American Children.* New York: Oxford University Press, 1995.

Primary Sources

Bremner, Robert H., ed. *Children and Youth in America,* vols. 1–3. Cambridge, Mass.: Harvard University, 1970–1974.

Reef, Catherine. *Childhood in America: An Eyewitness History.* New York: Facts on File, 2002.

Anthologies

Coontz, Stephanie, ed. *American Families: A Multicultural Reader.* New York: Routledge, 1998.

Fass, Paula S., and Mary Ann Mason. *Childhood in America.* New York: New York University Press, 2000.

Graff, Harvey. *Growing Up in America: Historical Experiences.* Detroit, Mich.: Wayne State University Press, 1987.

Hiner, N. Ray, and Joseph Hawes. *Growing Up in America: Children in Historical Perspective.* Urbana: University of Illinois Press, 1985.

Ethnic Families and Children

African Americans

David, Jay, and Bill Adler, eds. *Growing Up Black.* New York: Avon, 1992.

Franklin, Donna L. *Ensuring Inequality: The Structural Transformation of the African-American Family.* New York: Oxford University Press, 1997.

Gutman, Herbert. *Black Family in Slavery and Freedom, 1750–1925.* New York: Random House, 1977.

King, Wilma. *Stolen Childhood: Slave Youth in 19th Century America.* Bloomington: Indiana University Press, 1995.

Kotlowitz, Alex. *There Are No Children Here.* Garden City, N.Y.: Doubleday, 1991.

Patton Malone, Ann. *Sweet Chariot: Slave Family and Household Structure in Nineteenth-Century Louisiana.* Chapel Hill: University of North Carolina Press, 1996.

Schwartz, Marie Jenkins. *Born in Bondage: Growing Up Enslaved in the Antebellum South.* Cambridge, Mass.: Harvard University Press, 2000.

Stevenson, Brenda E. *Life in Black and White: Family and Community in the Slave South.* New York: Oxford University Press, 1997.

Asian Americans

Hong, Maria, ed. *Growing Up Asian American: An Anthology.* New York: Avon Books, 1994.

Immigrants

Berrol, Selma Cantor. *Growing Up American: Immigrant Children in America Then and Now.* New York: Twayne, 1995.

Ewen, Elizabeth. *Immigrant Women in the Land of Dollars.* New York: Monthly Review Press, 1985.

Glenn, Susan A. *Daughters of the Shtetl*. Ithaca, N.Y.: Cornell University Press, 1990.

Howe, Irving. *World of Our Fathers*. New York: Harcourt Brace Jovanovich, 1976.

Latinas/Latinos

Augenbraum, Harold, and Alan Stavins, eds. *Growing Up Latino: Memoirs and Stories*. New York: Houghton Mifflin, 1993.

De Jesus, Joy L., ed. *Growing Up Puerto Rican: An Anthology*. New York: Avon, 1998.

Griswold Del Castillo, Robert. *La Familia: Chicano Families in the Urban Southwest, 1848 to the Present*. South Bend, Ind.: University of Notre Dame Press, 1984.

Lopez, Tiffany Ana, ed. *Growing Up Chicana/o*. New York: Avon, 1994.

Native American

Riley, Patricia, ed. *Growing Up Native American: An Anthology*. New York: Avon, 1994.

Topical Studies

Adolescence, Youth, and Young Adulthood

Austin, Joe, and Michael Nevin Willard, eds. *Generations of Youth: Youth Cultures and History in Twentieth-Century America*. New York: New York University Press, 1998.

Buchmann, Marlis. *The Script of Life in Modern Society: Entry into Adulthood in a Changing World*. Chicago: University of Chicago Press, 1989.

Fass, Paula S. *The Damned and the Beautiful: American Youth in the 1920s*. New York: Oxford University Press, 1978.

Graebner, William. *Coming of Age in Buffalo*. Philadelphia: Temple University Press, 1990.

Graff, Harvey. *Conflicting Paths: Growing Up in America*. Cambridge, Mass.: Harvard University Press, 1995.

Greven Jr., Philip J. *The Protestant Temperament*. Chicago: University of Chicago Press, 1990.

Kett, Joseph. *Rites of Passage: Adolescence in America, 1790 to the Present*. New York: Basic Books, 1977.

Modell, John. *Into One's Own: From Youth to Adulthood in the United States, 1920–1975*. Berkeley: University of California Press, 1989.

Nasaw, David. *Children of the City: At Work and at Play*. New York: Oxford University Press, 1986.

Palladino, Grace. *Teenagers: An American History*. New York: Basic Books, 1996.

Age Consciousness

Chudacoff, Howard. *How Old Are You? Age Consciousness in American Culture*. Princeton, N.J.: Princeton University Press, 1989.

Adolescent Pregnancy

Luker, Kristin. *Dubious Conceptions: The Politics of Teenage Pregnancy*. Cambridge, Mass.: Harvard University Press, 1996.

Vinovskis, Maris A. *An "Epidemic" of Adolescent Pregnancy?* New York: Oxford University Press, 1988.

Adoption

Carp, E. Wayne. *Family Matters: Secrecy and Disclosure in the History of Adoption.* Cambridge, Mass.: Harvard University Press, 1998.

Boyhood, Manhood, Fatherhood

Ehrenreich, Barbara. *The Hearts of Men: American Dreams and the Flight from Commitment.* Garden City, N.Y.: Anchor Press/Doubleday, 1983.

Griswold, Robert. *Fatherhood in America: A History.* New York: Basic Books, 1993.

Rotundo, E. Anthony. *American Manhood.* New York: Basic Books, 1993.

Childbirth

Leavitt, Judith Walzer. *Brought to Bed: Childbearing in America, 1750 to 1950.* New York: Oxford University Press, 1986.

Childhood

Clement, Priscilla Ferguson. *Growing Pains: Children in the Industrial Age, 1850–1890.* New York: Macmillan, 1997.

Cross, Gary. *Kid's Stuff: Toys and the Changing Worlds of American Childhood.* Cambridge, Mass.: Harvard University Press, 1997.

Hawes, Joseph M. *Children between the Wars: American Childhood, 1920–1940.* New York: Macmillan, 1997.

Holt, Marilyn Irvin. *Children of the Western Plains: The Nineteenth-Century Experience.* Chicago: Ivan R. Dee, 2003.

Illick, Joseph. *American Childhoods.* Philadelphia: University of Pennsylvania Press, 2002.

Macleod, David. *The Age of the Child: Children in America, 1890–1920.* New York: Macmillan, 1998.

Mintz, Steven. *Huck's Raft: A History of American Childhood.* Cambridge, Mass.: Belknap Press of Harvard University Press, 2004.

West, Elliott. *Growing Up with the Country: Childhood on the Far Western Frontier.* Albuquerque: University of New Mexico Press, 1989.

West, Elliott, and Paula Petrick, eds. *Small Worlds: Children and Adolescents in America.* Lawrence: University Press of Kansas, 1992.

Zelizer, Viviana. *Pricing the Priceless Child: The Changing Social Value of Children.* Princeton, N.J.: Princeton University Press, 1994.

Child Rearing

Grant, Julia. *Raising Baby by the Book: The Education of American Mothers.* New Haven, Conn.: Yale University Press, 1998.

Hulbert, Ann. *Raising America: Experts, Parents, and a Century of Advice about Children.* New York: Alfred A. Knopf, 2003.

Stearns, Peter N. *Anxious Parents: A History of Modern Childrearing in America.* New York: New York University Press, 2003.

Wishy, Bernard. *The Child and the Republic: The Dawn of American Child Nurture.* Philadelphia: University of Pennsylvania Press, 1968.

Children's Rights

Hawes, Joseph. *The Children's Rights Movement: A History of Advocacy and Protection*. Boston: Twayne Publishers, 1991.

Contraception

Brodie, Janet Farrell. *Abortion and Contraception in Nineteenth-Century America*. Ithaca, N.Y.: Cornell University Press, 1997.

Gordon, Linda. *Woman's Body, Woman's Right: A History of Birth Control in America*. Rev. ed. New York: Penguin, 1990.

Courtship

Bailey, Beth L. *From Front Porch to Back Seat: Courtship in Twentieth Century America*. Baltimore: Johns Hopkins University Press, 1988.

Lystra, Karen. *Searching the Heart: Women, Men, and Romantic Love in Nineteenth-Century America*. New York: Oxford University Press, 1989.

Rothman, Ellen. *Hands and Hearts: A History of Courtship in America*. New York: Basic Books, 1984.

Death and Bereavement

Ariès, Philippe. *Western Attitudes toward Death: From the Middle Ages to the Present.* Baltimore: Johns Hopkins University Press, 1974.

Ariès, Philippe, et al. *Death in America*. Philadelphia: University of Pennsylvania Press, 1975.

Binski, Paul. *Medieval Death: Ritual and Representation*. London: British Museum Press, 2001.

Farrell, James J. *Inventing the American Way of Death, 1830–1920*. Philadelphia: Temple University Press, 1980.

Geddes, Gordon E. *Welcome Joy: Death in Puritan New England*. Ann Arbor, Mich.: UMI Research Press, 1981.

Gittings, Clare. *Death, Burial, and the Individual in Early Modern England*. London: Croom Helm, 1984.

Hallam, Elizabeth, and Jenny Hockey. *Death, Memory, and Material Culture*. New York: Berg, 2001.

Harding, Vanessa. *The Dead and the Living in Paris and London, 1500–1670*. New York: Cambridge University Press, 2002.

Houlbrooke, Ralph A. *Death, Religion, and the Family in England, 1480–1750*. New York: Clarendon Press, Oxford University Press, 1998.

Huntington, Richard, and Peter Metcalf. *Celebrations of Death: The Anthropology of Mortuary Ritual*. 2nd ed. New York: Cambridge University Press, 1991.

Jalland, Patricia. *Death in the Victorian Family*. New York: Oxford University Press, 1996.

Paxton, Frederick. *Christianizing Death: The Creation of a Ritual Process in Early Medieval Europe*. Ithaca, N.Y.: Cornell University Press, 1990.

Stannard, David. *The Puritan Way of Death*. New York: Oxford University Press, 1977.

Delinquency

Kunzel, Regina G. *Fallen Women, Problem Girls.* New Haven, Conn.: Yale University Press, 1993.

Odem, Mary E. *Delinquent Daughters: Protecting and Policing Adolescent Female Sexuality in the United States, 1885–1920.* Chapel Hill: University of North Carolina Press, 1995.

Schneider, Eric C. *In the Web of Class: Delinquents and Reformers in Boston, 1810s-1930s.* New York: New York University Press, 1992.

Divorce

Griswold, Robert. *Family and Divorce in California, 1850–1890.* Albany, N.Y.: SUNY Press, 1983.

May, Elaine Tyler. *Great Expectations: Marriage and Divorce in Post-Victorian America.* Chicago: University of Chicago Press, 1983.

O'Neill, William L. *Divorce in the Progressive Era.* New Haven, Conn.: Yale University Press, 1967.

Phillips, Roderick. *Putting Asunder: A History of Divorce in Western Society.* Cambridge: Cambridge University Press, 1988.

Riley, Glenda. *Divorce: An American Tradition.* Lincoln: University of Nebraska Press, 1997.

Domestic Violence

Gordon, Linda. *Heroes of Their Own Lives: The Politics and History of Family Violence.* New York: Viking Penguin, 1989.

Pleck, Elizabeth. *Domestic Tyranny: The Making of Social Policy against Family Violence from Colonial Times to the Present.* New York: Oxford University Press, 1987.

Emotions

Barker-Benfield, G. J. *The Culture of Sensibility: Sex and Society in Eighteenth-Century England.* Chicago: University of Chicago Press, 1992.

Bushman, Richard L. *The Refinement of America: Persons, Houses, and Cities.* New York: Knopf, 1992.

Kamensky, Jane. *Governing the Tongue: The Politics of Speech in Early New England.* New York: Oxford University Press, 1997.

Stearns, Carol Zisowitz, and Peter N. Stearns. *Anger: The Struggle for Emotional Control in America's History.* Chicago: University of Chicago Press, 1986.

Stearns, Peter N. *Battleground of Desire: The Struggle for Self-Control in Modern America.* New York: New York University Press, 1999.

Stearns, Peter N. *Jealousy: The Evolution of an Emotion in American History.* New York: New York University Press, 1989.

Stearns, Peter N., and Jan Lewis, eds. *An Emotional History of the United States.* New York: New York University Press, 1998.

Families and Public Policy

Grubb, W. Norton, and Marvin Lazerson. *Broken Promises: How Americans Fail Their Children.* Chicago: University of Chicago Press, 1988.

Sealander, Judith. *The Failed Century of the Child: Governing America's Young in the Twentieth Century.* New York: Cambridge University Press, 2003.

Family Celebrations

Gillis, John. *World of Their Own Making: Myth, Ritual, and the Quest for Family Values.* First Harvard University Press paperback edition. Cambridge, Mass.: Harvard University Press, 1997.

Luchetti, Cathy. *"I Do!": Courtship, Love, and Marriage on the American Frontier.* New York: Crown Trade Paperbacks, 1996.

Pleck, Elizabeth. *Celebrating the Family: Ethnicity, Consumer Culture, and Family Rituals.* Cambridge, Mass.: Harvard University Press, 2000.

Family Law

Bardaglio, Peter W. *Reconstructing the Household: Families, Sex, and the Law in the Nineteenth-Century South.* Chapel Hill: University of North Carolina Press, 1998.

Grossberg, Michael. *Governing the Hearth.* Chapel Hill: University of North Carolina Press, 1988.

Minow, Martha, ed. *Family Matters: Readings on Family Lives and the Law.* New York: New Press, 1993.

Girlhood, Womanhood, and Motherhood

Apple, Rima D., and Janet Golden, eds. *Mothers & Motherhood.* Columbus: Ohio State University Press, 1997.

Brumberg, Joan Jacobs. *The Body Project: An Intimate History of American Girls.* New York: Vintage, 1998.

Formanek-Brunell, Miriam. *Made to Play House.* New Haven, Conn.: Yale University Press, 1993.

Hunter, Jane H. *How Young Ladies Became Girls: The Victorian Origins of American Girlhood.* New Haven, Conn.: Yale University Press, 2002.

Jensen, Joan. *Loosening the Bonds: Mid-Atlantic Farm Women.* New Haven, Conn.: Yale University Press, 1986.

Osterud, Susan Grey. *Bonds of Community.* Ithaca, N.Y.: Cornell University Press, 1991.

Peiss, Kathy. *Cheap Amusements: Working Women and Leisure in Turn-of-the-Century New York.* Philadelphia: Temple University Press, 1986.

Ulrich, Laurel Thatcher. *Good Wives: Image and Reality in the Lies of Women in Northern New England, 1650–1750.* New York: Random House, 1991.

———. *A Midwife's Tale: The Life of Martha Ballard, Based on Her Diary, 1785–1812.* New York: Random House, 1991.

Hygiene and Cleanliness

Corbin, Alain. *The Foul and the Fragrant: Odor and the French Social Imagination.* Cambridge, Mass.: Harvard University Press, 1986.

Hau, Michael. *The Cult of Health and Beauty in Germany: A Social History, 1890–1930.* Chicago: University of Chicago Press, 2003.

Hoy, Suellen. *Chasing Dirt: The American Pursuit of Cleanliness.* New York: Oxford University Press, 1995.

Vigarello, Georges. *Concepts of Cleanliness: Changing Attitudes in France since the Middle Ages.* New York: Cambridge University Press, 1988.

Illegitimacy

Solinger, Rickie. *Wake Up Little Susie: Single Pregnancy and Race before Roe v. Wade.* New York: Routledge, 1992.

Infancy

Hoffert, Sylvia D. *Private Matters; American Attitudes toward Childbearing and Infant Nurture in the Urban North, 1800–1860.* Urbana: University of Illinois Press, 1989.

Meckel, Richard. *Save the Babies: American Public Health Reform and the Prevention of Infant Mortality, 1850–1929.* Ann Arbor: University of Michigan Press, 1998.

Infertility

May, Elaine Tyler. *Barren in the Promised Land.* New York: Basic Books, 1996.

Life Stages and the Life Cycle

Cressy, David. *Birth, Marriage, and Death: Ritual, Religion, and the Life Cycle in Tudor and Stuart England.* Oxford: Oxford University Press, 1997.

Manners and Deportment

Arditi, Jorge. *A Genealogy of Manners: Transformations of Social Relations in France and England from the Fourteenth to the Eighteenth Century.* Chicago: University of Chicago Press, 1998.

Bremmer, Jan N., ed. *A Cultural History of Gesture.* Ithaca, N.Y.: Cornell University Press, 1992.

Bryson, Anna. *From Courtesy to Civility: Changing Codes of Conduct in Early Modern England.* Oxford: Oxford University Press, 1998.

Hemphill, C. Dallett. *Bowing to Necessities: A History of Manners in America, 1620–1860.* New York: Oxford University Press, 1999.

Kasson, John F. *Rudeness & Civility: Manners in Nineteenth-Century Urban America.* New York: Hill & Wang, 1990.

Langford, Paul. *Englishness Identified: Manners and Character, 1650–1850.* New York: Oxford University Press, 2000.

Morgan, Marjorie. *Manners, Morals, and Class in England, 1774–1858.* New York: St. Martin's Press, 1994.

White, Shane, and Graham White. *Stylin': African American Expressive Culture from Its Beginnings to the Zoot Suit.* Ithaca, N.Y.: Cornell University Press, 1998.

Marriage

Coontz, Stephanie. *Marriage, A History.* New York: Viking, 2005.

Cott, Nancy. *Public Vows: A History of Marriage and the Nation.* Cambridge, Mass.: Harvard University Press, 2000.

Hartog, Hendrik. *Man and Wife: A History.* Cambridge, Mass.: Harvard University Press, 2000.

May, Elaine Tyler. *Great Expectations: Marriage and Divorce in Post-Victorian America.* Chicago: University of Chicago Press, 1980.

Stanley, Amy Dru. *From Bondage to Contract: Wage Labor, Marriage, and the Market in the Age of Slave Emancipation.* New York: Cambridge University Press, 1998.

Old Age

Achenbaum, W. Andrew. *Old Age in the New Land.* Baltimore: Johns Hopkins University Press, 1978.

———. *Shades of Gray.* Boston: Little Brown, 1983.

Fischer, David Hackett. *Growing Old in America.* New York: Oxford University Press, 1978.

Haber, Carole, and Brian Grattan. *Old Age and the Search for Security.* Bloomington: Indiana University Press, 1994.

Orphanages and Foster Care

Cmiel, Kenneth. *A Home of Another Kind: One Chicago Orphanage and the Tangle of Child Welfare.* Chicago: University of Chicago Press, 1995.

Hacsi, Timothy A. *Second Home: Orphan Asylums and Poor Families in America.* Cambridge, Mass.: Harvard University Press, 1997.

Halloran, Peter. *Boston's Wayward Children: Social Services for Homeless Children, 1830–1930.* Cranbury, N.J.: Fairleigh Dickinson University Press, 1989.

Zmora, Nurith. *Orphanages Reconsidered: Child Care Institutions in Progressive Era Baltimore.* Philadelphia: Temple University Press, 1994.

Sexuality

Adair, Richard. *Courtship, Illegitimacy, and Marriage in Early Modern England.* New York: St. Martin's Press, 1996.

Bailey, Beth L. *Sex in the Heartland.* Cambridge, Mass.: Harvard University Press, 1999.

D'Emilio, John, and Estelle Freedman. *Intimate Matters: A History of Sexuality in America.* New York: Harper & Row, 1988.

Francoeur, Robert T., ed. *International Encyclopedia of Sexuality,* vols. 1–4. New York: Continuum, 1997–2001.

Godheer, Richard. *Sexual Revolution in Early America.* Baltimore: Johns Hopkins University Press, 2002.

Harvey, A.D. *Sex in Georgian England: Attitudes and Prejudices from the 1720s to the 1820s.* New York: St. Martin's Press, 1994.

Hitchcock, Tim. *English Sexualities, 1700–1800.* New York: St. Martin's Press, 1997.

Hodes, Martha Elizabeth. *White Women, Black Men: Illicit Sex in the Nineteenth-Century South.* New Haven, Conn.: Yale University Press, 1997.

Laqueur, Thomas. *Making Sex: Body and Gender from the Greeks to Freud.* Cambridge, Mass.: Harvard University Press, 1990.

Horowitz, Helen Lefkowitz. *Rereading Sex: Battles over Sexual Knowledge and Suppression in Nineteenth-Century America.* New York: Alfred A. Knopf, 2002.

Moran, Jeffrey P. *Teaching Sex: The Shaping of Adolescence in the Twentieth Century.* Cambridge, Mass.: Harvard University Press, 2000.

Peiss, Kathy Lee, ed. *Major Problems in the History of American Sexuality.* Boston: Houghton Mifflin, 2002.

Thompson, Roger. *Sex in Middlesex: Popular Mores in a Massachusetts County.* Amherst: University of Massachusetts Press, 1986.

Single Parenthood

Gordon, Linda. *Pitied but Not Entitled: Single Mothers and the History of Welfare, 1890–1935.* Cambridge, Mass.: Harvard University Press, 1995.

3

The Body in Health, Disease, and Medicine

Jacqueline S. Wilkie

How have human bodies changed over time? How have people perceived their bodies and the bodies of others? How has treatment of the body changed? What caused these changes and how have they affected how people live their lives? And more importantly, how can we find answers to these questions?

HISTORICAL CHALLENGES IN STUDYING HEALTH, MEDICINE, AND THE BODY

Our body and its well-being are fundamental to how we see ourselves and how we function every day. We need bodies to work, play, muse, procreate, and generally interact in the world. The fact that all human beings have bodies that in the course of a life will experience health, disease, and decay is both a boon and a bane to studying the history of these phenomena. When we read Thucydides' account of the plague of Athens, we can imagine what it must have been like to both have the disease and see thousands dying around you. When we examine Michelangelo's artistic depiction of the ideal male form, we can appreciate its beauty. When we read the diary of a prospective mother in colonial New England, we can imagine the fear she might have experienced as she went into labor for the first time. Our humanity helps us think our way into the experiences of people in the past.

But therein also lies the danger. Bodies, like all parts of human life, have a history. Few in the developed world have experienced an epidemic in an era before the advent of modern antibiotics or intravenous fluids, so our reactions to something like the plague of Athens might be significantly different than those of both citizens and slaves in fifth century B.C.E. Athens. Mass advertising and modern media bombard us with mechanically perfected images of human bodies. These images, as well as changing sexual mores, probably lead us to view Michelangelo's famous statue of David differently than he did and differently than Victorians would have. The decline in maternal and infant mortality that has occurred since the eighteenth century has certainly altered the emotional meaning of childbirth.

Some contemporary critics charge that present-day people in western Europe, North America, and parts of industrialized Asia have become obsessed with the body, spending exorbitant amounts of money on indulging, maintaining, strengthening, and attempting to extend the life of the body. They suggest that modern industrialized society, with its focus on material accumulation and individualism, has led to both less willingness to accept the natural decay of the body and efforts to compensate for our disconnectedness from community and spiritual values through indulgence of the body. These pundits often point to less developed, non-Western, and past societies as models of more balanced— one might even say "healthier"—ways of seeing the body. This notion may tell us more about the critics than it does the history of the body.

The twentieth-century epidemiologist and medical philosopher Rene Dubos contended that all human societies in one form or another produce stories about other times or distant places in which people live more natural and, therefore, healthier, disease-free lives. He called this the "mirage of health." Dubos suggested that this notion about a perfect place where all the people are strong was rooted in a natural desire to live a pain-free life. He saw this as a fantasy because in a biological sense we grow physically fitter when our bodies are under stress. Our immune systems develop through exposure to germs that make us sick but don't kill us. Our skeletal, cardiovascular, and muscular structures gain strength from strenuous, but not overtaxing, exercise. Those who have the least experience of infectious disease are those who are most at risk from the microorganisms with which we share the planet. The history of the human body is, therefore, a dynamic one in which human bodies change through interaction with the natural and cultural environment.

Even the shape of the human body has a historical dimension. Much about our bodies, such as skin, eye color, arm length, and such, derives from our DNA, but what we inherit from our parents is simply the basis for what our bodies might be. Cultural factors interact with the basic biological information carried in genes to determine the ultimate shape of our bodies. The kinds of food available for consumption and how it is prepared impact the size of the body in significant ways. Rigorous exercise in childhood, or lack of, affects weight, height, and the onset of puberty. Disease patterns also alter the shape of the body. For example, many people even 100 years ago suffered from rickets, a childhood disease caused by soft bones. Yet now, few people in developed nations suffer from the bowed legs and other deformities related to rickets because of better overall nutrition, greater exposure to sunlight, and the introduction of foods reinforced with vitamin D. Conversely, people in developed nations today are more likely to be clinically obese, having a significantly high amount of body fat. Genetic inheritance, diet, and exercise all play a role in this development.

Such changes in the body seem to be fairly easy to document once someone pays attention to them. We can look at medical records and artistic and medical depictions of the body, and compare clothing and shoe sizes; we can even examine exhumed cadavers to illustrate the changes in the shape of the body over time and in different places. Still, even with modern scientific technology, determining how someone died or what caused spinal deterioration remains tricky. And this certainly tells us little about how people thought or felt about their bodies and disease.

Some changes in the shape of the human body are clearly the result of conscious attempts to sculpt the body in specific ways. Even before the advent of modern plastic surgery and the rise of the multimillion-dollar diet and exercise industry, people have attempted to shape and control the human body. Indeed, serious plastic surgery began over 2,000 years ago in India, with particular attention to reshaping the nose. Some cultures, such as that of ancient Sparta, focused on early physical training of the body to produce an ideal type. In the case of ancient Sparta, this meant creating a soldier with great strength and endurance, and fit wives and mothers for the defenders of the state.

Some of this effort to fashion the body has predominantly centered on beauty and appearance. Chinese foot-binding practices illustrate this tendency, but so too does the use of corsets in western European culture. Early feminist interpretations of both of these practices saw them as signs of the degree to which women in the past were treated as objects to be manipulated by male desire and power. More recently, historians have begun to rethink the ways in which women could have used these methods to assert their own agency and individuality. In terms of foot binding, in what ways did older women participate in the practice as a means of asserting the power of mothers-in-law within the family dynamic? To what extent did the decision to bind or unbind one's feet reflect an assertion of feminine agency, an attempt to take control of one's own life (at least in a small way)? Historians of western Europe have raised similar questions about corseting. One recent study (unpublished as of this writing) of female intellectuals in the Enlightenment has suggested that they embraced corsets as a means of resolving the conflict between current ideas about the disorderliness of the female body and their own claims to being rational people fully equal to men. In this case, the corset becomes a means of signaling the degree to which both the wearer's body and mind are disciplined and restrained.

Many early attempts to alter the body have been a means of self-expression. The history of tattooing and body piercing illustrates how complex this process may be. Until recently in western Europe and North America, only pierced ears was seen as appropriate for the middle and upper classes. Tattooing was associated with working-class men and was often seen as illustrative of their closer relationship with exotic or "savage" races. The decision to tattoo oneself then became a sign of one's occupation or of resistance to middle-class ideas. The increasing popularity of both tattooing and body piercing in recent times may illustrate a continuation of late-twentieth-century youthful rebellion as expressed through the body, but it may also illustrate the way in which globalization is a two-way street. In this case, western European and North American middle-class people adopt views of the body as a site for artistic expression from Polynesian and Asian cultures.

But explaining most of the changes in the body is not quite so straightforward as our study of bodies that have been purposefully fashioned. The chapter on economics and material conditions in this book, for example, notes that since the 1950s the average height of western Europeans has slightly increased, while that of Americans has not. In an era with a penchant for record keeping, this change is easy to document, but what are the differences between western European and American experiences that led to this change? Do European children get more rigorous exercise than American children? Do they have diets lower in fat? Or are they more likely to carry genes for tallness? And finally, what meaning might society make of such a difference? In this culture, height has often been associated with nobility and power; do increases in average height reinforce notions about the superiority of western European culture?

Answers to these kinds of questions require an interdisciplinary approach. Scientific findings about the causes and prevalence of disease can give us significant insights into what things might have affected people's bodies on a daily basis. They can help us make better guesses about what disease a specific outbreak may have been, and can tell us a lot about the sanitary and social interactions that may have contributed to the increased incidence of the disease. Epidemiological studies can help us trace the movement of and interaction among human populations through studying the transmission of disease or of interacting gene pools. Early historical theories about disease as an actor in human history have had to be altered as a result of new scientific findings about disease incidence and transmission. Historians of the body and disease need to be constantly alert to new scientific findings if their thinking about its history is to have any validity.

Still, as one medical historian has recently asserted, bench science best tells us about incidences of specific diseases in particular places among small groups of people. What it is less able to do is give us a big-picture view of the body and disease and how this has changed over a long period of time. Additionally, bench science tells us little about the way in which culture and human choice affected the body and how these changed. Nor can it tell us much about how people understood or experienced what was happening to their bodies.

There are some written records, many quite old, that can help us begin to decipher some of these issues. Each of these written sources has specific limitations. There is, for example, from almost every literate, civilized culture a considerable body of medical writing about the body and disease. If one can master changes in language (and technical language about the body and disease from the past is often very difficult to interpret), it is possible to begin to develop a sense of how people saw their bodies, what kinds of things happened to bodies on a regular basis, and the ways in which people tried to respond to crises. One of the problems with using medical works is that they focus primarily on disease, so we find out more about the human experience of crises than we do about everyday life.

Further, much of this writing is prescriptive. It tells people what they ought to do about their bodies and disease, but tells us little about what people actually did. For example, there is a considerable corpus of literature related to hygiene practices. We can ascertain what experts told people to do in terms of cleanliness and hygienic practices in ancient China, medieval Dar al Islam, nineteenth-century France, or the early-twentieth-century United States. But there is little evidence of what ordinary people actually thought and did about hygiene, because records of this are rare. Common people simply don't write about their daily habits. Some nineteenth- and twentieth-century anthropological studies of other cultures comment on the hygiene practices of their subjects, and social reformers in the industrialized world frequently make observations about the practices of the poor. The difficulty with these materials is that the writers frequently have ethnic and class blinders that make many of their observations suspect. And even if they are sympathetic toward their subjects, they may not fully understand what they are observing.

Cultural intellectuals have also produced materials that help us study the body and disease. From epic poems and other forms of literature, we can learn about the ideal warrior's body, how people overcame bodily limitations, what features of the body were considered sexually alluring, and how people reacted to bubonic plague and other epidemics. Drawings, sculptures, and paintings reveal to us both the development of artistic skill and how at least one group in society made sense of the body. For example, late medieval paintings of the Virgin Mary as the mother of mercy both depict an idealized adult female body and illustrate the fear of those threatened by bubonic plague. Since these paintings were often part of public religious rituals during times of crisis, they may have reflected more than the artist's personal point of view. Similarly, folk songs, grave markers, wills, diaries, and letters frequently give us glimpses at the meaning of death and disease among ordinary people.

Clearly, no single source tells us everything we want to know about the body, disease, and medicine in history. Historians in this field need to use many different kinds of sources to get a fuller picture of what happened, and need to be aware of the limits of each of their sources. They must also be alert to contemporary research about the body, disease, and medicine to better understand what may have actually happened in the past.

RELIGION, THE BODY, AND PERCEPTIONS OF WELL-BEING

Religious studies offer one fairly significant interdisciplinary approach to understanding the history of the body, disease, and medicine. Religious and philosophical ideas are among the most important cultural factors that affected people's understanding and treatment of the body. In many ways, all religions engage in bodily rituals that express dogma in human flesh and bone. Religious rituals incorporating symbolic tattooing, use of drugs, bodily prostration, bowing the head, and other prayer postures all link the individual human body to the spiritual. Many religions seek bodily purity as a symbol of, or a condition for, spiritual enlightenment.

In Buddhism, attaining nirvana requires freeing the self from desire, worldly suffering, and perpetual rebirth—all rooted in the body. According to the teachings of the Buddha, neither indulgence of bodily pleasures nor complete suppression of them through ascetic practices brings the enlightenment necessary for release of the soul. Indeed, complete denial of the body can itself become a desire that clouds the mind. Therefore, the Buddha suggested a middle way of moderation in which the seeker accepts the needs of the body, neither indulging them nor eliminating them. Indeed, the body and life are necessary for enlightenment. Buddhists also believe that some among the enlightened, bodhisattvas, choose to be reborn so that they can guide others toward understanding. Disease, in this outlook, is part of the worldly suffering from which the enlightened are freed and through which the seeker may find enlightenment. The Buddha himself was often described as a doctor whose "way" helped cure the ills of the world and the spirit.

The Chinese religious philosophy of Taoism holds that wholeness in body and soul leads to health, well-being, and long life. Through meditation and prayer, the believer seeks harmony between the spiritual and physical parts of one's being. Disease is seen as arising from inequality between the spiritual forces of the yin and the yang. The traditional Chinese medical system, particularly the practice of acupuncture, draws on this philosophy. In acupuncture, needles are inserted into specific parts of the body in order to manipulate the patient's chi, or life force, and restore balance.

Judaism, like the other major monotheistic religions that followed it, sees the body as a divine gift made in the image and likeness of God. The earliest Hebrew texts support the idea that it is only through the body, our senses, and the natural abilities of the mind that one can develop an intuitive understanding of God. Leviticus outlines hygienic and dietary restrictions that the people of Yahweh were to follow in order to please God. Historians of religion note that over time these ritual practices became increasingly intellectualized, particularly within the rabbinic tradition that arose in the Hellenistic period.

Some early historians of health asserted that these restrictions were actually sensible precautions that contributed to the health of the people of Israel. Beginning in the 1960s, anthropologists and others began to challenge this idea both by noting the way in which some of the practices were not necessarily healthful, and by comparing the tradition to body rituals in other religious systems. These scholars observed that the stated function in Leviticus 10:10, "to distinguish between the holy and the common, and between the unclean and the clean," parallels the use of taboos to create a hierarchical social order that sorts out members within the group and distinguishes adherents from outsiders. In other words, these are more about demonstrating that you belong to the group than they are about physical well-being. Nonetheless, these customs, like traditional practices in other cultures, continue to be described in the popular press and even in the academy as more natural and healthful ways of living.

The three major monotheistic religions—Judaism, Christianity, and Islam—all proclaim that the bodies of the dead shall one day be resurrected. Early Hebrew scripture asserted that the body and soul are indivisible and will be raised again together. Classical Greek rationalism introduced what came to be known as Platonic dualism, an idea that would challenge this belief and affect later Jewish, Christian, and Islamic ideas of the body. Platonic dualism posits a division between the material and immaterial world in which the unchanging immaterial world (the world of the *eidos*) is superior to the unstable material world. In religious terms this came to mean seeing the body and the soul as distinct entities.

Islam, unlike Christianity, has no doctrine of original sin and therefore sees the relationship between humans and God as an essentially positive one. Early Islamic thought concerning the body holds that harmony in the body reflects

God's merciful plan for humanity. Muslim teaching asserts that at the time of the apocalypse, the dead will be raised with their bodies in the same condition as when they died. In these bodies they will appear before God and be judged. This has led to an emphasis in Islam on maintaining the body in accordance with God's will and on ritual purity achieved through ceremonial washing and avoiding contact with unclean things, such as bodily fluids and unclean animals. The good Muslim is held responsible for the actions of his body, and traditional punishments for criminal behavior were frequently corporal, such as cutting off the hand of a thief or removing the tongue of a blasphemer. However, the Qur'an also teaches that illness is not the result of sinfulness nor a matter for shame. Caring for the ill is part of the charity required under *zakat*, one of the five pillars of Islam.

The rational philosophy and scientific thinking of the classical Greeks fascinated many medieval Islamic scholars. Some preserved the writing of the physician Galen. Galen combined the ideas of Hippocratic medicine—in particular, the notion that health in the body results from balance among four humors: blood, yellow bile, black bile, and phlegm. This notion of balance was well in keeping with the Islamic view of the relationship between the human body and God's plan. From Aristotle, Galen adopted the use of anatomic observation and classification, and from Plato, ideas concerning the nature of humans including mind/body dualism. This dualist thinking may have led some of the early Sufist writers to conclude that the body can be a distraction from seeking a personal relationship with God. These Sufists lived in austere seclusion from the rest of society and engaged in body whirling as a means of overcoming this.

Perhaps because of the influence of Platonic dualism on early Christian theologians, Christianity has often emphasized control of the appetites and a rejection of bodily pleasures. One controversial area concerning Christianity and the body revolves around questions of celibacy and ascetic denial of the body as a means of repentance. In the early Catholic Church, celibacy was considered a particular calling that only some were called to follow. There was no blanket requirement of celibacy for the priesthood before the Council of Elvira around 306. Nonetheless, marriage was often presented as inferior to celibacy. The degree to which the Catholic Church's adoption of sexual denial stems from the Gnostics in the late classical period and the degree to which it led to the church to reject birth control, to emphasize the virginity of Mary, and to establish a male, celibate priesthood remains a topic of heated debate. Medieval Catholic mystics often practiced what historian Joan Brumberg has called a divine anorexia, rejecting food as a means of achieving connection with God. In the second book of Dante's *Divine Comedy*, the metaphoric bodies of those repenting their earthly sin of gluttony are gradually fading away as they atone for their sin in Purgatory.

Some historians have suggested that the church became increasingly ascetic after Constantine was converted. One reason for this may have been that, as the church became the established religion of the state, its leading practitioners grew in wealth and power. Denial of the body, in this light, becomes a symbolic punishment to replace the earlier, very real persecution that Christians endured. Such an explanation seems compelling, though it does not fully account for earlier ascetics, nor does it explain the degree to which an emphasis on denying the body was extended beyond the halls of the powerful and the wealthy. Indeed, control of sexuality and dietary restrictions related to eating meat and ritual fasting were applied to struggling peasants as well as princes. The degree to which ordinary Catholics believed the body was a source of temptation is not clear. Some have suggested that the fasting rituals for Lent and other holy days might have been practical measures to eke out meager rations. But other evidence supports the idea that average practitioners may indeed have seen the body as a source of sinfulness. At the time of the Black Death, many peasants willingly participated in passion plays and flagellant rituals that expressed repentance for sin through mortification of the flesh.

Catholics were not alone in their emphasis on restricting the pleasures of the body. Though recent studies of Luther's letters to his wife reveal a hearty embracing of bodily appetites within the confines of marriage and family, many Reformation figures saw denial of the body as essential to the proper practice of Christianity. Protestants rejected the idea that good works that denied the body were necessary for salvation, but they emphasized restricting the desires of the body as part of their Christian calling. In this way of thinking, the body of the believer should visibly show the individual's faith: drunkenness, fat, and sexual indulgence all revealed that one was not at heart a true Christian or among the chosen. Evangelical protestant health reformers in the nineteenth-century United States, such as William Alcott and Sylvester Graham (inventor of the Graham cracker), emphasized stringent adherence to dietary guidelines as a means of purifying both the body and the soul. In the early twentieth century, advice authors for men emphasized what came to be called a "muscular Christianity," which emphasized manly vigor through exercise and sports as a means of demonstrating one's enlistment in the army of Christ.

Recent work on contemporary American Christianity reveals that body concerns remain linked to Christian ideology. At the turn of the twenty-first century, a spate of books and articles on slimness and diet as a Christian duty have hit the market. One tabloid headline shouted "Fat people don't go to heaven." A number of books offer to help the reader grow fit for God. Christian diet programs compete with secular programs such as Weight Watchers for the attention and money of the obese faithful. There has also been a renewed interest in masculine muscularity as a form of Christian expression. Artist Stephen Sawyer has produced images of Christ as a hyper-fit boxer ready to duke it out in the ring.

Though there is a clear association between religious and philosophical ideas and evolving concerns about the body, the degree to which religious commitment of any kind leads to particular behavior in daily life at any given time is debatable. Nineteenth-century Christian dietary reformers were in many ways indistinguishable from their non-Christian health-reformist counterparts. Late-twentieth and early-twenty-first-century Christian diet hucksters make up a small specialty niche in the very lucrative consumer diet market. The depiction of Christ as the epitome of muscular masculinity arises during times when traditional manliness was already at the forefront of public discourse. Finally, the degree to which religious ideas of the body have affected the actual behavior of believers is not clear. Despite the new attention to physical fitness as a sign of one's Christian devotion, recent sociological studies show a continuing strong geographic correlation between high levels of conservative Christianity and high levels of obesity within the United States.

THE BODY IN MODERN SOCIETY

Many studies of the history of the body in modern society take as their starting point the work of French historian Michel Foucault. Foucault proposed that beginning in the eighteenth century, the emergence of modern bureaucratic institutions illustrated a new approach to the body in Western society. To Foucault, the aim of these new institutions was the disciplining of the body. He claimed in his discussion of the evolution of prisons and punishment, "The body ... is caught up in a system of constraints and privations, obligations and prohibitions."[1] In Foucault's example, this disciplining of the body took place in varied settings—prisons, army barracks, hospitals, medical practices, and schools—but each followed the same pattern of examination of the body, observation of the body, and use of notions about what was normal in human bodies to implant the conception of the human body as a site of discipline.

Histories of manners seem to support Foucault's idea. For example, in the Middle Ages, adults in France generally blew their noses on their hands and expectorated both inside and outside. Gradually, the elite came to use handkerchiefs and refrained from spitting indoors. By the eighteenth century, people further down the social scale were being told to use handkerchiefs and to condition their children in this behavior as well. People were increasingly expected to control their bodies in public. Some historians believe that the middle classes were imitating elite behaviors because such standards distinguished one from the common and vulgar. Such manners were a social obligation and were not necessarily associated with health. The germ theory introduced health concerns into this understanding of manners. It certainly contributed to increased pressure on people to conform to social standards for expectoration and elimination, but public health campaigns against spitting and urinating in public simply continue a trend already part of Western culture.

Take, for instance, the increasingly stringent standards for hygiene and personal cleanliness. In premodern society, living a hygienic life meant maintaining balance in the body through generally living well. In this conception, health came from maintenance of harmony within the body and equilibrium between the body and the environment in which it lived. One's well-being came from a holistic interaction between person and place. Hygiene advice in this era was generally aimed only at the elite members of society. Beginning in the eighteenth century, we see the development of advice books for the middle classes that define hygiene as body regimens aimed at hardening the body so it could resist disease and improve character. John Locke in *Some Thoughts Concerning Education* proposed a hardening hygiene for children of cold water, cold air, and light clothing to toughen the body and spirit. In the nineteenth century, the notion that good hygiene consists of bodily regimens that people underwent for health and well-being gained considerable momentum. Proponents of these regimens encouraged people to exert control over diet, exercise, and bodily cleanliness. By the twentieth century, medical advisors, public health reformers, educators, parents, and modern advertising all emphasized seeing the body as a site of potential illness that needed to be properly fed, exercised, and cleaned if it were to maintain its health.

Some historians argue that people in modern Western society simply pay more attention to the body and its functions than premodern people did. It does seem fairly certain that the modern media pay considerable attention to the body and its appearance. Beginning in the late nineteenth century, advertisers joined health advisors and educators in focusing people's attention on the body in order to sell a wide variety of products from soap to deodorant to clothing. Though these ads changed their focus over time, becoming more visually striking and graphic, one of the overall themes of modern advertising related to the body was that one could tell a great deal about people from the appearance of their bodies.

All of this would be interesting but relatively uncontroversial if it weren't for the way in which the body's appearance and nature were used as a means of ordering human interactions and defining the value of particular groups of people. Ethnocentric ideas about bodies have had a long history. Hippocrates wrote about "Asiatic bodies," which begin generally more indolent and slothful than European bodies. Medieval authors wrote about Jewish bodies as sources of plague and illness, though this was countered by positive images of Jewish healers such as Maimonides.

Modern ideas at first glance might encourage a more open view of the body. After all, if one stayed clean, exercised, and disciplined the body in all the right ways, he or she ought to look the way "good" people looked and be able to move freely through society. French children were told that moral character came from good hygiene habits. The U.S. Americanization movement used hygiene instruction to turn European working-class immigrants into good Americans. According to this way of thinking, high standards of hygiene based on the manners of the white middle class created social order.

The germ theory of disease cause, which may have encouraged a decline in interpersonal intimacy even within families, also pushed forward the idea that there was equal opportunity in misfortune. As the title of Vanessa Northington Gamble's study of African American medical practice in the early-twentieth-century United States notes, Germs Have No Color Line. Indeed, much of the public health reform effort in Britain and the United States in the early twentieth century was aimed at providing working-class people with the means to achieve the levels of bodily discipline that middle-class people had already adopted. Some historians have described this as a form of social control, but many among the economically deprived embraced the new standards as opportunities for personal improvement for themselves and their families.

Still, the notion of "normal" bodies also held racial overtones. Some bodies, no matter how clean or fit, remained "abnormal" by social definition. In the United States, racial lines began to harden in the late eighteenth century. By the end of the nineteenth century, Irish immigrants, whose bodies (like those of African Americans) had previously been depicted in political cartoons as apelike, were now "white." And any person with even one distant ancestor from Africa was "black" or "Negro." African American leaders were well aware of this problem and offered hygiene instructions to their racial peers as a form of uplift. The most famous of these was Booker T. Washington's "gospel of the toothbrush." Unfortunately, in the racial climate of the United States, even strict adherence to the rules of hygiene did not free African Americans from the stigma of being by nature dirty, because of the cultural association between whiteness and purity.

Social Darwinists in Europe and the United States asserted that there were fundamental differences in human physiology that accounted for where one ended up both in the national social hierarchy and in the hierarchy of nations in the world. These ideas provided justification for both imperialism and eugenic laws. This association of the body with social fitness was central to the international social hygiene movement that had its roots in the pseudo-science of eugenics. Forced sterilization of people that eugenicists saw as genetically unfit focused on stopping unclean and corrupt bodies from reproducing and thereby continuing to pollute the species. Though racial hygiene went to the most horrific ends in Nazi Germany, it did not originate there. Laws to enforce reproductive hygiene were first initiated in the United States. By the 1930s, U.S. physicians and public agencies performed 2,000–3,000 forced sterilizations each year on those who were mentally ill, retarded, criminals, or members of racial minorities. During the Holocaust, the Nazis used the same kinds of legal codes to engage in mass murder of the Jewish, Gypsy, homosexual, and other "undesirable" populations. Nazi propaganda focused on controlling the bodies of women and preventing childbearing as the means of eliminating racial corruption and creating the master race.

Ideas about women's bodies and sexuality have an extensive history of their own. In 1990 historian Thomas Laqueur wrote a groundbreaking work in which he argued that Western attitudes toward women and sexuality have evolved. He claimed that in the classical world men and women were seen sexually as members of the same single sex, but male bodies were considered perfectly formed and female bodies fundamentally flawed or corrupted. After the Enlightenment a two-sex model, in which women were seen as opposites of men, came to dominate discourse about sexuality. While many historians continue to find this work compelling, others have noted that the idea that males and females are fundamentally different in their sexual natures is present in classical Greece and the Renaissance. Nor is it clear how much ordinary people knew or cared about the idea that males and females shared sexual characteristics.

Laqueur also argued that no matter which model of human sexuality a work asserted, all of them used their interpretation of the female body as a means of supporting the social subordination of women. Ministers argued in colonial New England that women's inferior bodies made them more earthy and in need of guidance from more-rational males. Though in the eighteenth century, feminist political philosopher Mary Wollstonecraft protested that it was society that made women's bodies, character, and minds weak, hers was not the prevailing view. In the nineteenth century, American doctors continued to argue that women were ruled by their bodies and girls should limit study during adolescence and menstruation. Studying difficult and taxing subjects such as physics at such times could lead to deformed ovaries or insanity. The manufacturers of Lydia Pinkham's opiate-laced patent medicine advertised it to parents as a cure for girls whose bodies collapsed under the pressure of studying math and history.

Wollstonecraft also noted that women were taught from an early age to care more about the appearance of their bodies than the fitness of their minds. Other historians have noted an eighteenth-century shift, initially in Europe, in rating women, rather than male aristocrats, as having particular responsibility for being beautiful. Women were to cultivate beauty as a means of captivating men who would protect and support them. It is certainly true that both masculine and feminine beauty is a significant part of the history of the body. Contemporary pundits would have us believe that judging women as worthy on the basis of their adherence to social standards of beauty is a modern phenomenon linked to mass advertising's creation of false, unattainable images of perfect human bodies. Historical study indicates that the degree to which we do this may be greater than in the past, but that judging women on the basis of their physical beauty has often been an important part of human social interaction at least among the elite.

What is different, of course, is what people see as beautiful. In traditional Hawaiian culture, the *ali'i*, or nobility, admired tall, physically strong, heavy-set men and women. The first Europeans to encounter them were often taken aback by their size and described them as giants. As western Europeans and Americans became more influential in the islands, paler, smaller, more delicate, and perchance underfed women became the model of beauty. Perhaps partly as a result of the Hawaiian nationalist movement, Hawaiian artists have begun to resurrect the traditional image of large, voluptious women as beautiful.

Clearly, many factors have affected the historical understanding of the human body. Religion, medicine, socioeconomic patterns, racial attitudes, notions of sexuality, and beauty all have an impact on the history of the body. Understanding this history may help us all accept the human body as a complex part of everyday life.

DISEASE IN HISTORY

Disease may indeed be a constant in human existence, but because human beings are part of a dynamic biological system, our experiences of disease and its impact on human society have an important historical dimension. Skeletal remains indicate that some diseases, such as chicken pox, have been part of human experience for a very long time, at least in Europe, Asia, and Africa. But most of the ailments humanity suffers from do not leave traces of themselves in human remains. Most of what we know about disease in the past comes from written records. As a result, historians of disease know more about epidemic disease than they do about endemic ailments since cultural elites often recorded such dramatic events. The *Epic of Gilgamesh* and the Hebrew Bible record a number of incidents of pestilence. Thucydides described in great detail the epidemic that struck Athens during the Peloponnesian War. Scholars in ancient China frequently recorded information on epidemic outbreaks. Bubonic plague figures largely in the literature of medieval Europe. Even in recent times epidemic diseases produce more records than our day-to-day ailments. The 1919 influenza pandemic spawned a varied and widely disseminated literature. And many have written about both the scientific study and the personal experiences of polio, cancer, and AIDS.

Many contemporary epidemiologists are fascinated by ancient descriptions of disease and have attempted to diagnose in modern terms what these ailments really were. Though this tends to be fairly antiquarian in its nature, it is also part of a continuing sense of how diseases play an important part in the political history of the world. Such scholars argue that ancient Athens might have been able to win the Peloponnesian War were it not for the plague. They raise questions about the role disease has played in the conduct of most prominent military conflicts. Certainly, prior to World War II most soldiers died from disease acquired in and spread by the movement of large armies than died of battlefield wounds. Other historians note that diseases affected the accomplishments of many great leaders, such as Alexander the Great, who died at a young age from an unknown ailment. Still, such studies give us little sense of how most people experienced disease in their everyday lives.

In the mid-twentieth century, epidemiologists and historians became concerned with discovering how nonepidemic diseases affected large populations. At first glance it appeared to historians of disease that the general pattern in western European and North American history was one in which infectious diseases, particularly those that attacked infants and children, accounted for the majority of mortality in preindustrial society. While these degenerative diseases, like some cancers and Alzheimer's disease, was the price we paid for the increased longevity of industrial society. It is certainly true that this account of disease incidence has considerable explanatory power.

Yet a number of questions about this pattern remain. Early historians of disease accepted that the decline in mortality in the modern era was the result of improved medicine, but by the 1970s and 1980s many epidemiologists argued that improvements in medicine had little to do with improved resistance to infectious disease before the introduction of antibiotics in the late 1930s. Thomas McKeown was one of the most influential of these scholars. As an epidemiologist and physician, McKeown was particularly concerned with discovering what caused this shift away from infectious disease in order to use this knowledge to improve health conditions in underdeveloped nations where infection remained a threat. He argued that improved nutrition of mothers and infants lay at the heart of this shift in disease burden, and he remained optimistic that reforms could prevent what he saw as the disease of poverty without great transfers of medical technology.

Though McKeown's work remains significant, his conclusions are now under serious challenge from both demographers and public health historians. These new studies indicate that in the eighteenth and nineteenth centuries, cultural changes affecting disease prevalence, public sanitary reforms, and improved nutrition all played a role in the declining impact of infectious disease. In the nineteenth century in particular, public health and sanitary reformers in England and the United States appear to have played a significant part in the eradication of serious infectious illnesses such as whooping cough, measles, scarlet fever, diphtheria, smallpox, typhoid, typhus, and tuberculosis. Though these reformers frequently held a scientifically mistaken theory that dirt caused contagion, their efforts to remove dirt also meant that exposure to germs, and therefore infection, decreased. Finally, recent work suggests that at least in the twentieth century, medical improvements have had a significant impact.

Other historians are exploring where other kinds of ailments fit into this more general picture of declining infection and increasing degeneration. As new scientific and historical evidence comes available, this earlier view of the shifting pattern of disease has had to be altered. For example, scientific evidence indicates that increases in some diseases, such as heart disease and diabetes, are probably the result of a combination of genetic inheritance, lifestyle decisions, and increased longevity. It also appears that low-grade, long-term inflammation in the body may contribute to deaths from heart failure. Other diseases, such as some forms of cancer, are now thought to have viral origins. In other words, they are caused by a combination of infection and degeneration that we do not fully understand. Longevity may be only one factor in the rise of diseases previously thought to be exclusively caused by degeneration.

Occupational and culturally induced ailments have also gained considerable attention during the last century, primarily because of the concerns of reformers about the harm being caused to people by industry and its byproducts. Recent studies suggest that a significant cost of modern manufacturing techniques is the harm it has caused to the human body, both in terms of direct injury and in the degradation of the environment. Public policy interests drive some of this concern with the harm caused by industry. Historical study of the public response to cancer incidence around the Love Canal in western New York reveals how the desire of residents and reformers to place blame often takes precedence in the historical records over careful epidemiological study. Clearly, understanding that chemical pollution may be only one of many factors causing a child's cancer is little comfort to a parent. Nor does the scientific understanding that such pollution is a necessary but insufficient factor in increased disease incidence mitigate the responsibility of chemical companies.

Still, this does not necessarily mean that this kind of disease is exclusive to modern industry. When we look at the past with our increased sensitivity to the ways in which what we do and how we do it may harm us, historians are now seeing incidents of this kind of disease in many places at many times. Hippocrates noted higher incidents of lead poisoning among miners. Traditional Chinese farmers suffered from particular kinds of parasitic infections due to working conditions. Historians of ancient Rome debate the degree to which lead poisoning from the water delivery systems may have sapped the energy of the republic and made it more susceptible to northern invaders. Are the higher rates of death from tropical ailments among European soldiers stationed in Africa, Asia, and the Caribbean during the Imperial Era a form of occupational illness?

As the question above illustrates, answers to demographic questions have serious political implications. One of the most politically volatile debates in terms of the impact of disease on history revolves around the epidemiological disasters that followed the first European encounters with the indigenous peoples of the Americas and the Pacific. From the end of the fifteenth century, as European people moved out of their home countries, they carried with them diseases to which they had developed a certain degree of immunity. As they traveled to the Western Hemisphere and throughout the Pacific, where people had been isolated for a long time from the ailments that were endemic to Africa, continental Asia, and Europe, European diseases killed scores of indigenous people. Demographic scholars estimate that the global population decline from these encounters was 20 to 1 in the first 100 years after contact, but these numbers remain educated guesses and are extremely controversial.

Take, for example, the experience in Hawaii. The travel accounts of the first Europeans who came to Hawaii provided the documentary evidence on which the first estimates of Hawaii's precontact population were calculated. These earliest estimates led to the conclusion that the total population was 250,000 to 400,000 in the entire island chain. Later demographers challenged the reliability of the travel accounts, which were in many ways biased by the travelers' failure to leave the coastline and their ethnocentric attitudes toward native peoples. This second generation of demographers used comparative techniques based on studies of disease impact in other Pacific islands as well as the archeological record. They proposed that the precontact population of Hawaii was around 800,000. Yet the controversy is not dead. Recently, scholars in the employ of the state government have asserted that comparison of Hawaii to islands in the eastern Pacific is invalid and, using the same archeological evidence and a reassessment of the early travel accounts, they have argued that the estimate of 250,000 to 400,000 is more accurate.

Within 100 years after first contact, the native population of Hawaii numbered only 48,000. Given this, what difference does it really make if the population was originally 250,000 or 800,000? Clearly, the demographic impact was devastating in either case. The reason that scholars still pursue these questions is largely the result of contemporary political concerns. The demographic tragedy made the government and the people of Hawaii susceptible not only to disease but to foreign domination. Hawaiian nationalists use the higher estimate of precontact population to bolster claims for greater political autonomy and the need for special status for those of indigenous descent. The different estimates also raise questions of moral responsibility. The amount of decline from the lower estimate to the 48,000 in the 1878 census can be explained as an "unintentional" genocide caused almost exclusively by disease, including infertility as a result of venereal infection. The greater decline might indicate that disease was only one factor and that more-intentional forms of genocide were also at work. Such questions are present in demographic debates about North and South America, Australia and New Zealand, and the other Pacific Islands.

Within the debate of the impact of global exploration on the transmission of disease, most of the attention has been on the impact of European diseases on indigenous peoples. When any attention was paid to the impact on European explorers, there seemed to be little to talk about, at least in the Americas and the Pacific. Indeed, there seemed to be a great irony that American foodstuffs such as maize and potatoes may have bolstered the European immunological advantage by improving their nutrition. Recently, historians of European imperialism in Africa and Asia have begun to reexamine the role that disease may have played there. British and French soldiers in the tropics had a rate of death due to disease that was twice that of their counterparts stationed in Europe. The pattern of disease incidence was different as well. British soldiers in the West Indies, Africa, and Southern India suffered disproportionately from diarrhea diseases, whereas in Britain, soldiers died more frequently from lung disease. These disease patterns led medical officers to engage in practical sanitary measures to combat the illnesses, including moving troops to higher ground and improving water supply and sewage systems. While the higher mortality rate did not undermine the imperial enterprise in the same way that European plagues devastated the population of the Americas and the Pacific, it did affect the structure of imperial governments and the conduct of local military affairs.

Clearly, disease has had a significant impact on the way people lived their daily lives. Though we are still trying to figure out how ordinary illnesses, such as colds, may have affected people, it is pretty clear that the major catastrophic illnesses described here had very important consequences for people. Among the powerful, prominent leaders died before they finished their work. Armies of conquest were stopped in their tracks by outbreaks of typhus or cholera. Ordinary lives were affected as well. The bubonic plague in Europe in the Middle Ages had long-term economic effects because it significantly reduced the population. The price of labor went up, formerly cultivated fields returned to woodlands and scrub, and those who survived appear to have become more pious. As entire populations were decimated by the introduction of new ailments, civilizations died out. In Hawaii, the native population was so quickly decimated that it was unable to maintain its traditional method of agriculture. Venereal diseases further compounded Hawaiians' difficulties by creating high levels of infertility that in turn may have heightened the Hawaiian desire for and indulgence of children. Modern American and European intellectuals may have grown more cynical about technology and human progress in the wake of both World War I and the influenza pandemic. Still, we are only beginning to understand the effects of harrowing epidemics in human history, and we know even less about the role of ordinary diseases in the day-to-day lives of average people.

While major patterns of disease, including epidemics, legitimately command the greatest historical attention, advances have also occurred in interpreting diseases that have a stronger cultural component. Late in the eighteenth century, for example, in western Europe and the United States, authorities began to identify a type of hysterical paralysis that particularly affected younger women. The disease, which had no apparent physical causation, may have reflected new concerns about facing public life, as urbanization and other developments generated rapid change and unfamiliar surroundings. The disease remained common until about the 1920s, when it virtually disappeared. Historians have also worked on explaining the origins of modern anorexia nervosa, first identified in the 1860s. There is a rich literature on outright mental illness and its treatment, including a clear decline in the tolerance for eccentric behavior in modern times and a corresponding tendency to label eccentric people as "ill." Cultural components of even clearly physical diseases—the different ways societies react to heart disease compared to cancer, for example, or the extent to which a disease is seen as a result of bad personal habits—merit attention as well. Finally, work on the history of modern dieting and the rise of obesity involves the food industry, body imagery, and larger issues of self-control in a complex combination.

MEDICINE IN HISTORY

The earliest efforts to understand the evolving role of medicine in history could best be described as celebratory tales of great doctors in Europe and America who were portrayed as heroic conquerors of disease. Many of these works were written by retired doctors, for doctors, about doctors. The titles reveal a great deal about this approach to the subject: *From Magic to Science*, *Stalkers of Pestilence* and (my favorite of this genre) *The Lame, the Halt and the Blind*. In this last account, real medicine begins with Hippocrates and Galen, or the classical Greek physicians. The ancient Greek practitioners were presented as both mistaken in their technical understanding of the mechanisms of disease and visionary in their laying the foundation on which modern medicine was built. Medicine then goes into decline from the end of the golden age of Athens until the Renaissance, when the great anatomists and physiologists began to trace and record the basic structure of the human body. After a side excursion into the early history of vaccination, such works then skip ahead to the mid-nineteenth century to Pasteur and Koch and the emergence of the germ theory of disease cause, at which point "modern progressive medicine" emerges. This is followed by great discoveries in diagnostic technology, such as the X-ray, and in surgical techniques including antisepsis and anesthesia. More-recent versions of this storyline add in the discovery of antibiotics and the emergence of medical specialties practiced in great hospitals. It is certainly true that many of the events historians in this mode described were of great benefit in the treatment of human disease. Nonetheless, the amusing and shocking tales these medical authors presented did not adequately explain much of what occurred in the history of medicine.

Even in the narrow field of great ideas in medicine there was considerably more going on than we previously understood. For example, even if we were to accept the argument that modern scientific medicine is a direct descendant of the classical Greek physicians, the story as told this way leaves out significant components to the tale. Some of these early medical histories attended to the Code of Hammurabi or the influences of ancient Middle Eastern civilizations on the development of Greek medicine, but most did not. Additionally, they frequently ignored the fundamental role played by Islamic scholars in the preservation, modification, and transmission of classical Greek medicine.

Islamic medical understanding, like much of the earliest work, was divided between scholarly philosophy about the nature of the body and disease that modified classical Greek ideas, and practical treatment based on observation and trial and error. Arabic writing incorporated the pursuit of health and religious purity. For example, Ibn Butlan, an Arabic Christian, in his eleventh-century *Almanac of Health* described the nature of the body and its ailments in terms of the need for balance among the four natural humors, but he also prescribed adherence to a diet determined by the individual's work and climate, regular exercise, sufficient sleep, daily washing, daily bowel evacuation, and weekly bathing in order to maintain health.

One of the most important challenges to the standard great-doctor history of medicine has been efforts to look at alternative systems with a more judicious eye. In the great-doctor accounts of the history of medicine, traditional and non-Western medical systems were portrayed as backward and superstitious approaches to be overcome by scientific efforts. Contemporary interest in alternative medicine has led to a reexamination of medical practices outside the Western tradition. Acupuncture has a long history, having been plied for over 2,000 years from the time of its origin in ancient China. By the seventh and eighth centuries A.D., it had spread from China to Korea and Japan, where it was an important component of mainstream medicine. European missionaries and merchants brought a rudimentary knowledge of acupuncture back with them in the sixteenth and seventeenth centuries. Though acupuncture was practiced by a number of doctors in Britain and the United States in the early nineteenth century, until the end of the twentieth century it was frequently treated as a form of quackery.

As Western medical missionaries began to enter China in the late nineteenth century, the effectiveness of traditional Chinese medicine, including acupuncture, was called into question. Several factors contributed to this. First, doctors trained in modern Western medicine were able to perform surgeries that were not possible within traditional Chinese practice. Additionally, the germ theory called into question some of the uses of acupuncture and traditional practices in the treatment of infectious illnesses. For example, in 1911 and 1921, bubonic plague broke out in Manchuria. During these outbreaks it became clear that Western methods (even before the advent of antibiotics) were more effective in halting the disease than traditional Chinese medicine. Indeed, it became clear that the use of acupuncture may have contributed to spreading the disease. Because of these and similar incidents, Chinese leaders began to establish schools of Western medicine to counter what many came to see as Chinese backwardness in the physical arts.

The case of traditional versus modern Western medicine in China illustrates how medicine is both a product of particular cultural circumstances and the way in which medicine can become an element in political discourse. Under the Guomindang in the early twentieth century, the development of Western medical systems was supported by cultural elites as a means of making China modern. In the early Communist regime, such an agenda was both politically and economically unviable. Communists created a system of "barefoot doctors" (probably comparable to the introduction of physician's assistants in the United States in recent times), who were trained in low-cost and low-tech public health interventions and in traditional Chinese medical practice. Only in urban areas were there Western-style hospitals, and even then they frequently relied on a combination of Western and traditional Chinese medicine. The political upheaval in China in the twentieth century also meant that many Chinese doctors fled to Europe and the United States and brought their traditional skills with them. As the limits of modern scientific medicine became more apparent in the West, attention turned to the methods of Chinese medicine. Though there is little scientific support for many of the claims of traditional acupuncture, many leading medical institutions in the United States and Europe have begun to incorporate an adapted form of acupuncture into their regimens, particularly for pain management and treatment of the inflammation common in arthritis.

The more sympathetic interpretation of acupuncture is part of an overall shift in the nature of historical studies of medicine. Great-doctor histories often assumed an automatic dispersion of great discoveries and inextricably link progress in medicine with improvements in health. In the post–World War II era, historians began to believe that the great-doctor approach of chronologically listing changes in medical science at the apex of the profession paid too little attention to the gap between discovery and widespread use of medical innovations. By the mid-twentieth century, other historians of medicine, particularly in Great Britain, expanded their narratives to include social influences on the development of medicine. In this approach, historians attended to both significant changes in medical ideas and practice and the role of medicine in society. These historians included changes in Western medical philosophy, descriptions of typical medical care, the evolution of medical education, and the activities of public health reformers. Others focus on the emergence and development of medical institutions such as medical schools, hospitals, medical insurance, government agencies, and pharmaceutical companies. Much of this still supported the idea of ultimate medical progress, but such historians attributed such progress to both scientific and social change.

Other efforts to understand medicine as a discipline have focused on the men who practiced the art every day and the efforts they made to change, perhaps to improve, their vocation. Research indicates that more than scientific or intellectual evolution brought about the tremendous change in medicine over the last few centuries. Some of the contemporary worship of medicine is the result of the active efforts of nineteenth- and twentieth-century medical practitioners to upgrade their own social and economic status. Studies show that medical men set out to improve public perceptions through associations to eliminate public disagreement, licensing to control entrance into the occupation, and educational standardization to raise the caliber of practice. While these efforts may not have been totally successful before the advent of scientific medicine, attention to such demonstrates the importance of these conscious attempts to professionalize medicine.

Some of this attention to the conscious efforts of physicians to elevate themselves among the professions arose from increasing discontent with medicine as it was practiced (a discontent that ordinary people may have expressed through increasing lawsuits against physicians for malpractice). One of the first studies of professionalization in the United States purposefully set out to discover how alternative medical systems were eliminated through physicians' conscious efforts, which some scholars saw as predominantly mercenary. Studies of medical societies in Wisconsin and England indicate that both self-interest and public concern played an important part in the establishment of medical associations. These historians conclude that economic self-interest was certainly a factor in the development of these associations, but they also served broader needs by providing doctors with a sense of comradery and establishing a means for bringing about medical and public health reforms that would benefit both society and medicine.

Such work provides a valuable description of the changing medical world of the late nineteenth century, in which early chiropractic practitioners, dietary reforms such as Sylvester Graham, proponents of hydropathy (treating disease with elaborate bathing systems), all challenged orthodox doctors and competed for the public's medical dollars. On the other hand, while research on medical sects indicates that irregular practitioners did lose some prestige and/or joined orthodox physicians with the advent of "scientific" medicine, this appears to be a *minor* issue in the history of irregular practice. Recent attention to alternative medicine indicates that sectarian medical practice continued to exist within some communities—such as the continued use of traditional midwives in Milwaukee, Wisconsin, well into the twentieth century—because it provided services to the community that orthodox care could or would not provide. In France, practitioners of alternative health systems, often described by standard medical treatise as quackery, persisted alongside orthodox practice despite medical efforts to eliminate these competitors. Studies of this phenomenon indicate that efforts to repress illegal practice played only a small role in spreading acceptance of official medicine among the French peasantry, and that higher standards of public education and urbanization were more important influences than medical police efforts.

Other historians of alternative practice are less concerned with efforts to eliminate it than with understanding what it tells us about people's understanding of medicine. The ineffectiveness of orthodox medical practice was at the center of the nineteenth-century struggle over the best kind of medicine for people to use. In ordinary practice in the era before antisepsis and sanitary measures, the most effective doctors were probably those who intervened the least in the body's own healing processes. Orthodox practice frequently consisted of heroic efforts that employed toxic substances (such as mercury in calomel), bleeding, and purging and leeching to combat acute illness. In many cases the cure may have been worse than the disease. Historians of medical systems rooted in the home have noted that, at first, physicians and domestic practitioners saw their roles as complementary, because doctors themselves realized the limits of what they could provide. Although nineteenth-century people accepted a subordinate role for what modern advertisers now call "doctor mom," they also recognized that patients and domestic caretakers would at times independently diagnose and treat.

In this light, professionalization efforts that defended against sectarian attacks may have had a positive outcome for the practice of medicine. They spurred orthodox physicians to more precisely delineate the responsibilities of the physician and improved the practice of medicine. In their attack on traditional heroic medicine, reformers emphasized practical, domestic responses to health crises. The proposed health solutions promised the patient greater personal control and better medical results than traditional medicine did. Physicians may have been pushed by this competition into incorporating the best from their challengers into their own practice.

Feminist analysis of medicine has also allowed us to see medicine as part of a cultural system. Some of the work in this area could best be described as great women doctors overcoming the opposition of the medical hierarchy and society in order to join the medical establishment or create new ways of treating patients. As such, it provided an important counter to the great male doctor mode of historical inquiry. But the most illuminating area of feminist research revolved around the ways in which cultural values entered into the relationships between doctors and patients.

One of the missing pieces in the history of medicine has been discovering what medicine meant to the patients. Studies of doctors and their female patients have been particularly fruitful in trying to fill in this gap. Pioneering feminist histories of doctors and their women patients in nineteenth-century Britain and the United States noted the way this interaction reflected and encompassed male attitudes toward women. Scholars suggest that in Britain, as the middle class came to demand medical care, the social status of doctors rose. Maintaining their newfound social rank as "gentlemen" required doctors to keep women "ladies." This led to medical theories concerning female weakness and efforts to exclude women from educational opportunities on this basis. In *Complaints and Disorders*, Barbara Ehrenreich and Deidre English proposed that the weakness nineteenth-century middle-class U.S. women adopted was the result of male doctors attempting to solidify their dominant position. In this interpretation, a form of psychological warfare was waged between doctors and their middle-class female patients. The male doctors are accused of using cures to maintain their own superiority that were little more than a symbolic form of rape.

A second generation of feminist research that presented a more balanced view of female treatment and male medical theory emerged in the 1980s. This approach agreed that doctors frequently described women as prisoners of their reproductive organs. Birth-control efforts threatened the male ethos of sexual domination by allowing women more control over themselves. But the majority of physicians steered a moderate course in their treatment of women. Society limited what male doctors could do to women in the same way that it allowed differential treatment of them. Other studies focused on the rise of gynecology and illustrated that the increased use of doctors in childbirth was the result of a complex interaction among professionalization efforts, changing family structures, new medical techniques and institutional developments, as well as women patients' own desire to have a pain-free childbirth. Finally, recent studies informed by gender theories related to individual agency indicate that female patients, though constrained by Victorian patriarchal attitudes and family structures, were strikingly self-assertive in seeking out doctors and medical treatments that conformed with their own desires. This parallels other studies that indicate that even in the unequal power relationship that exists in modern scientific medicine between the patient and the doctor, patients often exerted their own desires through continued self-treatment, doctor shopping, and simply not conforming to the prescribed treatments.

Another area of interest in terms of women and medicine explores the special place of nursing in the modern medical system. A few early studies presented "great nurses" as fairly romantic figures fulfilling feminine roles of providing care to the ill. By the 1980s standard histories of nursing turned their attention to the experiences of ordinary nurses within the increasingly bureaucratic world of the nursing school and hospital. The first of these studies describes diploma-based nursing schools in the United States as battlegrounds on which hospital managers and diploma-school superintendents contended over the disposition of student nurses. In these tales, hospital administrators, and doctors by association, are depicted as self-interested exploiters of nursing students. Nursing educators appear as selfless crusaders for student learning.

A second school of thought rejects this model of the diploma schools and shifts the focus from the relationship between nurse educators and hospital administrators to the work and values of the students and diploma-school graduates themselves. In this approach, nurses are divided into two distinct groups: the professionalizers, who fought to have nurses treated as specialized experts in their fields and who sought bachelor and graduate degrees in nursing, and "worker nurses," who operated from a craftwork orientation. Worker nurses celebrated their skills as nurses and were work centered in their activities and outlooks. Historians who approach nursing from this perspective argue that for most nurses, the feminine qualities associated with nursing were positive, not oppressive, features of their calling, and that the system of training met their needs for the development of work-oriented skills.

More-recent studies assert that this division between professionalizers and worker nurses is an inadequate explanation of what really went on. In these models there is no room for the ambiguity about occupational reform felt by nurses and administrators alike. These historians assert that the training school served the needs of both the hospital and the nurses, providing the hospitals with labor and the women with access to a socially acceptable occupation. Nursing schools provided hospitals with an orderly, efficient workforce in the late nineteenth and early twentieth centuries, when things seemed most chaotic. Additionally, a female workforce intensified the development of diploma schools by folding gender stereotypes into the equation. In this scenario, those involved believed that women were natural nurses and nursing became synonymous with the feminine.

The paradox for such historians is that hospital economics and the feminization of nursing, which at first served nurses' needs, eventually became barricades to reform of nursing by the mid-twentieth century. Nursing superintendents in this version remain professionalizers, but they are stymied by the very nature of their occupation. Therefore, we find nurse educators who sometimes embraced national professional goals, sometimes followed craft traditions, and frequently engaged in negotiations with hospital administrators over work hours, housing conditions, classroom space, and student nursing assignments that were both friendly and tense. Nursing research continues to explore the way in which nurses selectively wove together national professional standards with the needs of the home hospital and the students, all within a frame of feminine gender expectations and personal attachments that marked their lives.

One effect of the professionalization of modern medicine was the extension of medical authority in ways hitherto unknown. Doctors came to be seen as experts who had the necessary knowledge to comment on all things related to the body. All disease is in a way socially constructed. Leprosy was known in ancient times not as an illness to be combated, but as a sign that the individual was unclean in the eyes of God. Refusal to eat in medieval times was an ascetic or pietistic choice that expressed one's devotion to God. Today, anorexia nervosa is defined as a disease common to middle-class female adolescents. As a product of modern consumer society that requires social reform to combat, this disease is nonetheless placed under the control of physicians. In the not-so-distant past, overindulgence in alcohol or drugs was a moral problem, not a disease of addiction. Pregnancy and menopause were normal physical conditions, not ailments to be treated and controlled. An inability to put emotions into words was a normal function of masculine culture; it is now *normative male alexithymia*. With the rise in the status of doctors, more and more of the human condition came to be defined in medical terms.

The germ theory of disease cause was certainly used by physicians both to improve their delivery of care and to convince people to pay for their services. But doctors were not alone in selling specific etiology to the public. Advertisers for many different products defined new disease states—halitosis, for example—as a means of selling products like mouthwash and soap. And while doctors now assert that germs are often a necessary but not sufficient cause of illness (lots of people exposed to the same germs don't get sick, because of natural immunities or environmental conditions), manufacturers continue to tout products whose sole aim is to kill germs in order to keep oneself and one's family healthy.

Clearly, doctors are not solely responsible for the increasingly medicalized perception of the human body. Research on the rise of gynecology indicates that many women wanted things that medicine could offer and traditional midwifery could not, such as a less painful labor and the elimination of hot flashes. Social reformers and physicians worked together to convince people to engage in preventive medical practices such as vaccination, yearly checkups, regular dental care, and well-child care. Current research suggests that the public embraced some of these things because they saw an advantage in catching their own and their children's ailments early enough to ease suffering. Indeed, in Western society it seems clear that a significant part of this trend is the desire among people to avoid suffering.

The history of medicine, therefore, is one of evolving medical knowledge and changing medical practices, much of which improved people's daily lives but some of which may have harmed them. It is also a history of changing relationships between doctors and society, doctors and patients, and doctors and other medical practitioners. It is a history of changes in the delivery of medical care through hospitals in which other medical specialties, such as nursing, dietetics, and diagnostic technicians, now play such an important role. Finally, it is a history of ordinary people negotiating their way among traditional practices, alternative methods, and the medical establishment to use medicine in ways that meet their own needs.

DEATH, DYING, AND GRIEF

At one end of historical study of the body comes the need to study death, and here, too, there is a rich historical literature but also additional opportunity. Histories of death began to flourish in the 1960s and 1970s, when Western avoidance of death as a subject was coming under review. The subject has declined in interest a bit since, though there are a few dramatic new findings and interpretations, but it is likely to revive when death rates become more noticeable as part of aging industrial societies.

Death can be studied from various angles. Death rates and causes of death inevitably draw interest and link closely to the history of health and medicine. The demographic transition, completed in the West between 1880 and 1920, involved a dramatic reduction of infant deaths (accompanying lower birthrates). Other societies have moved or are moving in this direction since that time. Death also changed for adults. Infectious disease declined, thanks to changes in medicine, public health, and nutrition; and attention shifted to less visible, degenerative killers like heart disease, stroke, and cancer. Furthermore, the location of death moved from home to hospital, and doctors—death-fighters—rather than priests became the chief social agents dealing with death. Historians continue to explore what all these changes meant for the people involved. Did death become more remote and therefore scarier when it did occur? Interestingly, people who suffered deaths of loved ones (deaths prior to old age, in particular) often encountered less sympathy from others than had been true in the nineteenth century, and turned to Thanatos societies and other groups of strangers linked by their experiences. At the same time, new death practices arose, focused on elaborate funerals, cemetery plots, and viewings (including embalming of the corpse, introduced into Western funeral practice late in the nineteenth century); for many, these rituals seemed to satisfy the need to memorialize the dead. It was unusual death—among the young—or contemplation of one's own death that seemed most troubling amid the changing context for death. The idea of a "good death," definable in past times, may have become less accessible when death shifted to the unfamiliar surroundings of emergency rooms and efforts to prolong life at all costs.

All this raises a number of subjects and materials for study, both in traditional societies and in modern ones. Statistics on mortality bump up against the material culture of cemeteries—how they looked and where they were located. The agents who handle death, whether priests, doctors, or funeral home professionals, also warrant study, in terms of their outlook and social role. A good bit of attention has been devoted, more recently, to the history of emotions surrounding death. While death almost always leaves an emotional mark, societies vary and change in how they evaluate grief. Victorians in the nineteenth-century American and European middle class celebrated grief. Girls could even buy grief kits for dolls, complete with black clothing and caskets, to train them in appropriate emotion. But in the 1920s, Western society turned against grief, regarding excessive grief as a sign of mental imbalance; what was called "grief work" was a matter for psychiatrists. While this approach has moderated to some extent, many still worry that modern Westerners handle grief badly, trying to dismiss it. Further changes in burial practices, reducing formal mourning to almost nothing and increasingly (particularly in Europe) featuring cremation, produce other subjects that need interpretation from a historical perspective.

A final angle on death is, of course, the history of suicide, another really tough but essential topic that historians have explored to some extent. Suicide rates have almost certainly increased in modern societies (Japan as well as the West), particularly among youth and the elderly, and historical analysis may help determine why this is so, even as death more generally has declined. The history of death remains a topic somewhat separate from other concerns in the history of health and medicine, but it has its own richness and ultimately needs to be linked to the other aspects of the history of the human body.

CONCLUSION

Where does all of this leave us? First, in the last three decades, historians have done considerable work in recovering the history of the body and of its treatment. A considerable amount of basic research has been conducted. We know more about how the body has changed over time and how people perceived the body at any given point in time. We know more about the evolution of disease and its impact on human societies and events. We know much more about scientific understanding of and medical treatment of the body over time in many different places. We know more about how medicine as a field has evolved and how doctors and their patients interacted. Though some medical schools persist in teaching the great-doctor version of medical history, most historians of health and medicine now see this as a complex, socially constructed phenomenon.

Work on the history of death has also added a dimension to understanding modern medical practitioners.

We are beginning to sort out the ways in which cultural, economic, and political factors interact and affect the health of the body and its treatment. Still, much more needs to be done in this area. In the late twentieth century, historians of medicine disabused us of the notion that modern medicine was an unmitigated boon to humankind. They note the ways in which the practices of doctors both consciously limited the options of patients (e.g., regulating and decreasing the role of midwives in deliveries). Some suggest that doctors may have harmed patients both through the rise of impersonal bureaucratic structures and an overreliance on pharmaceutical and surgical intervention as well as encouraging cultural silence on and denial of death as a part of life. More-recent studies suggest that this much-needed reevaluation may have gone too far in blaming doctors. Indeed, some recent work notes that modern medicine created new options for people not previously available, such as well-child care. Medical specialization brought more of the human condition under medical scrutiny, but it also meant people could do something about physical conditions such as dental caries that were simply untreatable in the past. And we are beginning to discover the degree to which, despite all their efforts, doctors were unable to eliminate competitors for their services. Quackery persisted even in the most medically advanced cultures, and the penchant for self-dosing that nineteenth-century medical reformers tried to eliminate has in fact increased. This more complex view of our contemporary medical system requires further work.

Finally, we are beginning to understand the ways in which the spread of disease, medical treatment, and views of the body have evolved on a global scale. Historians are beginning to uncover the way in which the migration of people affects all of these. A recently published anthology brings together essays on women's bodies from around the globe. Many of these essays note the way in which views of women's bodies are all part of a "master narrative" of imperialism. Historians continue to dig into the history of the transmission of disease and its effect on political, economic, and social history in many parts of the world.

Still, much remains to be done. We know a great deal about specific diseases, specific depictions of the body, and specific medical practices in many places and times. There remain many places and times about which we know very little, either because historians of these places are more interested in political topics or because the evidence for body/medical history is hard to come by. We also know only a little about how regular people experienced these. Reconstructing the body, disease, and medicine in this place, these times, and among ordinary people requires both a new view of what is important in history and imagination in uncovering sources that speak to these issues. Finally, the sheer scale of the subject has complicated efforts at incorporating these into an integrated world history of the body or disease or medicine. It is difficult for any one historian to develop sufficient expertise in all of this to make any reasonable attempt at integration. Early efforts to produce such a global picture have often been attacked for getting things wrong about what happened at a local or regional level, creating a significant disincentive against doing integrative or comparative work. So the challenge of expanding our understanding of the history of the body in health, disease, and medicine remains real for future generations of historians. There is also a real need to integrate the major advances in our understanding of the history of body and of health with actual medical and social policy and with larger public awareness of the ways in which current health issues can be better interpreted when viewed as products of history.

NOTE

1. Michel Foucault, *Discipline and Punish: The Birth of the Prison,* trans. Alan Sheridan (New York: Vintage Books, 1979), 11.

FURTHER READING

On the body in history, see Mary Douglas, *Purity and Danger: An Analysis of Concepts of Pollution and Taboo* (London: Routledge, 2002); Michel Feher, ed., with Ramona Naddaff and Nadia Tazi, *Fragments for a History of the Human Body* (New York: Zone, 1989); Jessica Johnston, ed., *The American Body in Context: An Anthology* (Wilmington, Del.: Scholarly Resources, 2001); K. B. Roberts and J.D.W. Tomlinson, *The Fabric of the Body: European Traditions of Anatomical Illustrations* (Oxford: Oxford University Press, 1992); Tony Ballantyne and Antoinette Burton, eds., *Bodies in Contact: Rethinking Colonial Encounters in World History* (Champaign: University of Illinois Press, 2005).

On religion, see Sarah Coakley, ed., *Religion and the Body* (Cambridge: Cambridge University Press, 2000); YasuoYasuo Yuasa, *The Body: Toward an Eastern Mind-Body Theory,* ed. Thomas P. Kasulis, trans. Nagatomo Shigenori (Boulder, Colo.: NetLibrary, 1999); R. Marie Griffith, *Born Again Bodies: Flesh and Spirit in American Christianity* (Berkeley: University of California Press, 2004); Sander L. Gilman, *The Jew's Body* (New York: Routledge 1991); Uta Ranke-Heinemann, *Eunuchs for the Kingdom of Heaven: The Catholic Church and Sexuality* (New York: Penguin Books, 1992).

On care of the body, see Elaine N. McIntosh, *American Food Habits in Historical Perspective* (Westport, Conn.: Praeger, 1995); Virginia Smith, *Cleanliness* (London: Jonathan Cape, 2001).

On modern disciplining of the body, see Michel Foucault, *The Birth of the Clinic: An Archaeology of Medical Perception,* trans. A.M. Sheridan Smith (New York: Vintage Books, 1994); Michel Foucault, *Discipline and Punish: The Birth of the Prison,* 2nd ed., trans. Alan Sheridan (New York: Vintage Books, 1995); Michel Foucault, *The History of Sexuality,* trans. Robert Hurley (London: Penguin, 1990).

On sexuality, gender, and the body, see Roy Porter and Mikula s Teich, eds., *Sexual Knowledge, Sexual Science: The History of Attitudes to Sexuality* (Cambridge: Cambridge University Press, 1994); L.J. Jordanova, *Sexual Visions: Images of Gender in Science and Medicine between the Eighteenth and Twentieth Centuries* (Madison, Wis.: University of Wisconsin Press, 1993); Thomas Walter Laqueur, *Making Sex: Body and Gender from the Greeks to Freud,* Harvard paperback edition (Cambridge, Mass.: Harvard University Press, 1992); Catherine Gallagher and Thomas Laqueur, eds., *The Making of the Modern Body: Sexuality and Society in the Nineteenth Century* (Berkeley: University of California Press, 1987); Cynthia Eagle

Russett, *Sexual Science: The Victorian Construction of Womanhood*, first Harvard University Press paperback edition (Cambridge, Mass.: Harvard University Press, 1991).

On health, beauty, and the female body, see Barbara Ehrenreich and Deirdre English, *For Her Own Good: 150 Years of the Experts' Advice to Women*, Anchor Books edition (New York: Anchor Books, 1989); Debran Rowland, *The Boundaries of Her Body: Women's Rights in America* (Naperville, Ill.: Sphinx Publishing, 2004); Michael Hau, *The Cult of Health and Beauty in Germany: A Social History, 1890–1930* (Chicago: University of Chicago Press, 2003); Kate Mulvey and Melissa Richards, *Decades of Beauty: The Changing Image of Women, 1890's to 1990's* (London: Hamlyn, 2000); Julian Robinson, *The Quest for Human Beauty: An Illustrated History* (New York: W.W. Norton & Company, 1998); Noliwe M. Rooks, *Hair Raising: Beauty, Culture, and African American Women* (New Brunswick, N.J.: Rutgers University Press, 1996); Peter N. Stearns, *Fat History: Bodies and Beauty in the Modern West* (New York: New York University Press, 2002, rev. ed); Mary Lynn Stewart, *For Health and Beauty: Physical Culture for Frenchwomen, 1880s–1930s* (Baltimore: Johns Hopkins University Press, 2001); Jan Todd, *Physical Culture and the Body Beautiful: Purposive Exercise in the Lives of American Women, 1800–1870* (Macon, Ga.: Mercer University Press, 1998).

Two classic works by epidemiologists on the impact of disease in history available in reprint editions are Rene J. Dubos, *Mirage of Health: Utopias, Progress, and Biological Change* (New Brunswick, N.J.: Rutgers University Press, 1990); Hans Zinsser, *Rats, lice, and history: being a study in biography, which, after twelve preliminary chapters indispensable for the preparation of the lay reader, deals with the life history of typhus fever....* (New York: Black Dog & Leventhal Publishers, 1996). For a comprehensive survey, see Kenneth F. Kiple, ed., *The Cambridge Historical Dictionary of Disease* (New York: Cambridge University Press, 2003); Arno Karlen, *Man and Microbes: Diseases and Plagues in History and Modern Times* (New York: G.P. Putnam's Sons, 1995); Thomas McKeown, *The Origins of Human Disease* (Cambridge, Mass.: B. Blackwell, 1995); Charles E. Rosenberg, *Explaining Epidemics and Other Studies in the History of Medicine* (Cambridge: Cambridge University Press, 1992); Christopher Wills, *Plagues: Their Origin, History, and Future* (London: Flamingo, 1997).

Much work in this area focuses on specific diseases; what follows is a small sampling of these kinds of texts. Elizabeth Fee and Daniel M. Fox, eds., *AIDS: The Burdens of History* (Berkeley: University of California Press, 1988); Barbara Bates, *Bargaining for Life: A Social History of Tuberculosis, 1876–1938*, Studies in Health, Illness, and Caregiving in America (Philadelphia: University of Pennsylvania Press, 1992); James T. Patterson, *The Dread Disease: Cancer and Modern American Culture* (Cambridge, Mass.: Harvard University Press, 1987); Robert Proctor, *Cancer Wars: How Politics Shapes What We Know and Don't Know about Cancer* (New York: BasicBooks, 1995); Charles E. Rosenberg, *The Cholera Years: The United States in 1832, 1849, and 1866* (Chicago: University of Chicago Press, 1987); Sheila M. Rothman, *Living in the Shadow of Death: Tuberculosis and the Social Experience of Illness in American History* (Baltimore: Johns Hopkins University Press, 1995); Susan Sontag, *Illness as Metaphor; and, AIDS and Its Metaphors*, first Picador USA edition (New York: n.p., 2001); James C. Whorton, *Inner Hygiene: Constipation and the Pursuit of Health in Modern Society* (New York: Oxford University Press, 2000).

For general works on the debate over disease, geographic mobility, and political domination, the touchstone work is William Hardy McNeill, *Plagues and Peoples* (New York: Anchor Books/Doubleday, 1998). Another central figure in this area is Alfred Crosby. See Alfred W. Crosby Jr., *The Columbian Exchange: Biological and Cultural Consequences of 1492,* 30th anniversary edition, with forewords by J. R. McNeill and Otto von Mering (Westport, Conn.: Praeger, 2003); Alfred W. Crosby, *Germs, Seeds & Animals: Studies in Ecological History* (Armonk, N.Y.: M.E. Sharpe, 1994). Others in this area include Jared M. Diamond, *Guns, Germs, and Steel: The Fates of Human Societies* (New York: W.W. Norton & Co., 1999); Henry F. Dobyns, *Their Number Become Thinned: Native American Population Dynamics in Eastern North America* (Knoxville: University of Tennessee Press, with the Newberry Library Center for the History of the American Indian, 1983), includes an essay with William R. Swagerty as coauthor. For studies that take the perspective of disease interaction in terms of the experiences of both the indigenous and the immigrating populations, see Philip D. Curtin, *Disease and Imperialism before the Nineteenth Century* (Minneapolis: University of Minnesota, 1990); Philip D. Curtin, *Disease and Empire: The Health of European Troops in the Conquest of Africa* (Cambridge: Cambridge University Press, 1998); Philip D. Curtin, *Migration and Mortality in Africa and the Atlantic World, 1700–1900,* Variorum Collected Studies Series (Aldershot, Hampshire, England: Ashgate/Variorum, 2001); Philip D. Curtin, *Death by Migration: Europe's Encounter with the Tropical World in the Nineteenth Century* (Cambridge: Cambridge University Press, 1989); Bruce Fetter, ed., *Demography from Scanty Evidence: Central Africa in the Colonial Era* (Boulder, Colo.: L. Rienner Publishers, 1990).

On the history of medicine, see Irvine Loudon, ed., *Western Medicine: An Illustrated History* (Oxford: Oxford University Press, 2001); Lawrence I. Conrad et al., *The Western Medical Tradition: 800 BC to AD 1800* (Cambridge: Cambridge University Press, 1995); Thomas McKeown, *The Role of Medicine: Dream, Mirage, or Nemesis?* 2d ed. (Oxford, Eng.: Blackwell, 1979).

On Asian, Arabic, and Jewish medicine, see Pen Yoke Ho and F. P. Lisowski, *A Brief History of Chinese Medicine,* 2nd ed. (Singapore: World Scientific, 1997); Gwei-djenand Joseph Needham Lu, *Celestial Lancets: A History and Rationale of Acupuncture and Moxa,* with a new introduction by Vivienne Lo (London: RoutledgeCurzon, 2002); Toby E. Huff, *The Rise of Early Modern Science: Islam, China, and the West,* 2nd ed. (New York: Cambridge University Press, 2003); David C. Lindberg, *The Beginnings of Western Science: The European Scientific Tradition in Philosophical, Religious, and Institutional Context, 600 B.C. to A.D. 1450* (Chicago: University of Chicago Press, 1992); Max Meyerhof, *Studies in Medieval Arabic Medicine: Theory and Practice,* Collected Studies Series (London: Variorum Reprints, 1984); Franz Rosenthal, *Science and Medicine in Islam: A Collection of Essays,* Collected Studies, CS 330 (Aldershot, Hampshire, England: Variorum, 1990); Joseph Shatzmiller, *Jews, Medicine, and Medieval Society: Joseph Shatzmiller* (Berkeley: University of California Press, 1994).

Thomas Neville Bonner, *Becoming a Physician: Medical Education in Britain, France, Germany, and the United States, 1750–1945* (Baltimore: Johns Hopkins University Press, 2000); George Rosen, *A History of Public Health,* expanded edition, introduction by Elizabeth Fee, biographical essay and new bibliography by Edward T. Morman (Baltimore: Johns Hopkins University Press, 1993); Charles E.

Rosenberg, *The Care of Strangers: The Rise of America's Hospital System* (Baltimore: Johns Hopkins University Press, 1995); Paul Starr, *The Social Transformation of American Medicine* (New York: Basic Books, 1982); Nancy Tomes, *The Gospel of Germs: Men, Women, and the Microbe in American Life* (Cambridge, Mass.: Harvard University Press, 1999); James C. Whorton, *Nature Cures: The History of Alternative Medicine in America* (Oxford: Oxford University Press, 2002).

On the history of women in medicine, see Judith Walzer Leavitt, *Women and Health in America: Historical Readings*, 2nd ed. (Madison, Wis.: University of Wisconsin Press, 1999); Martha N. Gardner, *Midwife, Doctor, or Doctress?: The New England Female Medical College and Women's Place in Nineteenth-Century Medicine and Society* (N.p., 2002). Judith Walzer Leavitt, *Brought to Bed: Childbearing in America, 1750 to 1950* (New York: Oxford University Press, 1986); Regina Markell Morantz-Sanchez, *Conduct Unbecoming a Woman: Medicine on Trial in Turn-of-the-Century Brooklyn* (Oxford: Oxford University Press, 2000); Regina Markell Morantz-Sanchez, *Sympathy & Science: Women Physicians in American Medicine*, with a new preface by the author (Chapel Hill: University of North Carolina Press, 2000).

For a pictorial history on nursing, see M. Patricia Donahue, *Nursing, the Finest Art: An Illustrated History*, 2nd ed. (St. Louis, Mo.: Mosby, 1996). For the early debate over the nature of nursing, see Barbara Melosh, *"The Physician's Hand": Work Culture and Conflict in American Nursing* (Philadelphia: Temple University Press, 1982); Susan Reverby, *Ordered to Care: The Dilemma of American Nursing, 1850–1945* (Cambridge: Cambridge University Press, 1987).

For more recent interpretations of nursing, see Ellen D. Baer et al., eds., *Enduring Issues in American Nursing* (New York: Springer, 2002); Diana J. Mason and Judith K. Leavitt, eds., *Policy and Politics in Nursing and Health Care*, 3rd ed. (Philadelphia: W.B. Saunders, 1998); Monica E. Baly, *Nursing and Social Change*, 3rd ed. (London: Routledge, 1995); Darlene Clark Hine, *Black Women in White: Racial Conflict and Cooperation in the Nursing Profession, 1890–1950*, (Bloomington: Indiana University Press, 1989); Joan Roberts and Thetis M. Group, *Feminism and Nursing: An Historical Perspectives on Power, Status, and Political Activism in the Nursing Profession* (Westport, Conn.: Praeger, 1995).

On mental illness and psychosomatic diseases, see Joan Jacobs Brumberg, *Fasting Girls: The Emergence of Anorexia Nervosa as a Modern Disease* (Cambridge, Mass.: Harvard University Press, 1988); Gerald Grob, *The Mad among Us: A History of the Care of America's Mentally Ill* (New York: Free Press, 1994); Edward Shorter, *A History of Psychiatry: From the Ear of the Asylum to the Age of Prozac* (New York: John Wiley & Sons, 1997). See also Peter N. Stearns, *Fat History: Bodies and Beauty in the Modern West* (New York: New York University Press, 1997).

On death and dying, see Philippe Ariès, *The Hour of our Death* (New York: Knopf, 1981); Philippe Ariès and David E. Stannard, *Death in America* (Philadelphia: University of Pennsylvania Press, 1975); Gary Laaderman, *Rest in Peace: A Cultural History of Death and the Funeral Home in Twentieth-Century America* (New York: New York University Press, 2003). On changes in grief, see Peter N. Stearns, *American Cool: Constructing a Twentieth-Century Emotional Style* (New York: New York University Press, 1994).

4

History of Daily Life: Popular Culture, Religion, Science, and Education

Lynn Wood Mollenauer

In 1829, handbills distributed around the city of London invited the public to visit the Egyptian Hall in Piccadilly Square to view the latest of nature's marvels exhibited within: the conjoined twins, Chang and Eng. The appearance of the 18-year-old twins (after whom the term *Siamese twins* was coined) caused an absolute sensation. Accounts in the London *Times* heightened already-avid public interest. The "lively, cheerful, and intelligent" twins, the paper enthused, "swim across the room with all the ease and grace of a couple skillfully waltzing, and seem never to have any difference of intention of purpose which can give pain to their band of union, by making them draw opposite ways." The twins were connected, wrote the reporter, by "a cartilaginous ligament of several inches in length and in circumference … proceeding from the breast-bone, just above the pit of the stomach … [T]he necessities of life have taught them to turn half round, so that they appear side by side, with an inclination inwards, and with each arm about the neck or body of the other."[1]

Paying the equivalent of 50 cents apiece, Londoners flocked to daily shows during which Chang and Eng displayed their connective tissue, performed acrobatics, and carried the heaviest member of the audience around the theater. Interest in the twins' anomaly came from all quarters, from members of the working classes to the members of the royal family. London's fascination with Chang and Eng even became the subject of a satirical poem by Edward Bulwer Lytton that mocked the crowds who eagerly overpaid for show tickets and souvenirs.[2] Commemorative pamphlets that described the twins' life histories and photographs (called *cartes de visite*) were available for sale at the shows. A typical photograph shows Chang and

Eng standing side by side in a richly furnished parlor, each wearing a fashionable dark suit that was cut so as to allow their connective tissue to be seen. Other pictures of the twins portrayed them engaging in respectable and gentlemanly pursuits: driving in their carriage, hunting, even playing badminton.

The details of the twins' biography were well known in the nineteenth century. The brothers were born in 1811 in a town outside of Bangkok, Siam (now Thailand). Their birth caused great consternation in Siam; fearing that they were an augury of misfortune, King Rama II initially ordered that the infants be put to death. (The order obviously was never carried out.) When the brothers turned 17, an American named Captain Abel Coffin and his British partner persuaded them that they could make a fortune by exhibiting them-

Chang and Eng as they appeared in the *Cartes de visite* sold at their shows. Note their fashionable clothing and elegant surroundings. Courtesy of the Library of Congress.

selves in the West. "The Siamese Double Boys," as their new managers billed them, reached the city of Boston in 1829 and began an exhausting tour of concert halls and theaters across the United States and into Canada, Europe, and South America. In each new city, Chang and Eng submitted to a medical examination by local authorities to demonstrate the validity of their anomaly. Such doctors' reports, extensively quoted in local newspapers, not only countered accusations of fakery but also provided valuable publicity.

After 11 years on tour, Chang and Eng retired. The life that they created for themselves was almost startlingly conventional in nineteenth-century America. The brothers settled in a small town in North Carolina, became citizens of the United States, adopted the name Bunker, and took up first shopkeeping and then farming. They bought a plantation and slaves, married (unconnected) sisters, and raised families of 11 and 10 children, respectively. Financial losses, however, necessitated a return to public exhibition during the 1850s and again after the

Civil War. The famous showman P. T. Barnum managed their post–Civil War engagements. He exhibited Chang and Eng in his American Museum in New York City and sponsored their final tour of Europe.

The brothers died within hours of each other in 1874. As two of the most famous people in the country (and indeed the Western Hemisphere), Chang and Eng had their deaths reported on the front page of the *New York Times*. Weeks later, their bodies were brought to the Mütter Museum of Philadelphia, where two doctors appointed by the city's College of Physicians performed autopsies. Chang and Eng's shared liver, preserved in a jar of formalin, remains in the collection of the museum.

Why did Chang and Eng become so famous? Were Chang and Eng unique, or did other people with anomalies also exhibit themselves? How was their appearance understood in the nineteenth century—as a warning of divine displeasure, as evidence of the wondrous fecundity of nature, or as the unfortunate result of a chromosomal abnormality? Why was the exhibition of people with such disabilities not seen as inappropriate, exploitative, or demeaning, as it came to be in the twentieth century? What sort of people—men, women, upper class, lower class—attended Chang and Eng's daily performances? To answer the questions posed above requires attention to the shared values, religious beliefs, scientific knowledge, and education of the people of Victorian England and America. The study of why Chang and Eng were—and remain, as a quick Internet search for their names attests—objects of fascination therefore serves as a useful entry into a consideration of popular culture and all that it encompasses.

The study of popular culture opens up a broad vista into the daily life of the past. Its exploration necessitates attention to almost all aspects of lived experience, from work to family life to religious belief, because those experiences and attitudes shape the ways in which people make sense of their world. Historians have drawn on the tools of folklorists, economists, and sociologists in order to access this past-lived experience. In particular, they have relied on the methods of anthropologists such as Clifford Geertz and Mary Douglas. In order to avoid writing anachronistic history (an account that looks for the present in the past), these scholars try to emphasize the strangeness of past practices by thinking of the past as a foreign country; they envision the past as a place that is utterly different from, and yet accessible to, the present.

To understand the term *popular culture,* we must first clarify how scholars define culture itself. Peter Burke, a noted historian of early modern Europe and one of the first to analyze popular culture, describes culture as "a system of shared meanings, attitudes and values, and the symbolic forms (performances, artifacts) in which they are expressed or embodied."[3] Historians understand the study of culture in much the same way that anthropologists do, as an enterprise that attempts to assess the values, the judgments, the perceptions—in short, the worldview—held by the members of a society. This worldview, though, is not seen as separate from economic or social relations but rather as intimately connected to them. As the cultural historian Roger Chartier writes, "All practices are 'cultural' as well as social or economic, since they translate into action the many ways in which humans give meaning to their world. All history, therefore— whether economic, social, or religious—requires the study of systems of representation and the acts the systems generate … Describing a culture should thus involve … the totality of the practices that express how it represents the physical world, society, and the sacred."[4] In the simplest terms, then, culture can be thought of as everything that is *not* nature; it is how human beings attribute meaning to what they perceive with their senses.

The historians who pioneered the study of popular culture initially employed the term to refer to the worldview shared by the members of the most populous group in society. They sought to uncover the ways in which ordinary people made sense of their universe by studying their literature (both written and unwritten), social activities, and pursuits. Ordinary people have been variously termed "non-elites," "the masses," or the "subordinate classes." In early modern Europe, for example, this group included artisans, women, peasants, children, and the indigent. Clearly, though, such as characterization of popular culture depends on an understanding of elite culture; the unofficial culture of the masses is negatively defined against the official culture of the elite. The elite can be most readily described as those in positions of authority within their society. In early modern Europe, those people included nobles, judges, government officials, and members of the church hierarchy.

As subsequent historians pointed out, there are two major failings in this conception of a strict dichotomy between popular and elite culture. First of all, the model is monolithic. It does not distinguish between groups either within "the people" or "the elite," but erases regional, ethnic, gender, religious, and occupational differences. Would eighteenth-century peasants from the south of Italy necessarily have the same worldview as sixteenth-century artisans in the Netherlands? Did noblewomen in Meiji Japan share the attitudes of their male counterparts? Do male factory workers in twenty-first-century Detroit always see eye to eye with female clerical workers in Raleigh? Attention to the plurality of cultural practices within and between groups leads to a more nuanced understanding of both popular and elite culture. Secondly, the use of the term *popular culture* implies a strict divide between the culture of the rich and powerful and that of ordinary people. More recently, scholars have come to understand that an insurmountable gulf between the two did not exist. Many now prefer to use the term *vernacular culture* rather than *popular culture*. By doing so, they seek to emphasize that many of the values, perceptions, and judgments prevalent in a certain place and time are fluid and circulate among all members of a society, whether those people are rich or poor, educated or illiterate, powerful or powerless.

The workings of this concept of vernacular culture can be seen in the example of Chang and Eng. The large audiences that crowded into the conjoined twins' performances represented a cross-section of nineteenth-century society. When the twins exhibited themselves in London and elsewhere, factory workers as well as members of the nobility eagerly packed into the shows. Chang and Eng's socially mixed audiences were in this way similar to the London theater audiences of 250 years earlier, when people from the top to the bottom of the social ladder together attended performances of Shakespeare's plays at the Globe Theater. Because the twins were so well known on both sides of the Atlantic, their image became a potent cultural metaphor that was used to convey messages that could be easily grasped by most members of their society. In antebellum America, when the country was debating the prospect of Southern secession, both separatists and those in favor of the union sought to sway public opinion with political cartoons. Images of the conjoined twins were taken up by both sides of the debate. Separatists' cartoons depicted the two as an unnatural monster, while unionists' idealized the connection between the brothers as a happy symbol of the bond between the states—"one and inseparable, now and forever," in the words of the Massachusetts senator Daniel Webster.[5]

Even historians who emphasize the shared nature of vernacular culture, however, acknowledge that the modern period is marked by a growing disparity between elite and popular culture. This is sometimes characterized as a deliberate withdrawal of the elite classes from popular culture. While elites in 1500 had eagerly shared in the activities of the popular classes (such as festivals and participation in Carnival celebrations), by 1800 the nobility, upper clergy, and bourgeoisie largely abandoned both popular pursuits and popular beliefs. This growing disparity between popular and elite culture could have very material consequences. One can see this clearly demonstrated in the history of belief about witches in early modern Europe. At the beginning of the age of the great witch hunts (approximately 1500 to 1700), most Europeans, regardless of their place in society, regarded witches as real and dangerous threats to the Christian community. While popular beliefs about the power of witches and the dangers that they posed remained stable over the time period (as evidenced by witness testimony in witch trials), the educated classes came to view witchcraft with increasing skepticism. By the start of the eighteenth century, the judges who had once encouraged the prosecution of accused witches now contemptuously dismissed accusations as the product of ignorant superstitions. They began to refuse to try accused witches as criminals at all.

Many scholars have argued that elites deliberately distinguished themselves from those further down the socioeconomic ladder largely because they sought to justify their dominant position in society. Members of the bourgeoisie promoted a set of values and enjoined a code of behavior meant to demonstrate their moral, intellectual, and even physical superiority over the members of the lower classes. In the eighteenth and nineteenth centuries, therefore, elite interest or participation in an enterprise lent it an air of respectability. While the showmen who promoted the exhibition of anomalies emphasized elite interest in the acts in order to attract popular audiences, the elite critics of such exhibits sought to discourage their peers by associating interest in anomalies with the superstitious, the uneducated, and the irrational. The Enlightenment philosopher David Hume, for example, sneered that freak shows were antithetical to "sense and learning."[6]

For historians, locating sources that provide insights into the daily life of ordinary people in the past can be challenging. This is particularly true of the premodern era, before the advent of printing (about 1500), the spread of literacy, and widespread access to primary education in the West. Certainly, many more textual sources for elite culture can be found—historically, elites (particularly elite men) have had better access to education than have the popular classes (or elite women). Educated, literate men left written records; most members of the popular classes scarcely appear in the historical record at all. Even works that might at first glance appear to be written by or intended for a popular audience may be misleading. For example, the sixteenth-century authors of shepherd's calendars (a type of literature similar to today's farmer's almanacs) claimed that the folk wisdom contained in their works had been dictated by actual sheep herders. The books included instructions on when to plant and harvest crops for verisimilitude, but in fact, most almanacs were written by and for members of the urban elite. Even the king of France, Francis I, owned one.

To access evidence of popular culture, then, historians have had to be creative. Some scholars have turned to letters, diaries, and journals kept by members of the educated classes. Others have made use of the few written documents that do note details of daily life, such as marriage contracts, tax documents, and wills. The most useful of written documents may be judicial records, for these contain the actual statements of ordinary men and women taken down word for word by court clerks. Another point of entry into the worldview of the past is through oral culture—the stories, ballads, folklore, and even the rumors that were communicated by word of mouth. Still another approach has been to study collective action, to analyze the meanings of rituals, riots, or rebellions in order to discover what some historians have termed the "logic of the crowd."

Collections of personal writings—diaries, journals, or letters—can offer a rare glimpse into the vernacular culture of the past. While these sources cannot provide an unmediated view of popular culture, literacy was not restricted to the upper echelons of society. Premodern peasants were unlikely to send their children to school, but urban dwellers of middling means could and did. In fifteenth-century German towns, for example, girls were taught to read and write in the vernacular and do simple sums (as these were the skills they were likely to need as participants in family businesses). Such an education allowed an ordinary woman from Nurenberg, like Magdalena Behaim, to correspond with her husband, Balthasar Paumgartner, while he traveled for business. Their letters to one another illuminate almost every aspect of their lives, exchanging news about their ailments and illnesses, business transactions, and the doings of their relatives and their son. By reading the couple's correspondence, historians have been able to learn about not only the ways in which Magdalena and Balthasar spent their days, but what they thought about as they did so and the religious beliefs that gave their lives structure and meaning.

Wills and tax records have also proved to be significant sources for historians. One study of Renaissance Italy used wills to assess how women defined their families. Although women were subsumed into their husband's lineages upon marriage, an analysis of the bequests left to members of their natal families revealed that strong ties continued to bind women to their families of origin. Another particularly rich source of information about the daily life of ordinary Italians during the Renaissance is the Florentine *catasto* of 1427, a census that assessed the tax value of each of the 60,000 households in the city. Each head of household in Florence was required to submit the names and ages of all family members, including servants; to report annual income; and to record every household asset, from number of hearths in the home (a means of calculating the size of the house) to moveable goods. Armed with this economic data, scholars have been able to demonstrate, for example, the material consequences of the low value accorded women during the Renaissance. According to the *catasto,* the overall sex ratio of adult men to women in fifteenth-century Florence was 110 to 100. This is a surprising finding, because in most known populations, the sex ratio is 105:100 at birth, with women constituting a majority of the population by adulthood. It is possible that daughters in fifteenth-century Florence may have been left off the lists of family members, perhaps forgotten because they had been placed in convents or were in service in other households. However, statistical analysis of population figures from the *catasto* reveals that female infant mortality was far greater than male infant mortality in the city (and was probably due to inferior treatment, as female babies are more likely to survive infancy than are males). It also shows that girls were abandoned in far greater numbers than boys (70% of the babies in the city's foundling hospital were girls). The low proportion of women in the represented population may even be a silent witness to social acceptance of the practice of female infanticide.

Judicial records are another important source for those seeking insights into popular culture. Trial transcripts are almost the only place in which verbatim statements by ordinary, often illiterate men and women were recorded. In fact, judicial records have been used so extensively for studies about commoners in Spain, England, the Low Countries, Italy, France, and Germany that some criticism has been made that the entire body of knowledge historians possess of popular culture is in fact knowledge of criminal culture. There is, admittedly, a kernel of truth in this assessment. However, a trial involves many more people than the one accused of a crime. Witnesses, not under legal scrutiny themselves, testified to the character of the accused or the deeds they saw him or her commit; judges asked questions that revealed their own assumptions; criminals themselves echoed the values of their society in the arguments that they offered to win acquittal or mercy. Crimes by definition transgress legal boundaries. In so doing, they delineate what actions or behaviors a society deems acceptable.

Mining the information found in judicial records for information about popular culture resulted in one of the most comprehensive pictures of daily life in the past, the groundbreaking *Montaillou: The Promised Land of Error,* by Emmanuel Le Roy Ladurie. The inhabitants of Montaillou, a village in the south of modern-day France, were the focus of an inquisition launched at the beginning of the fourteenth century. The Roman Catholic pope charged a Dominican monk named Jacques Fournier (who later became Pope Benedict XII) to root out the adherents of a heretical group known as the Cathars. Between 1318 and 1325, Fournier interrogated over one hundred villagers suspected of Cathar sympathies. Each villager's deposition was transcribed by a clerk and then entered into an official register. As they responded to the inquisitor's questions about their religious beliefs, the people of Montaillou described their daily lives in extraordinary detail, from the composition of their diets to their practice of delousing family members on rooftops. Furthermore, their testimonies revealed their worldview more broadly: their concepts of time and space, sexual mores, and beliefs about the origins of the cosmos.

Certainly, scholars need to approach inquisitorial registers, like all judicial records, carefully. All the information contained within them reflects the perceptions of the orthodox clerics of the time and the documents themselves were recorded by church officers and preserved by the church. It has even been argued that the judges themselves "created" heretics because they often relied on standardized inquisitorial manuals for the questions they asked during their interrogations. Men and women whose nonconformist beliefs may have had very little to do with the inquisitors' preconceived definitions of heresy were nonetheless labeled heretics as a result. Additionally, the inquisitors and those they questioned had very different agendas. While the inquisitors' agendas may seem readily apparent—a desire to extend church control over a particular region motivated most—those of the men and women testifying before them is more complex. Some, certainly, sought to be absolved and reintegrated with the church, while others, less penitent, sought to survive their encounter by making false abjurations. Still others sought martyrdom, which they believed would confirm the truth of their beliefs. The task facing the historian, when sifting through inquisitorial records, is to sort out which is which.

Historians have also looked to recover the everyday experiences of the popular classes of the past by analyzing oral traditions. Some scholars, for example, have sought to understand the worldview shared by the twentieth-century Japanese by analyzing the country's many legends celebrating the failed hero, a man whose honesty, sincerity, and sense of personal honor propelled him toward a spectacular personal failure. Caution is warranted when using such sources from the premodern era, however, because it was members of the upper classes who compiled popular sayings, songs, and stories into written collections. They were corrected by editors and altered to suit the tastes of a new, elite audience. Furthermore, elites often published folk sayings simply to disprove them, as did the sixteenth-century French doctor Laurent Joubert in his *Erreurs Populaires*. Collections of proverbs and folktales, therefore, are best thought of as texts that are several steps removed from an unmediated popular culture.

However, they still remain valuable texts for those historians who take into account the dangers of this sort of oblique approach to the worldview of urban artisans or peasants. European folktales, for example, collected by Charles Perrault in France and the Brothers Grimm in Germany during the eighteenth century, have been shown to demonstrate the centrality of food in peasant culture. In a time and place when the majority of the population could almost never eat their fill and meat was a luxury eaten only once or twice a year, food loomed large in the collective imagination. When characters in these folktales were given wishes, as was the heroine of a French version of *Cinderella*, they almost always wished first for a square meal. Beauty itself was defined by access to food—in an age of scarcity, beautiful heroines were always plump.

Sometimes canonical works of literature can be fruitfully analyzed as folktales as well. The one hundred stories of Boccaccio's *The Decameron* can provide a window into the vernacular culture of the men and women who lived in the cities of early Renaissance Italy. The tale of Brother Onion, for example, illustrates both the genuine religiosity and the anticlericalism that was so widespread in the fourteenth century. (Anticlericalism is a point of view that criticizes the conduct of the clergy without questioning the doctrine or theology of the Catholic Church.) The story of Brother Onion concerns a crafty monk who swindles a group of naïve peasants out of their few coins by promising to show them a feather that he claims was plucked from the wing of the Angel Gabriel. When a prankster replaces Brother Onion's parrot feather with some lumps of coal, the monk announces that a great miracle has taken place, for Gabriel has replaced his feather with an even holier relic, the charcoal used to roast St. Lawrence. Boccaccio's tale celebrates the triumph of Brother Onion more than it criticizes his method of collecting donations for the church.

To better understand how folktales might reveal the attitudes, concerns, and beliefs of a society, consider the modern American folktales, or urban legends, that you may have heard (or even seen disproved on the A&E network show *Mythbusters*). Most Americans today, even from opposite ends of the country, are familiar with stories about alligators in the sewers or tales about ghostly hitchhikers. Folklorists who have investigated these legends assert that they divulge much about modern American culture. For several decades now, for example, the legend of the "Kentucky Fried Rat" has circulated in the United States. Variations abound, but the core of the story entails an unfortunate fast-food customer who bites into a deep-fried rodent rather than the expected piece of chicken. In an era when Americans eat at restaurants more than ever before, the "Kentucky Fried Rat" story gives voice to concerns about food safety, the carelessness and impersonality of big business, and the social consequences of abandoning the traditional ritual of the family dinner. Like ballads and fairy tales of earlier times, modern American folklore is passed from one person to another in casual conversation and group situations such as the office "water cooler" or children's slumber parties. But unlike the stories of early modern Europe, the mass media and the Internet also have a role in dissemination. Even films can serve as a means of transmission, such as the *Urban Legend* series of horror movies directed by Jamie Blanks.

Finally, historians have expanded their definition of "text" in their search for popular culture. Rather than restricting their understanding of text to the written word, they have come to think of texts as a variety of forms of communication, whether written, oral, or symbolic. Attention to "reading" the meanings of gestures, festivals, rites, and ritual has opened up accounts of collective action to historical inquiry. These studies seek to understand who participated in riots, joined mobs, or took part in popular rebellions and what those participants sought to express and achieve by doing so. In some cases, incentives for turning to violent collective action can seem readily apparent to the modern historian even without corroborating documentation. Rebels protesting food shortages or tax increases expressed economic concerns that continue to be relevant today. For example, the imposition of an onerous poll tax in late-fourteenth-century England provoked a widespread peasant revolt. The peasants communicated their dissatisfaction by burning local tax records, marching on London, and lynching the government officials they considered responsible for the new tax. The leaders of the revolt then met with King Richard II and presented demands for lower rents, higher wages, and the abolition of serfdom in writing. Language and action, in this case, can be easily read.

But how can historians read popular actions that do not seem to have any connection to modern experience? How does one make sense, for example, of a Roman mob responding to news of Pope Paul IV's death in 1559 by storming the offices of the Inquisition and decapitating the statue of the pontiff on the Capitol? And how does one interpret the fact that such pillages took place whenever a pope died during the Renaissance era, and that the riots followed a certain script known to all participants? Here, once again, the work of anthropologists has been of great use. Using insights gleaned from cultural anthropology, historians of popular culture have paid particular attention to symbolism and ritual in order to understand the ways in which the members of a society thought about their world. The ritual pillages of Renaissance Rome, scholars have found, took place during periods of transition when the normal rules of law and order were suspended. The period of time between the death of a sitting pope and the election of his successor, referred to as Vacant See, was such a liminal moment because all government functions in the Papal States were in abeyance. (During the Renaissance, the pope was not only the spiritual leader of the Roman Catholic Church but a head of state who ruled over a territory in the middle of the Italian peninsula.) While the actions of the mob that ritually punished Paul IV's statue might initially appear to be merely the opportunistic indulgence of criminal behavior, the crowd acted on specific targets that symbolized the pope's rule —the papal palace, the records of his government, his statue—and thereby communicated their sense that the unpopular pope had violated the reciprocal obligation that existed between rulers and the ruled.

Much of the vocabulary of ritual gesture employed by premodern men and women was drawn from the religious rites that they either observed or participated in. Religion is essential to understanding the worldview of the past, for it shapes how people invested their world with meaning. Scholars have therefore sought to comprehend how ordinary men and women interpreted the events around them by studying popular religious beliefs and practices.

The study of monsters has once again proved a fruitful area of inquiry in this regard. Had Chang and Eng Bunker been born three hundred years earlier, their anomaly would have been understood in a dramatically different way. In the nineteenth century, Londoners did not attribute any particular religious significance to Chang and Eng's appearance but saw the twins as wondrous evidence of nature's diversity. In sixteenth-century Europe, however, the birth of conjoined twins was interpreted as a prodigy, a sign or omen sent by God. Prodigies, or unusual occurrences, signaled divine displeasure with the world and warned of dire consequences for humanity's sins. Floods, earthquakes, comets, rains of blood—all foretold catastrophic events such as the death of kings and the outbreak of wars. Prodigies also had apocalyptic connotations, as evinced in an often-quoted biblical passage that predicted that the end of the Babylonian Exile of the Hebrews would be heralded when

the sunne shal suddenly shine againe in the nighte, and the moone thre times a day. Blood shal drop out of the wood, and the stone shal give his voice … There shal be a confusion in many places, and the fyre shal oft breake forthe, and the wilde beastes shal change their places, and menstruous women shal beare monsters.[7]

Monstrous births too, as the above quotation indicates, signified God's censure. Popular and elite classes alike shared the conviction that monsters represented a perversion of nature, God's perfect creation. God clearly permitted abnormalities to exist only to serve as warnings to humankind to repent for their sins.

Monsters consequently served as potent cultural metaphors during the Protestant Reformation. Protestant as well as Catholic propaganda portrayed the appearance of monsters or misbirths as evidence of God's wrath. The 1523 birth of a blind calf in the city of Freiburg, with a bald patch on its head and a large flap of skin on its back resembling a monk's cowl, therefore touched off a flurry of interpretation among competing theologians. The unfortunate beast was dubbed the Monk-Calf and became the subject of a number of illustrated pamphlets. Martin Luther himself published a pamphlet that identified each feature of the Monk-Calf as a symbol of an abuse perpetuated by the Catholic church.

Evidence of the religiosity that infused the worldview of men and women in the past can be located in the same types of sources used to find out about popular culture. For example, the letters of the sixteenth-century couple Magdalena and Balthasar, discussed earlier, indicate that they understood each of the events of their lives, from a lucrative business deal to the death of their only child, as the work of an omnipotent being whose will was ultimately beyond the comprehension of mortals. Diaries such as the one kept by Samuel Pepys, a high-ranking civil servant in seventeenth-century England, or the journal kept by the eighteenth-century Massachusetts minister John Cleveland similarly attest to their authors' faith in an ultimately benevolent, if inscrutable, Providence.

Wills, too, provide valuable clues about religious beliefs. They have proved particularly helpful to historians seeking to determine the extent of underground religious practices. For example, when Catholicism was forbidden by law in sixteenth-century England, Catholics could no longer practice or acknowledge their faith openly. How, then, can historians determine the extent of Catholic belief? They have looked to sources that were likely to escape the notice of contemporary authorities. The author of one study of religious practices of sixteenth- and seventeenth-century English villagers focused on the sections of wills that commended the testator's soul to God. The language in which testators consigned their souls, she found, frequently betrayed religious conviction. For example, a Catholic might leave his or her soul to "Almighty God, the Blessed Virgin Mary, and the whole company of Heaven." A Puritan, on the other hand, would never mention the Virgin Mary or the saints. Instead, he or she might request that the soul pass on to "Almighty God and his only Son our Lord Jesus Christ, by whose precious death and passion I hope only to be saved."[8]

The danger of using wills to determine religious conviction is that testators did not always write up their wills themselves; wills were often written by scribes for the illiterate or incapacitated. In such cases, the religious convictions of the scribe, rather than the testator, would be responsible for the language employed in the will. To overcome this obstacle, the author of the study not only identified the villagers who served as scribes for their neighbors but she also distinguished among the particular scribes' formulae for the commendation of the soul. She was therefore able to determine if the religious beliefs expressed in the will were indeed the testator's or the scribe's.

Probably no component of popular religious belief has been the subject of more historical research than that of witchcraft and magic. Aside from the intrinsic interest many take in the subject, the study of witchcraft also allows a privileged look into the worldview of the past. Judicial records (which constitute much of the contemporary sources available to the historian) offer evidence of the hopes, fears, attitudes, and opinions of ordinary men and women. Sometimes referred to as the "witch craze," the dramatic upsurge in European witch trials between

1450 and 1750 has in particular drawn the attention of scholars. While nearly all premodern societies believed in witchcraft and made some attempt to control it, only in early modern Europe (and the English colony of Massachusetts) did those beliefs lead to large-scale hunts and mass executions. Over the course of three centuries, about 100,000 people (three-quarters of them women) were tried, and between 40,000 and 50,000 were executed for the crime of witchcraft. The problem that has plagued historical inquiry is that the components of witchcraft belief are so complex and the motivations behind accusations of witchcraft are so varied that the subject simply defies generalization. While many early studies of witchcraft sought to identify the root cause of the persecution of witches, pointing to compelling possibilities such as misogyny or state-building or a pathological response to economic hardship, no single reason can satisfactorily explain the witch hunts in their entirety. The best of recent scholarship offers multicausal explanations that consider the interplay of judicial, social, economic, cultural, and religious factors.

Of late, historians have become increasingly interested in ascertaining the extent of religious orthodoxy among ordinary men and women. Until the 1970s, many scholars assumed that an understanding of religious belief in the past could be achieved by assessing official doctrine and theology. They supposed that sources such as the writings of church officials, the decisions of church councils, sermons, and confessional manuals would reveal the religious beliefs and practices of ordinary men and women. The instruction provided by the Roman Catholic Church in the seventeenth century, for example, was thought to have been absorbed if not wholesale, at least nearly so, by the body of the faithful. More-recent scholarship has analyzed the reception and appropriation of official doctrine. It acknowledges that the promulgation of rules and decrees may not necessarily indicate how ordinary people interpreted them. What was said, in other words, was not necessarily what was heard. Evidence of popular religiosity suggests that the men and women of the popular classes freely adapted the teachings of church officials to suit their own needs and experiences.

One of the first scholars to describe how religious teachings could be so appropriated was the Italian historian Carlo Ginzburg. Using the techniques of microhistory (the microhistorical method seeks to uncover broad social trends and discern collective mentalities by closely analyzing the experiences of individuals—their relationships, their decisions, their opportunities—in history), Ginzburg brilliantly reconstructed the worldview of a sixteenth-century Italian miller named Menocchio. He sought to explain how Menocchio came to claim during his heresy trials before the Venetian Inquisition that the cosmos, including God and the angels, had been created out of an inchoate mass, just like worms spontaneously appeared in cheese. Menocchio's understanding of the universe and its origins astounded his judges. Trained theologians themselves, they reacted with incredulity when Menocchio, an avowed Catholic, declared that he did not know as basic a tenet of his faith as the Ten Commandments. Ginzburg convincingly argues that Menocchio's belief system reflected a traditional pre-Christian and materialist cosmology shared by the peasants of his region. Menocchio's worldview served as a filter for the religious books he read: the miller appropriated only those details that seemed to substantiate his preexisting conception of the universe.

Evidence of popular appropriation of official religious doctrine has been found by scholars studying all corners of the globe. Some syncretic religions, such as *voudoun* in Haiti, have their roots in such practices of appropriation. Brought to the Caribbean by slave traders in the seventeenth and eighteenth centuries, West Africans blended their own religious traditions with European and Carib religious beliefs. *Voudoun* (commonly referred to as "voodoo") was the result of this fusion. It fused the religious traditions of early modern Africans (primarily peoples from Yoruba, Dahomey, Loango, Ashanti, and Mandingo) with Catholicism to form something entirely new.

As they have considered the gaps between officially sanctioned religious doctrine and actual practice, historians have also turned their attention to the efforts on the part of the elite to ensure religious orthodoxy. Members of the elite classes sought to instruct their inferiors in Christian belief not only out of missionary zeal for the salvation of souls but because those teachings reinforced the social hierarchy. Obedience to God, they taught, entailed obedience to one's social superiors. Scholars have characterized these attempts to police popular religious belief as the practice of social disciplining. Social disciplining describes the process by which elites imposed their views on the popular classes and demanded adherence to, and deference toward, elite values. The concept of social disciplining has been critical to the study of popular culture generally because it helps to explain the persistence of patterns of social and economic domination.

Science, like religion, informs the ways in which people see their universe and their place within it. By the eighteenth century, scientists who once would have agreed that monstrous births were evidence of divine wrath were more inclined to view misbirths as natural phenomena subject to scientific scrutiny. The meaning of monsters, for professors such as those from the newly-established *Académie des Sciences*, was not to be found in scripture or biblical exegesis but would be revealed by rational inquiry into comparative anatomy and embryology. This sea change in the understanding of the natural world, in which the reasons for natural events were to be sought solely in the investigation of natural causes, has been the subject of much scholarly attention as historians of science have attempted to explain the origins of the modern, secular worldview.

For the past several decades, historians of science have been deeply interested in assessing how scientific paradigms, or intellectual frameworks, have shaped the worldview of people in the past. Scholars have sought to analyze exactly how and why a revolution in the understanding of the physical universe came about. Until perhaps 30 years ago, historians of science concentrated their efforts on composing an intellectual history of the development of modern science. They charted its evolution by tracing a genealogy of scientific advances, from the theories of Aristotle down to those of the present day. The scholars engaged in this enterprise sought to identify the discoveries that caused educated Europeans to alter their view of the purpose and construction of the heavens, the correspondences between the celestial sphere and earthly events, and the role of God within the system. The story was usually told sequentially, with the ideas of one prominent thinker inspiring his intellectual heir's leap to the next crucial discovery, until the (inevitable) revolution was accomplished. Neither the personality of the scientist, nor the circumstances of his discoveries, nor the worldview he shared with his contemporaries was taken into account.

The history of the Scientific Revolution, therefore, was recounted in the following way. The story began in medieval Europe. Educated Europeans imagined the cosmos in much the same terms as Aristotle had conceived of it a millennium before. Aristotle described a geocentric universe in which a series of tight-fitting concentric crystalline spheres encased a stationary earth. Each crystalline sphere held a heavenly body: the moon, a planet, the sun, or the fixed stars. As the crystalline spheres fit tightly together, like a series of gears, the movements of the outermost sphere, the primum mobile, caused the inner ones to rotate in turn. In this Christian universe, the area beyond the primum mobile was God's abode, a space filled with light, warmth, and the music of the spheres. In the sublunary sphere (the area below the moon's orbit, which included the earth), corruption and imperfection reigned. In contrast, the heavens that rotated around the earth were fixed, unchanging, and perfect. Thus despite its central location, the earth was the cesspool of the universe, with hell at its core. Human beings lived at the very center of the universe, and it was the very worst place to be.

According to this genre of intellectual history, a series of scientific discoveries in the sixteenth and seventeenth centuries forced Europeans to alter this Aristotelian picture of the universe. The first of these, Nicolas Copernicus's challenge to the geocentric universe, described in his posthumous *On the Revolution of the Heavenly Spheres*, went largely unheeded. (It does, after all, defy the evidence of the senses to maintain that the earth revolves around the sun or that the earth rotates on its axis at a speed of 18 miles per second.) Aristotle's cosmos was dealt a stronger blow in 1577, however, when the Danish astronomer Tycho Brahe observed a comet flying above the moon's orbit—in the heavens imagined to be fixed and unchanging—instead of through the sublunary sphere. At the beginning of the seventeenth century, Galileo's refinement of the telescope (he did not invent it, but improved the design) led to the discovery of new stars and the moons of Jupiter, bringing the concept of the immutability of the heavens further into question. Galileo's work also suggested that the heavens were as imperfect as the earth when he observed sunspots and moon craters. Once Galileo's contemporary Johannes Kepler proved that the earth and the planets wheeled elliptically around the sun according to mathematical laws, and Isaac Newton hypothesized that all bodies in the universe—earth, moon, stars, and planets—were bound by the same laws of physics, the geocentric view of the universe finally gave way. These scientific advances transformed the worldview of premodern Europeans. Where medieval men and women had seen the hand of God behind celestial phenomena and events on earth, those at the beginning of the eighteenth century believed that natural laws accounted for such things. God came to be envisioned as a divine clockmaker who constructed the delicate mechanism of the universe according to the laws of gravity, motion, and inertia, but could not intervene in his creation once he had started its motor.

After the pioneering work of Thomas Kuhn, however, historians of science began to ask different questions of their material. In *The Structure of Scientific Revolutions*, Kuhn analyzes how and why scientific paradigms change over time. He set out to understand not the triumph of the heliocentric view but the resistance to it. Like their contemporaries, according to Kuhn, scientists are socialized to embrace the dominant paradigm. Change is strenuously, if irrationally, resisted because it requires the destruction of the prevailing worldview. He argues that only repeated and prolonged challenges to a paradigm, challenges that demonstrate the existence of more and more anomalies within an accepted system, bring about change. The obstinacy with which early modern Europeans held fast to their vision of a geocentric and magical cosmos, even in the face of overwhelming contradictory evidence, was therefore in keeping with the ways in which change in worldview comes about.

A more recent trend in scholarship is the use of the tools of social history and anthropology to situate scientific discoveries in time and place, analyzing them in their social and cultural context. This approach also imagines scientific knowledge as a cultural product. The enterprise of science, many historians have come to argue, is not simply an inevitably successful quest for the advancement of knowledge about the natural world. Scientists are shaped by their society and culture, and therefore the questions that they ask and the assumptions that underlie their research are historically contingent. One notable example of this historiographical trend, for example, places Isaac Newton's understanding of the universe and his quest for knowledge in the context of his intense religiosity. For as Newton wrote in the *Principia*, "this most beautiful system of the sun, planets, and comets, could only proceed from the counsel and dominion of an intelligent and powerful Being."[9]

Other recent work in the history of science considers the ways in which science has served as an arbiter of social questions. In the eighteenth century, philosophers such as John Locke and Immanuel Kant found the justification for their views regarding man's "reason and dignity" in nature. Individual freedom and equality were due mankind, they argued, on the basis of natural law. Following their lead, subsequent liberal theorists argued that nature and its law was an irrefutable authority upon which all social convention should be based. Therefore, if social inequalities were to be justified, scientific evidence was needed to demonstrate that human nature was not uniform, but varied according to sex, race, and class. Accordingly, eighteenth-century scientists "discovered" that female skeletons possessed smaller skulls and wider pelvises than males. They claimed the differences were indisputable evidence of women's intellectual inferiority; this highly interested interpretation was then used to justify the exclusion of women from full legal and political rights. As an article on male and female skeletons in the most famous work of the Enlightenment, the *Encyclopédie*, asserted, "All these facts prove that the destiny of women is to have children and to nourish them."[10]

Denis Diderot and Jean d'Alembert's monumental *Encyclopédie* included articles on not only the structure of the human skeleton but 60,000 other subjects as well, from cannibalism to textile dyeing. Diderot's self-avowed project was to enlighten the human race, "to collect knowledge scattered over the face of the earth to present its general outlines and structure to the men with whom we live."[11] In one (multivolume) work was contained more information than any education could possibly provide. But as the quotation about female destiny indicates, the instruction offered in the *Encyclopédie* was entirely shaped by the worldview of its authors. In this, the *Encyclopédie* enlightenment project is in keeping with educational programs across time and place.

Historians studying education first turned their attention to institutions of learning. They traced the development of the university system, the spread of primary schools, and the consequences of changes in curricula. Taken as a whole, their research has demonstrated the extent to which access to even the rudiments of learning was dependent on class, sex, and even religious affiliation. Literacy rates are often relied on to tell the story. At the end of the seventeenth century in France, 29 percent of men and 14 percent of women were literate. By the end of the next century, 47 percent of men and 27 percent of women could read and write. The same time period saw a great increase in literacy among male artisans in particular; in the southern city of Marseilles, male literacy rates jumped from 28 to 85 percent by 1789, but female literacy remained low at 15 percent. The vast majority of peasants (75%), however, remained illiterate.

However, as an increasing number of scholars have pointed out, literacy rates alone did not determine the access that people had to written culture and formal institutions are not the only site of pedagogical enterprise. Books and pamphlets, for example, reached a far larger audience than merely the literate percentage of even the early modern population. European society was heavily dependent on oral communication, so those who were illiterate would have had printed material read aloud to them by those who were able to do so. Broadsheets, or cheap illustrated pamphlets, were probably the most common form of written text available. Inexpensive enough to be purchased by all but the very poor, they combined visual imagery and printed text in both Latin and the vernacular in order to appeal to the broadest possible audience, from the illiterate to the university educated. Religious reformers therefore attempted to win over adherents with printed propaganda that painted their opponents in the blackest possible terms, as Luther did when he asserted the Monk-Calf was a manifestation of God's anger over the abuses of the Catholic church.

The impact of religious change on educational institutions has also been the focus of considerable scholarship. Studies of the pedagogical programs enjoined by religious leaders during the Protestant Reformation, for example, have sought to discover if the reformers' rhetoric about the importance of literacy and learning had any discernable impact on lay education. After 1525, religious authorities in Protestant Germany called for the establishment of primary schools for both girls and boys, as ministers urged their congregations to learn to read the scriptures. Historians of education conclude that religious persuasion did in fact affect access to schools; educational opportunities for children in Catholic areas tended to lag behind those in Protestant regions. By the end of the seventeenth century, almost 95 percent of parishes in Saxony had schools for boys and 40 percent had them for girls as well.

A number of scholars have devoted their energies to exploring the educational opportunities available to women in the past. Unsurprisingly, in those periods of time when women were denied full legal and political participation, education was largely a masculine endeavor. One study of late sixteenth-century Venice found that a quarter of the boys in the city were enrolled in a school, compared with only 30 girls.[12] While access to primary school education did increase for both sexes during the early modern period, historians have found that opportunities for girls lagged far behind those available to boys. Not only were there many fewer schools for girls, but the educational programs that they offered were quite limited in time as well as quantity. In Germany, boys were taught advanced mathematics and to read and write Latin. Girls were taught to sew, to perform some simple arithmetic, and to read and write in the vernacular. Furthermore, girls attended classes only one or two hours a day, for one or two years. Because girls attended school for such a short period of time, and because reading and writing were taught sequentially rather than simultaneously, girls frequently left school without learning how to write at all.

Attention to contemporary notions about who should receive an education and what form that education should take has been shown to be quite revealing about the worldview of people in the past. Teaching German girls to read but not to write dovetailed nicely with contemporary notions about the proper role of women in society. Reading the works of (male) classical and Christian authors was to help women inculcate notions about appropriate feminine behavior; writing might only encourage women to express their own ideas. As a 1552 ordinance from a girls' school in Mecklenburg, Germany, explained, the purpose of girls' education was "to habituate girls to the catechism, to the psalms, to honorable behavior and Christian virtue, and especially to prayer, and make them memorize verses from Holy Scripture so that they may grow up to be Christian and praiseworthy matrons and housekeepers."[13] In Renaissance Italy, those women who did succeed in attaining the equivalent of university educations (achieving fluency in Latin and Greek, for example) were viewed as having compromised their femininity.

Pedagogical practice, scholars have demonstrated, is informed by attitudes regarding class as well as gender. The writings of educational reformers clearly articulated their understanding of the educational enterprise. In eighteenth-century England, for example, a writer named Hannah More, who founded a charity school for the poor, described its program: "My plan of instruction is extremely simple and limited. They learn on week days such coarse work as may fit them for servants. I allow no writing for the poor. My object is to train up the lower classes in habits of industry and piety."[14]

Historians of education have not only turned their attention to the academic subjects considered appropriate for certain groups but have also sought to understand how educational programs served to socialize students. Schooling was not merely intended to drill a certain number of facts into children's heads, but to teach them the conventions of proper social behavior as well. Following in the footsteps of the sociologist Norbert Elias, scholars interested in the impact of etiquette have argued that the adoption (or imposition) of an elite code of manners by members of the popular classes was part of the "civilizing process" that shaped the modern world. When the humanist Desiderius Erasmus wrote *De civilitate morum puerilium*, or *Manners for Children*, in 1530, Elias argues, he helped to launch this civilizing process. The widely copied work went into hundreds of editions over the next three hundred years. Good manners, for Erasmus, entailed systematic restraint not only over speech but over the expression of emotion and the comportment of the body. In some ways, historians have pointed out, Erasmus's program was an equalizing one, for it was available to educated people regardless of their socioeconomic status. Although no one can choose his country or his father, the humanist wrote, everyone can acquire virtue and good manners.[15] Other scholars argue, however, that such manuals testify to a growing divide between popular and elite culture. As would later writers, Erasmus contrasted refined behavior with that of peasants: "To blow your nose on your hat or clothing is rustic, and to do so with the arm or elbow befits a tradesman."[16] The ability to follow an intricate code of manners increasingly differentiated popular from elite classes over the course of the early modern period.

Many observers may find popular culture easier to handle for recent history than for earlier periods, particularly premodern eras. After all, evidence about popular culture surrounds us at almost every turn. Newspapers and other media comment on the latest popular trends. Polls tell us, or seem to tell us, what people think about all sorts of subjects, from religion to consumer life. We know what the schools teach in contemporary societies. Widely purchased products and shows would seem to indicate popular taste in other areas.

Yet all sorts of interpretive challenges remain, and some new ones are added. We still need to use various stories and rituals to obtain insights into certain aspects of popular belief. We still need to look at complex relationships between elites and masses. With the rise of modern consumerism and modern media, often accompanied by new attitudes about sexual display, elites and ordinary people frequently shared certain interests. But it was also true that elite observers consistently criticized popular taste. Elites also issued masses of prescriptive literature, trying to define how people should raise their children or manage their health. This prescriptive literature—for example, pregnancy manuals like *What to Expect When You're Expecting*—provides important evidence about popular culture, at least when it is widely circulated. But of course people did not necessarily agree with the prescriptions down the line, so we still need independent evidence about what people actually believed and how they interacted with official recommendations about topics such as family or health. Commercialization provides another challenge, this one even newer. It is relatively easy to study consumer fashions, like dance crazes or musical trends; it is far more difficult to determine what they suggest about actual popular beliefs and values. Most historians agree that popular culture does not change nearly as often as fads do, and that people are able to enjoy new media styles, for example, without necessarily being heavily influenced by them. But sorting out more fundamental trends remains difficult, in part, because the sheer amount of evidence is so overwhelming.

New divisions add further complications. Although it is not necessarily entirely new, many historians argue that a distinct youth culture began to emerge in the twentieth century, and some even refer to a "global" youth culture by the beginning of the twenty-first century. So it may be necessary to consider age-specific values when discussing popular culture. The revival of religion from the 1970s onward that has taken place in many countries around the world, including the United States, raises questions about what contemporary religion means to ordinary believers. It also prompts inquiry into its relationship to older religious values and to other aspects of contemporary culture, such as consumerism and science. Successful studies of earlier manifestations of popular culture demonstrate that it is essential to delve beneath the surface when examining religion, to weigh what religious leaders say against other kinds of evidence of what ordinary people seem to believe. But this task, never easy, may be harder when we lack the advantage of historical perspective.

Popular beliefs continue to evolve, though they often retain strong traces of earlier values. Even magic has not disappeared from popular culture in the contemporary world—spells of love magic, for example, are easily found on the Internet. The nature of evidence about popular culture certainly changes. Some of the analytical requirements, however, including getting beneath the surface, dealing with ritual expressions, and coping with complex interactions between elites and wider publics, carry over from earlier periods. Indeed, experience from assessing previous manifestations of popular culture may assist in evaluating more-recent outcroppings. In today's America, for example, conjoined twins are no longer interpreted as a warning of divine disapprobation, as testament to nature's fecundity, or seen as suitable for exhibition in freak shows. Social convention holds that the display of people with physical anomalies is in bad taste at best and exploitative of the handicapped at worst. However, the birth of conjoined twins continues to be the subject of much public fascination. The intense media coverage they inspire typically focuses on medical and scientific issues and emphasizes that their anomaly is the result of a chromosomal abnormality that can be medically resolved by advanced surgical techniques, albeit at great financial and emotional cost. But what assumptions underlie such reporting? And are the twins on display nonetheless?

NOTES

1. Quoted in Richard D. Altick, *The Shows of London* (Cambridge, MA: Belknap Press of Harvard University, 1978), 261.

2. Edward Bulwer Lytton, *The Siamese Twins: A Satirical Tale of the Times with Other Poems* (New York: J&J Harper, 1831).

3. Peter Burke, *Popular Culture in Early Modern Europe* (New York: Harper and Row Publishers, 1978), prologue, 1.

4. Roger Chartier, *The Cultural Uses of Print in Early Modern Europe,* trans. Lydia G. Cochrane (Princeton, NJ: Princeton University Press, 1978), 11.

5. Quoted in "Webster Daniel." *Encyclopedia Britannica* from Encyclopedia Britannica Online. http://o-search.eb.com.unclc.coast.uncwil.edu.80/eb/article-9076397 (Accessed August 15, 2005).

6. Quoted in Heather McHold, "Diagnosing Difference: The Scientific, Medical, and Popular Engagement with Monstrosity in Victorian Britain" (Ph.D. diss., Northwestern University, 2002), 60.

7. 2 Esd., v.4–8 (Geneva Version), quoted in Lorraine Daston and Katherine Park, "Unnatural Conceptions: The Study of Monsters in France and England in Sixteenth- and Seventeenth-Century France and England," *Past and Present* 92 (August 1981): 25.

8. Margaret Spufford, *Contrasting Communities: English Villagers in the Sixteenth and Seventeenth Centuries* (New York: Cambridge University Press, 1974), 320.

9. Quoted in Timothy Ferris, *Coming of Age in the Milky Way* (New York: Doubleday, 1988), 121.

10. Quoted in Londa Schiebinger, "Skeletons in the Closet: The First Illustrations of the Female Skeleton in Eighteenth-Century Anatomy," *Representations* 14 (1986): 68.

11. Quoted in Margaret C. Jacob, *The Enlightenment: A Brief History with Documents* (New York: Bedford/St. Martin's, 2001), 157.

12. Paul F. Grendler, *Schooling in Renaissance Italy: Literacy and Learning, 1300–1600* (Baltimore, Md.: The Johns Hopkins University Press, 1989).

13. Quoted in Gerald Strauss, "The Social Function of Schools in the Lutheran Reformation in Germany," *History of Education Quarterly* 28 (1988): 198.

14. Quoted in Jackson J. Spielvogel, *Western Civilization* (Toronto: Thompson Wadsworth, 2006), 494.

15. Edward Muir, *Ritual in Early Modern Europe* (Cambridge: Cambridge University Press, 1997), 120.

16. Quoted in Norbert Elias, *The History of Manners,* trans. Edmund Jephcott (New York: Pantheon Books, 1978), 144.

FURTHER READING

On the history of sideshows in nineteenth-century England, see Heather McHold, "Diagnosing Difference: The Scientific, Medical, and Popular Engagement with Monstrosity in Victorian Britain," (Ph.D. diss, Northwestern University, 2002); and Richard D. Altick, *The Shows of London* (Cambridge, MA: Belknap Press of Harvard University Press, 1978). For an analysis of the ways in which images of Chang and Eng were used to convey political and social messages, see Allison Pingree, "America's 'United Siamese Brothers': Chang and Eng and 19th-century Ideologies of Democracy and Domesticity," pp. 92–114, in *Reading Monsters/Reading Culture,* ed. J.J. Cohen (Minneapolis: University of Minnesota Press). On the display of human anomalies in modern America, see Robert Bogdan, *Freak Show: Presenting Human Oddities for Amusement and Profit* (Chicago: University of Chicago Press, 1988). Of particular interest is the Web site dedicated to P.T. Barnum's American Museum, at which the showman exhibited many of the nineteenth century's most famous human anomalies, including General Tom Thumb and Chang and Eng Bunker, "The Lost Museum," http://www.lostmuseum.cuny.edu/home.html.

On the history of popular culture, see Peter Burke, *Popular Culture in Early Modern Europe* (New York: Harper & Row Publishers, 1978), the essays of Natalie Zemon Davis, *Society and Culture in Early Modern France* (Stanford, CA: Stanford University Press, 1975), and Roger Chartier, *The Cultural Uses of Print in Early Modern France,* trans. Lydia G. Cochrane (Princeton, NJ: Princeton University Press, 1978).

The correspondence of a sixteenth-century German couple is the basis of Stephen Ozment's *Magdalena and Balthasar: An Intimate Portrait of Life in 16th-Century Europe Revealed in the Letters of a Nurenberg Husband and Wife* (New Haven, CT: Yale University Press, 1986). One of the few collections of letters written in English during the fifteenth century is the Paston family correspondence, available as *The Pastons: A Family in the War of the Roses,* ed. Richard Barber (Rochester, NY: Boydell and Brewer, 1993). The multivolume diary of Samuel Pepys is gradually being posted on the Web. The first years of his diary are available at "The Diary of Samuel Pepys," http://www.pepysdiary.com.

For a consideration of European folktales, see Robert Darnton, *The Great Cat Massacre and Other Episodes in French Cultural History* (New York: Norton, 1980). Ivan Morris considers the meaning of Japanese legends in *The Nobility of Failure: Tragic Heroes in the History of Japan* (New York: Meridian, 1975).

The history of witchcraft has received a great deal of attention from scholars. For excellent introductions to the field, see Brian Levack, *The Witch-Hunt in Early Modern Europe* (New York: Longman Publishing, 1994); Robin Briggs, *Witches and Neighbors: The Social and Cultural Context of European Witchcraft* (New York: Penguin Books, 1996); and Stuart Clark, *Thinking with Demons: The Idea of Witchcraft in Early Modern Europe* (Oxford: Oxford University Press, 1997). In his highly influential *Religion and the Decline of Magic* (New York: Charles Scribners' Sons, 1971), Keith Thomas compares early modern English witchcraft beliefs with those from twentieth-century West Africa. On the only large-scale witch hunt in colonial America, see Stephen Boyer and Paul Nissenbaum, *Salem Possessed: The Social Origins of Witchcraft* (Cambridge, MA: Harvard University Press, 1974). On the persistence of magical beliefs into the twentieth century, see Begnt Ankarloo and Stuart Clark, eds., *Witchcraft and Magic in Europe: The Twentieth Century* (Philadelphia: University of Pennsylvania Press, 1999).

For a comprehensive analysis of the Florentine *catasto*, see David Herlihy and Christiane Klapisch-Zuber, *Tuscans and Their Families* (New Haven, CT: Yale University Press, 1985). The full text of the *catasto* is available on the Web at http://www.stg.brown.edu/projects/catasto/overview.html. Laurent Joubert's *Erreurs Populaires* is available in a modern translation by Gregory David de Rocher, *Popular Errors* (Tuscaloosa: University of Alabama Press, 1989) and is the subject of Natalie Zemon Davis's essay, "Proverbial Wisdom and Popular Errors," in *Society and Culture in Early Modern France* (Stanford, CA: Stanford University Press, 1975). The folklorist Jan Harold Brunvand has extensively written on urban legends in modern America; for an introduction to his work, see *The Vanishing Hitchhiker: American Urban Legends and Their Meanings* (New York: Norton & Co., 1981).

For a microhistorical approach to popular culture that brilliantly explores the worldview of a sixteenth-century Italian peasant, see Carlo Ginzburg, *The Cheese and the Worms: The Cosmos of a Sixteenth-Century Miller,* trans. John and Anne Tedeschi (Baltimore: Johns Hopkins University Press, 1980). Another important work of microhistory is Natalie Zemon Davis, *The Return of Martin Guerre* (Cambridge, MA: Harvard University Press, 1983). The historians of the French *Annales* school seek to write "total history" that emphasizes the continuities of everyday life from the Renaissance to the Enlightenment. For an example of this socioeconomic approach, see the pioneering work of one of the preeminent *Annales* historians, Emmanuel Le Roy Ladurie, *The Peasants of Languedoc,* trans. John Day (Chicago: University of Illinois Press, 1974). The same author also wrote the magisterial *Montaillou: The Promised Land of Error,* trans. Barbara Bray (New York: George Braziller, 1978).

On the use of inquisitorial records as historical sources, see Carlo Ginzburg, "The Inquisitor as Anthropologist," in *Clues, Myths, and the Historical Method* (Baltimore: Johns Hopkins University Press, 1989) and Renato Rosaldo, "From the Door of His Tent: The Fieldworker and the Inquisitor," in *Writing Culture: The Poetics and Politics of Ethnography,* ed. James Clifford and George E. Marcus (Berkeley: University of California Press, 1986).

The anthropologist whose work on ritual has most influenced cultural historians is Clifford Geertz; see "Thick Description: Toward an Interpretive Theory of Culture," in *The Interpretation of Cultures: Selected Essays* (New York: Basic Books,

1973) for a précis of his concept of "thick description." On current ritual theory, see David Kertzer, *Ritual, Politics, and Power* (New Haven, CT: Yale University Press, 1988). Edward Muir analyzes the early modern European experience in *Ritual in Early Modern Europe* (Cambridge: Cambridge University Press, 1997). For a brilliant reading of the ways in which religious ritual shaped collective action, see Emmanuel Le Roy Ladurie, *Carnival in Romans*, trans. Mary Feeney (New York: George Braziller, 1979).

On the evolution of the meaning of monsters in popular and elite culture, see the influential article by Lorraine Daston and Katherine Park, "Unnatural Conceptions: The Study of Monsters in France and England in Sixteenth- and Seventeenth-Century France and England," *Past and Present* 92 (August 1981): 20–54. The two authors have completed a longer work on the same subject, *Wonders and the Order of Nature, 1150–1750* (New York: Zone Books, 1998).

For information about the role of religion in daily life, see the works of John Bossy, particularly *Christianity in the West, 1400–1700* (Oxford: Oxford University Press, 1985) and "The Counter-Reformation and the People of Catholic Europe," *Past and Present* 47 (1970): 51–70. Also noteworthy are Margaret Spufford, *Contrasting Communities: English Villagers in the Sixteenth and Seventeenth Centuries* (New York: Cambridge University Press, 1974) and Christopher Jedry, *The World of John Cleveland: Family and Community in Eighteenth-Century New England* (New York: Norton and Co., 1979). The seminal work on *voudoun* is Melville Herskovitz, *Life in a Haitian Valley* (New York: Knopf, 1937).

On the history of science, see the seminal work by Thomas Kuhn, *The Structure of Scientific Revolutions* (Chicago: University of Chicago Press, 1962). A traditional narrative of the Scientific Revolution is A. Rupert Hall, *The Revolution in Science, 1500–1700* (London: Longman Publishing, 1983). Stephen Shapin emphasizes the role played by contingency and social context in the Scientific Revolution; see his book, coauthored with Simon Schaffer, *Leviathan and the Air Pump: Hobbes, Boyle, and the Experimental Life* (Princeton, NJ: Princeton University Press, 1985). For an explication of the connections between natural science and science, see William Eamon, *Science and the Secrets of Nature: Books of Secrets in Medieval and Early Modern European Culture* (Princeton, NJ: Princeton University Press, 1994). On scientific knowledge as a reflection of social and cultural forces, see Londa Schiebinger, *The Mind Has No Sex? Women in the Origins of Modern Science* (Cambridge, MA: Harvard University Press, 1989).

On literacy and learning, see R. A. Houston, *Literacy in Early Modern Europe: Culture and Education, 1500–1800* (New York, Longman Publishing, 1989); Anthony Grafton and Lisa Jardine, *From Humanism to the Humanities: Education and the Liberal Arts in Fifteenth- and Sixteenth-Century Europe* (Cambridge, MA: Harvard University Press, 1986); and Rosemary O'Day, *Education and Society, 1500–1800: The Social Foundations of Education in Early Modern Britain* (New York: Longman Publishing, 1982). A rather negative assessment of the impact of the Protestant Reformation on education is Gerald Strauss, *Luther's House of Learning: Indoctrination of the Young in Luther's Germany* (Baltimore: Johns Hopkins University Press, 1978). The impact of the printing press on European culture, particularly on religious and scientific understanding, is treated in Elizabeth Eisenstein, *The Printing Revolution in Early Modern Europe* (Cambridge: Cambridge University Press, 1983).

On manners, the seminal work is Norbert Elias, *The Civilizing Process: Sociogenetic and Psychogenetic Investigations*, trans. Edmund Jephcott, ed. Eric Dunning et al. (Malden, MA: Blackwell Publishers, 1994). See also Jorge Arditi, *A Genealogy of Manners: Transformations of Social Relations in France and England from the Fourteenth to the Eighteenth Century* (Chicago: University of Chicago Press, 1998).

The manual *What to Expect When You're Expecting*, a highly prescriptive guide to pregnancy by Arlene Eisenberg and Heidi E. Murkoff (New York: Workman Publishing, 2002), is the subject of some criticism in works such as that by Naomi Wolf, *Misconceptions: Truth, Lies, and the Unexpected on the Journey to Motherhood* (New York: Anchor Books, 2003).

5
Material Culture and Daily Life

Julie Richter

INTRODUCTION

Students of material culture treat objects—furniture, clothing, ceramics, buildings, kitchen utensils, and agricultural tools—as historical resources to be analyzed and interpreted, not just as items to be catalogued and admired. The practice of seeing objects as primary documents helps students of daily life to learn about the meanings that various objects had to the men, women, and children who used these objects each day.

The field of material culture flourishes because it enables academic historians and historians at museums and historic sites to expand our knowledge about people of *all* social levels. Artifacts from archaeological excavations provide evidence of tools that poor men and women used each day as they labored to feed their families. Pieces of broken dishes, kitchen utensils, seeds, and bones yield clues about the food that people ate and the way in which they ate their meals. Stains in the soil indicate the small size of the wooden structures that were home to men, women, and children at the bottom of the social ladder. Recovered artifacts also shed light on the lives of slaves who labored for masters throughout Great Britain's 13 North American colonies. Slaves used a combination of items brought from Africa and objects they acquired, such as clothing and food, to create a material culture that preserved elements of their African backgrounds.

At the upper end of the social scale, the prosperous few used material possessions as symbols of their status, wealth, and lifestyle. Beginning in the late seventeenth century and continuing into the eighteenth century, it became easier for the wealthy to purchase more consumer items because Great Britain, France, and the Netherlands began producing a wider range of household items and personal goods. The flood of goods available for purchase on both sides of the Atlantic changed daily life. As a result of the Consumer Revolution, wealthy families had more clothes, furniture, prints, paintings, serving trays, dishes, and tea sets in their homes.

Members of the middling rank also took part in the Consumer Revolution because the increased level of production lowered prices for many items. Artisans, craftsmen, and farmers added a few luxuries to their daily lives. Most colonial families had a teapot and a few teacups by the third quarter of the eighteenth century. Middling people bought a few prints to hang on their walls, enough eating utensils for each family member, and individual dishes, bowls, and glasses.

Material objects became caught up in the tensions between Great Britain and its North American colonies. During the latter part of the 1760s and the early 1770s, colonists from Massachusetts to Georgia decided to stop importing certain goods from Great Britain to protest what Patrick Henry called "taxation without representation." As a result, consumer goods—especially tea—became inseparable from political events that led to another revolution, the American Revolution. This chapter focuses on the material world of Peyton Randolph, a prominent Virginian who served as the president of the First and Second Continental Congresses, to examine daily life in his Williamsburg household. A variety of material culture sources—architectural evidence, archaeological artifacts, and material possessions listed in the inventory of Randolph's estate— provide details about the way Randolph and his wife, Betty, used their home as a public symbol of their status and as their private space for daily activities. Material culture also yields information about the work that Randolph's slaves did each day in his house.

PEYTON RANDOLPH'S INVENTORY

On January 5, 1776, Betty Randolph asked Billy, a male slave dressed in green and crimson livery, to open the front door of her house. Three Williamsburg residents—the printer and city mayor John Dixon, a merchant named William Pierce, and the saddler Alexander Craig—entered the dwelling that stood on Market Square in the heart and center of the eighteenth-century city. Dixon, Pierce, and Craig met on that day to inventory—to list and value—the personal property that Peyton Randolph had in his Williamsburg household. Randolph, the Speaker of Virginia's House of Burgesses and the president of the First and Second Continental Congresses, died in Philadelphia on October 22, 1775.[1] In the eighteenth century, an inventory served an important legal purpose.[2] The document written by Dixon, Pierce, and Craig was a legal record of Peyton Randolph's personal possessions. When these men finished their work, they gave the inventory to Betty Randolph. As her husband's executrix, Betty Randolph took the record of the items in the Williamsburg household as well as the inventories of possessions at two plantations in James City County and one plantation in Charlotte County to the York County Courthouse on July 15, 1776. Thomas Everard, the clerk of the court, recorded the three documents and returned the originals to Betty Randolph. The widow Randolph used the three inventories to manage Peyton Randolph's estate and to keep track of the bequests she transferred to Randolph's heirs during her lifetime and the legacies that family members received after Betty Randolph's death in early 1783.

The Randolph inventory is more than a list of furniture, dining and cooking utensils, bedding, agricultural tools, and slaves. Today, the inventory is one piece of the puzzle that historians, curators, architectural historians, and archaeologists put together to furnish the house and to interpret daily life for all members of the Randolph household: Peyton and his wife, Betty, their niece Elizabeth Harrison, and Randolph's 27 enslaved men, women, and children. The other pieces include architectural information about the dwelling and other buildings on the property, artifacts recovered from archaeological excavations, and primary documents about the Randolph family and the gentry lifestyle in eighteenth-century Virginia. Together, these puzzle pieces provide a context for our examination of daily life at the Randolph house and a key to understanding the meaning(s) that Randolph's material objects had for the different people—white and black—who used them.

We will begin our study of daily life at the Randolph house with an examination of the dwelling itself and the other buildings on the property. An overview of the house and its history will help us to see and understand the landscape Peyton Randolph created on his urban property. Evidence from written records, architectural studies, and archaeological excavations will help us answer the following questions: When and why did Peyton Randolph renovate the house his father bought in the early 1720s? What did the house mean to the Randolph family and their slaves? How did the house define and shape their lives?

This view of Peyton Randolph's home from Market Square includes the reconstructed covered walkway and kitchen-laundry-quarters building that stands behind the main part of the house. Reprinted with permission of the Colonial Williamsburg Foundation.

Next, we will turn to the inventory of personal property in Randolph's Williamsburg household to learn about the meaning that items such as furniture, eating utensils, and decorative accessories had in the daily lives of the Randolphs and their slaves. We'll study Randolph's personal possessions in the rooms in which he and other household members used these items. Our examination of these objects in the spaces in which they were used will help us to answer another set of questions: How did household members use these objects in their daily lives? How did Peyton and Betty Randolph spend their days? Where did the 27 enslaved men, women, and children work? What did John Dixon, William Pierce, and Alexander Craig leave off Randolph's inventory and why? Answers to these two sets of questions will help us re-create daily life in Peyton Randolph's Williamsburg household.

THE SETTING—WHITE AND BLACK LANDSCAPES AT THE RANDOLPH HOUSE

Daily life in the Randolph house emerges in part from a study of the house, the history of the structure, and details about other buildings on the property. John Dixon, William Pierce, and Alexander Craig knew details about the dwelling even though they did not record any of this information. Dixon, Pierce, and Craig remembered that the dwelling had been Peyton Randolph's home since his father, Sir John Randolph, bought the property. They also knew that Peyton Randolph made substantial changes to his boyhood home in the early 1750s and that it was one of the largest private buildings in eighteenth-century Williamsburg.

As a younger man, Alexander Craig had seen the house where Peyton Randolph lived as a child. In 1724, John Randolph bought two half-acre lots on the north side of Market Square. Randolph, his wife, Susannah, and their two young sons, Beverley (b. 1720) and Peyton (b. 1721), moved into the frame house on the corner of North England and Nicholson streets because it was better built than the structure that stood 36 feet to the east on the adjoining lot.

The dwelling that John Randolph purchased was a prominent part of the Williamsburg landscape in the early 1720s. This structure was one of a small number of two-story dwellings in the city, and its asymmetrical, three-bay (or opening) design was fashionable when William Robertson built the house between 1715 and 1718. Robertson paid close attention to the exterior finish of the dwelling. This builder included a classical cornice[3] over the front door, and it is likely that the house had double-hung sash windows, an expensive item in the first part of the eighteenth century. A red-brown paint covered the exterior of the building.

A visitor entered the Randolphs' home through the door that faced North England Street (a north–south street). Inside the house, this person found himself or herself in the entry in the southwest corner of the dwelling. The entry served as a barrier to a visitor who was not a friend or a family member. A social inferior or a stranger conducted his or her business in the entry—the main public space in an early eighteenth-century gentry dwelling—and then left the house.

In contrast, friends and family members walked through the entry to the Randolphs' private rooms on the first floor: a hall in the southeast corner, a dining room to the northwest corner, and a room in the northeast corner of the house. The hall was a multipurpose space in many houses in the 1720s. Families might work, eat, and sleep in the hall in their dwelling. The size of the Randolph house allowed the family to use the hall as a space for talking and visiting with guests. Susannah Randolph might have taught her daughter, Mary (born 17??), to sew in this room. John Randolph could also have used the hall as his law office and library. The Randolphs ate their meals in the dining room in the dwelling's northwest corner. John and Susannah Randolph might have used the northeastern room as their bedchamber. A stairway in the entry led from the first floor to three rooms on the second floor. The four Randolph children—Beverley, Peyton, John (born c. 1727), and Mary—slept in the three bedchambers on the second floor.

A close look at the interior of the house reveals that this dwelling was both fashionable and unfinished. Few early eighteenth-century Virginia houses had a room that a family reserved for dining or a space that served specifically as an entry. Architectural evidence indicates that Robertson left the walls of all four downstairs rooms unplastered and that one could see the house's framing. Two upstairs rooms—the northwest room over the dining room and the southeast room over the hall—had plaster walls and the ceiling had also been covered with plaster. Robertson did not include finishing touches such as baseboards,[4] cornices, or chair boards[5] in either of these two rooms. The third upstairs room had plaster on the walls, but not on the ceiling.

Architectural evidence indicates that John Randolph did not improve the interior of his house during his lifetime. Randolph did, however, make additions to the yard behind this dwelling. He had workers construct at least four outbuildings north of the main house. Indentured servants and slaves cooked the family's meals in the kitchen. Black laborers and white laborers cured meats in the smokehouse and made butter in the dairy. A tenant lived in a small house on the northern edge of the Randolph property. This renter grew some of his own food in four planting beds near the tenement.

The frame house, in spite of the unfinished nature of its interior, suited Randolph. He bought eight adjoining lots to have enough space to construct outbuildings for domestic work and to give his property the appearance of a small plantation. The exterior of the dwelling indicated that Randolph was an important member of the Williamsburg community in the second quarter of the eighteenth century. Most importantly, the location of the house placed Randolph in the center of Williamsburg and a short distance from the important public buildings in the city. Randolph lived about a half mile west of the Capitol, where he served as a member of the House of Burgesses, the Attorney General for the colony, and Virginia's Treasurer. He also argued cases in the General Court in the Capitol and earned the reputation as the colony's most distinguished lawyer. In 1732, John Randolph became the only colonial-born Virginian to be knighted in recognition of his services to the British Crown.

Randolph and his family attended church services at Bruton Parish Church, about a quarter-mile walk from their home. From Bruton Parish Church, which still stands on Duke of Gloucester Street, it is another quarter mile to the College of William and Mary, at the western end of Williamsburg. John Randolph sent his sons, Beverley, Peyton, and John, to attend classes in the Philosophy School at the college, as he had done from 1709 to 1711.

Sir John Randolph died on March 7, 1737/8, and his will was probated in Virginia's General Court on April 28, 1738. Randolph left his Williamsburg house, two plantations in nearby James City County, and his household servants and slaves to his wife, Susannah, during her lifetime, and then to his son Peyton. Randolph also gave Peyton his "whole collection of books with the cases in which they are kept hoping he will betake himself to the study of the law."[6]

Peyton Randolph followed in his father's footsteps. After Randolph completed his studies at the College of William and Mary, he traveled to London to study law. In 1743, Randolph returned to Virginia and became a licensed attorney. A year later, Randolph received an appointment to be the colony's Attorney General. He celebrated his 24th birthday in 1745 and took over management of his estate: the Williamsburg house, two plantations in nearby James City County, indentured servants, and enslaved blacks. Randolph married Betty Harrison on March 8, 1745/6, and the couple lived in the dwelling. Lady Susannah Randolph lived in either the family house with her son and daughter-in-law or in a small building at the north end of the lot.

In the 1750s, Peyton Randolph made changes to the house that Williamsburg residents called "Mr. Attorney's." Randolph renovated his dwelling during a building boom in Williamsburg. In 1748, the members of the House of Burgesses decided, by a two-vote margin, to keep Virginia's capital in Williamsburg and rebuilt the Capitol, which had burned in late 1747. A number of gentry leaders reinforced the importance of Williamsburg by purchasing lots and buildings in the city and renovating existing structures. During the 1750s, Governor Robert Dinwiddie had a ballroom and supper room added to the Governor's Palace, the proprietor of the Raleigh Tavern added the Apollo Room to his building, and Henry Wetherburn enlarged the tavern that bears his name today. George Wythe moved into a new two-story Georgian-style brick home on Palace Green, built by his father-in-law, Richard Taliaferro. William Ludwell built an impressive two-story brick building on Duke of Gloucester Street, which he used as a rental property. Wythe's neighbor, Thomas Everard, renovated his Palace Green dwelling, and Doctor George Gilmer updated his home.

The timing of the renovation indicates that Randolph, a prominent Williamsburg resident, wanted a house that reflected his position in the city and the colony. Randolph also wanted to reflect the changes that had taken place in Williamsburg during his lifetime. As a child, Randolph lived in a city that was Virginia's political and commercial center; by midcentury, Williamsburg was also Virginia's social center.

The work at Randolph's house took place in two distinct phases. In 1751, during the first phase, Randolph had workmen plaster all of the ceilings in the house. Laborers covered the walls in the entry, in the stairway, and in the second-floor space over the entry with chair board–height wainscoting[7] and plaster above. On the first floor, paneling extended from the floor to the ceiling in the hall, the dining room, and the northeastern room. On the second floor, workers added floor-to-ceiling paneling in two rooms. Randolph decided to have wallpaper added to the third upstairs room. In addition, Randolph had the northeastern room covered in oak wainscoting from floor to ceiling to indicate that it was the most important, private room on the second floor. Peyton and Betty Randolph would have used this space as their bedchamber. Downstairs,

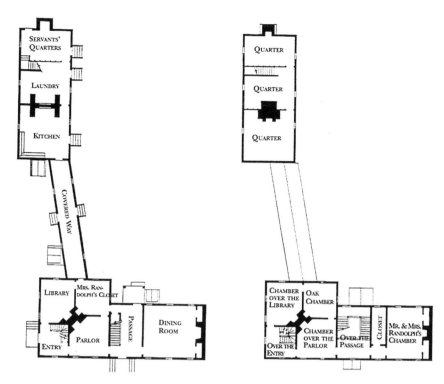

The floor plan of Peyton Randolph's remodeled home includes the original house, the passage and eastern wing added in the 1750s, and the reconstructed covered walkway and kitchen-laundry-quarters building. Reprinted with permission of the Architectural Research Department at Colonial Williamsburg. Drawing by Mark R. Wenger.

Randolph planned to continue to use the hall as his main room for entertaining guests. He had workers add paneled wooden keystones over each of the four windows in the hall. The 1751 set of renovations that Randolph made to his home helped to finish the building that William Robertson built in the late 1710s. Four years later, Randolph began the second, extensive remodeling phase. These changes indicate that the frame dwelling that met Sir John Randolph's needs was not sufficient for Peyton and Betty Randolph. Also, the timing of the second set of renovations suggests that Lady Susannah Randolph had died and that her son was the owner of the house.

First, Randolph had workers add an eastern wing to the 1715–1718 frame house. The renovated house had seven bays, three on each side of a new front door. Randolph decided to have his house face out onto Market Square, not North England Street—a sign of the importance of this section of Williamsburg. By midcentury, Market Square was the most important civic area in the city.

A visitor to the remodeled Randolph house entered the dwelling through an eight-foot-high door in the new passage in the center of the building. Virginia's gentry began to include central passages in their homes in the 1720s. The passage was a long, narrow hall in the center of a house that provided access to rooms from the front of the dwelling to the back. It also served as waiting space for social inferiors who went to the Randolph house on business. The Randolphs might have opened both the front and back doors of the house to take advantage of cooling breezes during Williamsburg's hot, humid summers.

Once inside the renovated house, a guest saw a grand stairway that led to the dwelling's second floor. A large window on the dwelling's rear wall lit the passage and the stairway. The first-floor section of the passage as well as the stairwell had wallpaper above the chair board. The second-floor portion of the passage had floor-to-ceiling paneling and served as circulation space that connected the two parts of the house.

The new wing had a spacious dining room east of the new passage. The new dining room was the largest room in the house. It had a marble mantle on the eastern wall and a built-in buffet (or closet) on each side of the mantle for storage. The Randolphs used the large chamber over the dining room as their bedroom. Three nearby closets provided storage space. The two new rooms in the eastern wing had floor-to-ceiling wainscoting that was similar to the wainscoting in the original portion of the house. The addition had walnut doors, as did the first-floor doorways in the old section of the dwelling. Many of the doors were hung with brass hinges topped with acorn-shaped finials. Woodwork throughout the interior of the house was painted a red-brown.

The rooms in the first floor of the old wing had new functions. The hall became an elegant parlor for the entertainment of family and friends. Peyton Randolph used the old dining room as his study. Betty Randolph added a desk and a bookcase to the northeast room, which might have served as her mother-in-law's bedchamber at the end of her life. The old entry and the old stairway to the second floor became part of the family's private area and allowed the Randolphs, family members, and slaves to go to the second floor without using the new stairway in the public portion of the house.

In the 1750s, Randolph also had workers make major changes to the area behind his house. First, he asked the laborers to take down the outbuildings—the kitchen, dairy, smokehouse, and tenement—that his father had added to the property in the 1720s. Next, Randolph had workers build two sets of outbuildings: a U-shaped group of buildings directly behind the house and a second group of buildings at the northern end of his property.

Randolph used the two groups of buildings to re-create the world in which his urban slaves lived and worked. He gathered much of his household's domestic work and workers into a new building. The main domestic building was a new two-story brick kitchen, which measured 20 feet wide and 48 feet long. This structure also included a laundry on the first floor and living space for some of Randolph's slaves on the first and second stories. A 35-foot-long covered walkway at the building's southeast corner connected it to the main house. This covered walkway hid slaves as they walked from the outside work areas to the house and also protected food as slaves carried meals from the kitchen to the dining room. Randolph's kitchen is the largest kitchen known to have stood in eighteenth-century Williamsburg, and it was larger than the frame house that Sir John Randolph bought in 1724. There was also a dairy, a smokehouse, and several storehouses near the kitchen building.

Peyton Randolph stored perishable food, wine, and spirits in a vaulted cellar located below the kitchen. On the building's first floor, the large internal chimney had seven-and-a-half-foot-wide fireplaces for cooking in the kitchen and washing in the laundry area. This internal chimney also heated a large room over the kitchen and a room over the laundry. These two rooms served as quarters for some of Randolph's slaves. An external chimney on the building's northern end heated a room on each of the kitchen's two floors. Perhaps Randolph's slaves used the first-floor space as a gathering area and the second-floor room for sleeping.

A marl walkway led from the U-shaped domestic buildings near the house to a group of outbuildings on the northern edge of the property. The buildings at the back of Randolph's yard had a coarse, rough appearance. This set of buildings included a storehouse for grain and the tools used by slaves who labored on Randolph's rural plantations. The northern end of the backyard also had a stable large enough for Randolph's horses, carriage, and carts.

Several of Randolph's slaves probably lived in the sizable stable farther north on England Street, and others may have occupied unheated storage buildings on the lot. The granary and the western wall of the lumber house lined up with the western wall of the kitchen-laundry-quarters building. Randolph added a fence along the edge of his property to separate his home and support buildings from North England Street.

In the 1750s, Randolph re-created both the white and black landscapes on his Williamsburg property. The extensive changes Randolph made to his house and to his yard lead one to wonder why Randolph remodeled his house and backyard instead of building a new house and accompanying outbuildings, as his younger brother, John, did at the southern end of England Street. John Randolph's new home, Tazewell Hall, was an impressive two-story brick Georgian dwelling at the southern end of England Street. The youngest Randolph brother had room in his backyard to place his outbuildings in a symmetrical arrangement.

Perhaps Peyton Randolph did not want to move from Market Square—the center of Williamsburg activities in the middle of the eighteenth century—or tear down his childhood home to build a new house to reflect his social and political standing. It is also possible that Randolph showed a practical side when he decided to renovate his home, since he had already paid for the first set of improvements to the structure. Also, he wanted his house to remain an important part of the Williamsburg landscape, as it had been during his father's life.

Architectural evidence indicates that Randolph made some economizing decisions during his second, major remodeling project. He had workers use bricks from the old kitchen in the foundation of his house's new east wing as well as the new kitchen structure. The exterior of the house was painted red-brown. The decision to paint his house in a brick color cost Randolph less money than if he had his dwelling's exterior covered with bricks. Williamsburg builders used bricks in the city's public buildings as a sign of permanence, and many of Virginia's gentry had brick homes to indicate their wealth and social status. An analysis of the paint indicates that Randolph let the exterior of his house weather and did not have it repainted during his lifetime. As a supporter of the nonimportation agreements before the American Revolution, Randolph could not have imported paint to touch up the outside of his house or to repaint the dwelling in white, the color that became the fashionable color for gentry houses, parish churches, and county courthouses in the third quarter of the eighteenth century.

Randolph made both fashionable and personal choices on the interior of his house. The brass hinges with decorative finials, wallpaper in the stairwell and passage as well as an upstairs bedchamber, expensive oak doors, and the large dining room with the marble mantle were quite fashionable in the 1750s. The floor-to-ceiling paneling, especially the oak paneling in the northeastern room on the second floor, was a sign of Randolph's wealth. By the mid-eighteenth century, however, many wealthy Virginians wainscoted the lower portion of the walls and had the upper portion either plastered or covered with wallpaper.

The fashionable and personal choices Peyton Randolph made to his house reflect the fact that he had public and private parts of his life. Randolph used his dwelling to show Williamsburg residents and visitors to Virginia's colonial capital that he was a member of the gentry and an important official. Peyton and Betty Randolph used three rooms in their house—the passage, the dining room, and the parlor—as public spaces to receive and entertain guests.

The Randolphs also led private lives in their home. Peyton and Betty Randolph had their personal space at the back of the house and on the dwelling's second floor. Peyton Randolph engaged in discussions about law and politics in his library. Betty Randolph managed her household from the space known as "Mrs. Randolph's Closet."[8] Overnight guests could use the old stairway to reach beds on the second floor. The Randolphs slept in the large bedchamber in the new wing of the house.

The re-created backyard was also part of Randolph's private life. Slave women cooked, washed clothes, mended garments, and taught enslaved girls how to live and work in a gentry household in the two-story brick kitchen. People could not see slaves carry food from the kitchen to the house via the covered walkway. Male slaves tended to Randolph's horses, kept his carriage in order, and ran errands between the Williamsburg house and the nearby James City County plantations. Few people could see Randolph's slaves as they worked in the backyard behind his renovated dwelling.

THE MATERIAL WORLD OF THE RANDOLPH HOUSEHOLD

At first, it appears that John Dixon, William Pierce, and Alexander Craig listed Peyton Randolph's personal possessions in a random order. That is to say, the inventory appears to be a long list of objects that do not seem to belong together. However, after a careful examination, it is apparent that Dixon, Pierce, and Craig did record Randolph's possessions in a room-by-room manner as they moved from the house to the outbuildings and back again.

On January 5, 1776, Dixon, Pierce, and Craig walked from the passage in the center of the dwelling and began their work in the Randolphs' dining room in the east wing of the house. As was the custom for Virginia's gentry, Randolph had two large rectangular tables in his dining room, so as many as 12 people could sit on mahogany chairs and enjoy a meal and conversation. The Randolphs and their visitors sat down for dinner—the main meal of the day—between 2 p.m. and 3 p.m. Supper, a lighter meal of meats and sweets, was served at 9 p.m. An enslaved butler prepared drinks on the sideboard table against one of the walls. Food could be set on three additional tables until it was time for waiters to serve the meal on the family's blue and white china. Archaeological evidence indicates that the Randolphs and their guests ate beef in addition to some pork, mutton, and veal. On occasion, they had a meal of fish, poultry, or wild fowl. An analysis of the bones also reveals that the Randolphs and their guests ate meat from domestic animals raised on the James City County plantations as well as cuts of meat purchased at Williamsburg's public market in Market Square.

During a meal, guests around Randolph's table would have noticed the carpet on the floor because the floors in many eighteenth-century Virginia homes were untreated pine boards. Four mirrors—two each on the north and south walls—reflected light from candles and helped to brighten the room during evening meals. When the family's blue and white china, coffee cups, beer glasses, sugar dish, water glasses, wine glasses, and punch glasses were not in use, Betty Randolph stored them in one of the two built-in buffets (closet) that flanked the fireplace. The other buffet held knives, forks, and other silver utensils.

The appraisers left the dining room, returned to the passage, turned right, and proceeded to the back door. Once outside, Dixon, Pierce, and Craig walked to the back of Randolph's property and entered the stable. Randolph kept a chariot, harnesses, a phaeton (a four-wheeled horse-drawn vehicle), and 3 carts (including a tumbrel, or farm tipcart). The stable was large enough to hold 5 chariot horses, 3 horses to pull carts, a riding horse, a mare and her colt, and 2 cows.

Next, the men stopped at the storehouse and noted that this building contained a parcel of lumber. It is likely that Randolph stored a variety of items—scythes, saws, wools, flax, hemp, frying pans, 25 bushels of salt, sacks, and tallow—in an outbuilding before he sent these items to his plantation in Charlotte County. Randolph's Charlotte County slaves grew wheat and spun cotton and flax.

The appraisers walked out of the storehouse and retraced their steps along the marl walkway to the house. The men entered the dwelling through the back door. Dixon, Pierce, and Craig noted that Betty Randolph stored linens—tablecloths, towels, napkins, sheets, pillowcases, and cloths to protect the top of the sideboard—in the closet under the stairway in the passage.

Next, Dixon, Pierce, and Craig followed the passage toward the front door, turned to their right, and entered the parlor. They soon realized that the parlor had the most expensive and elaborate furnishings in the entire house. A mirror hung over the fireplace, and two fire screens helped to direct the heat from the fire into the parlor on cold winter days and to cover the fireplace during the summer months. A "Sett of Ornamental China" decorated the mantle over the fireplace.[9] Craig and Dixon knew that the value of this china set—20 pounds—was almost as much money as a journeyman craftsman made in a year. A fashionable Wilton carpet covered the floorboards and added to the elegance of the parlor.

The Randolphs used the parlor as a place to entertain guests after supper in the dining room. Twelve mahogany chairs lined the perimeter of the room, ready to be pulled up to the card table for a game. During the day, Betty Randolph also invited friends and family members to sit on these chairs when they gathered around the two tea tables for a drink and some conversation. As the wife of one of Virginia's leading patriots, Betty Randolph served coffee, not tea, to her guests. It is possible that the Randolphs sat in the parlor on some mornings at about 8 a.m. or 9 a.m. for breakfast. The parlor was much smaller than the dining room and a fire would have warmed this room much faster on a cold winter morning.

The next items on the inventory, a black walnut press and 9 spinning reels, suggest that the appraisers remembered that they had not noted the presence of the press in the passage or the spinning reels in the storehouse. After adding these items to the inventory, the men turned their attention to the contents of a room they described as Mrs. Randolph's Closet. In this instance, "closet" means private room. The low value of the items in the room—less than 20 pounds total—indicates that it was a place for work and not for entertainment. Dixon, Craig, and Pierce noted that the room had "a dressing table and Glass," 6 "old Chairs," "a small Cabinet," and 1 "Sett old Blue damask Curtains." It is possible that Lady Susannah Randolph used the room as her bedchamber during the last years of her life. After her mother-in-law's death in the mid-1750s, Betty Randolph could have had the bed removed and added "a Desk and Book Case" to the room.[10] Betty Randolph wrote letters to friends and family, kept track of household expenses, and managed the work of the domestic slaves while she sat at her desk in this space at the back of her house. It is likely that the bookcase on her desk held a copy of a popular cookbook—Hannah Glasse's *The Art of Cookery Made Plain and Easy*—as well as several books of recipes she copied. Betty Randolph would have consulted her collection of recipes and checked the supply of food stored in the cellar beneath the brick kitchen as she planned meals for her family and guests.

Dixon, Craig, and Pierce opened a door on the north wall of Mrs. Randolph's Closet and entered the covered walkway, which connected the Randolph house to the brick kitchen-laundry-quarters building. On their way to the kitchen, the appraisers walked past a warming pan, a pair of scales and weights, and 2 spinning wheels. Once in the kitchen, the men noted that there were a variety of kitchen utensils that Betty, the Randolphs' cook, used to prepare food. Betty and the enslaved women and girls who helped her in the kitchen had pewter plates and dishes, 6 kettles, stew pans, fish kettles and covers, skillets, mortars for grinding spices, and frying pans. Two spits for roasting meat hung near the fireplace. The kitchen also included shelves for the copper and tin utensils, an iron ladle, a chopping knife, a flesh fork, 8 sauce pans, 5 cake molds, and a colander to drain liquids. The only food items that Dixon, Pierce, and Craig listed were 100 pounds of brown sugar and 150 pounds of coffee. Perhaps the kitchen had a space for items that needed to be washed. The appraisers found 11 chamber pots, 3 wash basins, 35 wine glasses, and 8 beer glasses.

Next, Dixon, Pierce, and Craig examined the contents of the nearby dairy. The items these men found—8 stone butter pots and 7 milk pans—indicate that the Randolph slaves milked the five cows in the property's stable area. After carrying the milk to the dairy, these slaves poured milk into the milk pans, set the pans down to allow the cream to rise, skimmed the cream off the top of the milk, and then churned the cream into butter for the family.

It is likely that there was a storehouse near the kitchen building that contained a variety of items that Randolph planned to issue to his slaves. The appraisers counted 4 spades, 29 hoes, and 6 scythes and sharpening stones. The 7 "dutch blankets" and 4 pairs of "Coarse Shoes" were probably stored on a shelf.[11] Dixon, Pierce, and Craig also found textiles that Randolph purchased to be made into clothing for his slaves. The appraisers measured 35 yards of green cloth, 40 yards of cotton, 10 yards of crimson cloth, about 30 yards of green plains, and 20 ells

(45 inches per ell) of oznaburg. Randolph ordered the green cloth and the crimson fabric to be made into suits of livery for his personal slave, Johnny, as well as his butler, Billy, and Watt, his coachman.[12] He intended the green plains—a coarser, nappier material than that used for livery—to be made into clothes for slaves whose work did not take them off his property. Male slaves had a jacket and a pair of breeches made of plains, and female slaves wore a jacket and a petticoat made from this fabric. Rural slaves in James City County and Charlotte County wore clothes made from oznaburg, a coarse linen fabric.

Before returning to the dwelling, the appraisers noted that Randolph had wine, empty jugs, butter, candles, oil, 30 gallons of rum, lumber, and soap jars in the cellar beneath the kitchen. The variety of items kept in the kitchen and the other outbuildings in Randolph's backyard indicates that these spaces were truly work areas. The many items in this part of the Randolph property were not as neatly organized as were the public areas of the house.

After the appraisers finished their work in the Randolph yard, they returned to the house via the covered walkway. They walked through Mrs. Randolph's Closet to get to the room Peyton Randolph used as his work space. Randolph had six mahogany book presses to hold his extensive collection of books, which Dixon, Craig, and Pierce valued at 250 pounds. Randolph could consult the law books he inherited from his father, Sir John Randolph, as he prepared for court cases. He also had a writing table and a paper press where he kept important letters and papers from getting wrinkled. He might have moved a chair from Mrs. Randolph's Closet into his library when he sat at his writing table to review reports from the overseer at his plantation in Charlotte County and to manage the work of his slaves at his two James City County plantations. The presence of a clock suggests that Randolph was a busy man who needed to keep track of time and wanted to be ready to talk to visitors and Virginia's political leaders when they called on him. Randolph found some time to play backgammon with friends and family members at the two backgammon tables in this room.

Dixon, Craig, and Pierce left Peyton Randolph's library and walked to the space that had been the entry to the original frame house. The entry held an old pine table, 6 mahogany chairs, and a lantern. This space appears to have been a storage area. The low value of the mahogany chairs—just 2 pounds—indicates that they were extra chairs that could be moved in case the Randolphs needed places for guests to sit. The table was probably a round table, not a more fashionable square table.

Having finished their work on the first floor, the appraisers turned their attention to the items in the rooms on the second story. The men left the old entry, walked through the parlor to reach the passage, and then proceeded up the main stairway. Though they did not list it in the inventory, Dixon, Craig, and Pierce saw the expensive wallpaper above the chair board as they climbed the stairs. Perhaps they stopped on the landing between the two floors and looked out the large, arched window to see the outbuildings in the backyard and slaves walking between these outbuildings as they worked.

Once on the second floor, Dixon, Craig, and Pierce walked to the bedchamber in the house's east wing. Peyton and Betty Randolph used this large room over the dining room as their bedchamber. This room contained two bedsteads, or bed frames. Each bedstead had high posts so that the bed curtains could hang on rods between the posts. The Randolphs hung curtains around their beds for extra warmth during the winter months and netting for protection from mosquitoes during the summer. Each of the room's four windows had a set of curtains. The low value (20 shillings) of the "old Carpet" on the floor in the main bedchamber indicates that it was not nearly as fashionable or as new as the Wilton carpet on the parlor floor.[13] Betty Randolph might have moved one of the room's six mahogany chairs in front of the dressing table so she could look in the mirror as she got dressed each morning. Perhaps Peyton Randolph sat in another chair as Johnny, his personal slave, rinsed a razor in the china basin and shaved him and then helped him get dressed.

Betty Randolph kept a variety of items in the closet next to the main bedchamber. The list of linens included a set of calico curtains, 5 quilts, a chintz (printed cotton) bedcover, 7 bolsters, 9 pillows, 8 feather mattresses, 4 hair mattresses, 10 counterpanes (embroidered quilts), 3 wool counterpanes, 6 new blankets, 7 old blankets, 76 yards of Irish linen, and 1 piece of fustian dimity (a strong fabric made of cotton and linen). Betty Randolph had bedding for summer and winter months for herself and Peyton in addition to family members who might visit. She probably stored these expensive items—valued at 103 pounds and 10 shillings—in the four "old Trunks."[14]

The upstairs closet also had a corner cupboard where Betty Randolph kept some of her most expensive tableware. The corner cupboard's shelves held syllabub (a sweet drink of milk or cream beaten with either wine or liquor) glasses, jelly glasses, 4 trays, 8 water glasses, 22 wine glasses, 3 glass candlesticks, a tea board, and 3 globe candlesticks. Betty Randolph also had "a parcel [of] physick"—medicine for the entire household—in her closet and 100 pounds of white sugar.[15] Betty Randolph, like other gentry women, kept expensive textiles, tableware, medicine, and kitchen supplies near her bedchamber so she could control who had access to them.

After totaling the items in the closet, the appraisers walked through the short hall over the passage and the chamber over the parlor before they entered the oak-paneled chamber in the northeast corner of the original house. This bedchamber was almost as expensively furnished as the bedchamber used by Peyton and Betty Randolph. The oak-paneled room had a bedstead, bed curtains, and window curtains, valued at 10 pounds. A mahogany press to hold clothes, 4 mahogany chairs, a dressing glass, carpet, and tools to tend a fire totaled almost nine pounds. Betty Randolph's 13-year-old niece, Elizabeth Harrison, used this room after she moved to Williamsburg following the 1772 death of her father (and Betty's brother), Henry Harrison.

Dixon, Craig, and Pierce noted that the two remaining upstairs rooms had inexpensive items. The northwest room over the library contained a pine table and looking glass, 3 old chairs, 2 bedsteads, a fender (a low metal frame or screen placed in front of a fireplace), and 3 chairs, all of which the appraisers valued at just 3 pounds and 5 shillings. The items in the chamber over the parlor in the southeast corner—a bedstead, an old chest of drawers, a pine table, and a floor cloth—were worth 2 pounds and 10 shillings. The inexpensive bedsteads and furniture in these two upstairs rooms suggest that they were bedchambers for Betty Randolph's younger brothers and nephews when they attended classes at the College of William and Mary. The presence of two floor cloths in the original section of the house indicates that the floor's untreated pine boards were worn after nearly 60 years of use.

The appraisers left the last upstairs chamber and returned to the first floor of the house. Dixon, Pierce, and Craig then proceeded to the cellar under the original portion of the dwelling. There they noted that Randolph stored agricultural tools—5 hoes, a dung fork, a garden rake, and a spade. The men also found a pair of money scales, 8 dozen bottles, a "parcel [of] old Casks and Tubs," "About 100 Bushels dust Coal," and a steel mill.[16] Perhaps the three appraisers returned to the parlor to tally the list of items that they had recorded. They valued Randolph's personal property at 1,578 pounds, 14 shillings, and 6 pence.

Dixon, Pierce, and Craig then added a list of the enslaved men, women, and children who lived and worked at the Randolph house. They began the list with men and boys: Johnny, Jack, Billy, Watt, Breeches, Ben, Caesar, George, Henry, Sam, William, Bob, a second male named Caesar, and a boy named Watt. Next, they wrote the names of women, girls, and young boys: Eve, Charlotte, Aggy, Succordia, Little Aggy, Kitty, Betsy, Lucy, Katy, Peter, and Betty. After they added Roger and Moses to the list, the appraisers noted that they valued these 27 slaves at 1,305 pounds. The total appraised value of Peyton Randolph's Williamsburg estate was 2,883 pounds, 14 shillings, and 6 pence.

Peyton and Betty Randolph used the many objects in their Williamsburg household to show visitors to their home that they were part of Virginia's gentry. The Randolph home contained many fashionable items: the wallpaper in the passage and the stairway, the marble mantle in the dining room, the brass hinges on doors, the Wilton carpet on the floor in the parlor, and the china stored in the buffet. Peyton and Betty Randolph participated in the Consumer Revolution when they purchased fashionable, elegant objects for their dwelling. Randolph also burned coal, not wood, to heat his home.

One of Williamsburg's most elegant houses also contained many practical items. The Randolphs kept old furniture for the upstairs bedchambers, which family members used during their years at the College of William and Mary. Both Betty and Peyton Randolph had utilitarian furniture and objects in their work spaces at the back of the original house. Betty Randolph furnished Mrs. Randolph's Closet as her work space and Peyton Randolph did the same in his library.

All of Randolph's personal possessions, whether fashionable or practical, depended on the labor of the slaves he owned. Profits from the wheat, corn, and tobacco grown by enslaved men on Randolph's Charlotte County plantation helped to pay for material objects in the Williamsburg house. Randolph also gained money from the sale of livestock—cattle, hogs, and sheep—raised in Charlotte County. Enslaved women and girls spun wool sheared from the sheep as well as cotton and flax.

Closer to home, Randolph counted on the labor of his James City County slaves to raise some of the food that he needed to feed members of his Williamsburg household. Randolph's enslaved laborers grew corn, wheat, oats, and barley. Slave men cut timber that Randolph sold to Williamsburg residents for fencing around their lots. Other Williamsburg families burned wood cut from Randolph's James City County plantations in their fireplaces. Slaves also raised cattle, hogs, and sheep in James City County. Peyton Randolph sold some of the meat from these animals to people who lived in Virginia's colonial capital. Moses, the Randolphs' carter, carried other cuts of beef, pork, and mutton from the nearby plantations to Williamsburg, where Betty used the meat in an elegant meal for the Randolphs' guests or made sure that it was cured in the smokehouse.

Randolph depended on the labor of his urban slaves to make his house a place that reflected his position at the top of Virginia's society, and to tend to the family's daily needs. Betty used the many cooking utensils in the kitchen as she prepared meals for the family and any guests at the house. Johnny spent his day attending to Peyton Randolph's personal needs, and Eve did the same for Betty Randolph. Watt made sure that the family carriage was ready to take Randolph to meetings or to visit friends. Moses carried goods between the Williamsburg household and the nearby James City County plantations. Enslaved women and girls cleaned the house, washed clothes, made candles, churned butter, and tended small vegetable and herb gardens. An old woman named Succordia watched the young children so that their mothers could do their daily work in the household and in the backyard. Male slaves ran errands in Williamsburg and to plantations in the surrounding rural area.

Randolph's enslaved men, women, and children worked in all areas of the house and the backyard each day. Perhaps Randolph knew that his attempt to create a white and black landscape could not succeed, because he could not make a clear distinction between his family and his slaves. The covered walkway between the dwelling house and the brick kitchen joined the two landscapes into one interconnected household.

WHAT DID THE APPRAISERS LEAVE OUT OF PEYTON RANDOLPH'S INVENTORY?

It is likely that John Dixon, William Pierce, and Alexander Craig spent most of January 5, 1776, at the Randolph house as they listed and valued the personal possessions Peyton Randolph owned at the time of his death. They walked through each room in his dwelling house and each of the outbuildings on his property. In spite of the appraisers' attention to detail, we know that they failed to list and value Peyton and Betty's jewelry and clothing, personal accessories, and the portraits that hung in the parlor. Why did Dixon, Pierce, and Craig leave these items off the inventory? Did the men feel they were not important? Did they neglect to record items associated with Betty Randolph because she was a woman? Did the Randolph slaves have any personal possessions?

Many appraisers did not list clothing and jewelry in inventories because it was assumed that a wife could have possession of her clothing after the death of her husband. Peyton Randolph did specify that Betty was to have "all her wearing Apparel rings and Jewels."[17] It is possible that Randolph planned to leave his clothes to his younger brother. However, John Randolph was a loyalist who left Williamsburg for England before his brother's estate was settled.

Betty Randolph documented some of the items that Dixon, Pierce, and Craig "missed" when she wrote her will and codicil. Her nephew Edmund Randolph inherited "the Family Picture ... and his uncles seal which I wear to my Watch." Elizabeth Harrison, the niece who slept in the oak-paneled room on the second floor, inherited "all my wearing Cloths my miniature Picture of my dear

Husband [and] my Watch." Betty Randolph also left her "dressing Table and Glass that stands in my Chamber and the Cabinet on the Top of the Desk" to Elizabeth Harrison. Nephew Benjamin Harrison received "four silver candlesticks called the new ones which were given me by my grandmother Harrison." Another niece, Lucy Randolph, received the books that her aunt kept in the bookcase in her closet.[18]

Why did Dixon, Pierce, and Craig fail to include the family portraits and Peyton Randolph's seal on the inventory? It is possible that Betty Randolph followed the appraisers through her house and persuaded them that the portraits and seal had value only to family members. In addition, Betty Randolph might have told the men that these items were her personal property (even though Virginia law did not allow married women to own property in their own name) and that they did not belong on a list of her husband's possessions.

Virginia law also stated that slaves could not own property. However, the appraisers did not list the clothes, shoes, or socks that Randolph's urban slaves had at the time their owner died. Unlike the uniform appearance of the oznaburg shirts, breeches, jackets, shifts, and petticoats worn by rural slaves in Virginia, Randolph's urban slaves wore clothing that reflected their position in his household and the work they did each day. Slaves who worked in the vegetable and herb garden or tended the horses and cattle near the stable probably wore clothes made from green plains, as did Moses when he carried goods between the Williamsburg dwelling and the James City County plantations. Slaves whose work required them to greet visitors in the Randolph house, serve meals in the dining room, or run errands in town wore finer clothes. Billy wore livery when he opened the dwelling's front door for guests, as did Watt when he drove the Randolph carriage. Watt and a postilion (a rider who accompanied the carriage) also wore hats. Johnny, in his role as Randolph's personal slave, had fine clothing to reflect both his status in the household and that of his master. It is likely that Betty Randolph's personal slave, Eve, and the other female slaves who worked in the house wore stays under their shifts and petticoats.

Clothing, whether made from oznaburg, plains, or wool, reminded Randolph's slaves of their status each day. This group of enslaved men, women, and children were able to acquire possessions in addition to the items Randolph issued to them each season and the straw pallets they used as their beds. Written records reveal that Johnny, Billy, and Watt received tips when they ran errands for Randolph. Other male slaves might also have received tips. It is possible that the Randolphs gave their slaves money during their lives. In her will, Betty Randolph left money to be "divided among the Servants that shall attend me in my House as they shall deserve."[19]

The tips that slaves received meant that they had money they could use to purchase goods in the public market or from Williamsburg's merchants. Dixon, Pierce, and Craig did not note the presence of any personal possessions in the kitchen-laundry-quarters building or the other outbuildings on the Randolph property. Again, Betty Randolph might have persuaded the appraisers that her slaves owned a few possessions and these items were not part of her husband's estate.

What kind of material possessions might Randolph's slaves have had? They might have bought ribbon, buttons, or brightly colored fabric to personalize the plain clothing that they wore. It is possible that the enslaved women and girls had some cowry-shell jewelry that they or a relative brought to Virginia as a reminder of life in Africa. It is possible that male slaves made bedsteads to raise pallets off the floor as well as tables and chairs to make their spartan living space more comfortable. A shelf could have held dishes, plates, and mugs. There could have been several books or a copy of the *Virginia Gazette* in the kitchen building because at least four of Randolph's slaves—Little Aggy, Roger, Sam, and Johnny—knew how to read. Enslaved men, women, and children might have gathered to play card games or to roll dice. Children might have spun tops or used a stick to roll hoops in the yard. Adults might have smoked tobacco in a clay pipe as they passed on stories about Africa and talked about their work and lives in the Randolph household.

It is possible that Randolph's urban slaves knew their daily lives differed from the experiences of the slaves who worked on their master's plantations in James City County and Charlotte County. The most obvious difference between urban and rural slavery in eighteenth-century Virginia was that in an urban setting, a large number of slaves lived in close proximity in a relatively small area. Not even the largest plantation ever had the number of slaves who lived in Williamsburg in the third quarter of the eighteenth century. On the eve of the American Revolution, just over half (52%) of the city's population of almost 1,900 residents was black.

Urban slaves, including the men, women, and children owned by Randolph, lived and worked in close proximity to their masters each day. Enslaved workers who labored on distant plantations might see their masters a few times a year. Unlike the plantation world,

A look at the inside of the quarters area shows the crude finish of the interior walls and some material objects that Peyton Randolph's slaves might have used to create their own personal space within this building. Reprinted by permission of the Colonial Williamsburg Foundation.

where the usual relations between black and white tended to be limited to that of slaves with an owner or overseer, urban slaves saw a variety of whites of various backgrounds, statuses, wealth, and even national backgrounds. Williamsburg's enslaved residents had to learn how to deal with a multitude of whites. In a similar way, urban whites dealt with more slaves who were not their own, and over whom they had no direct control.

Williamsburg's slaves experienced the harsh realities of life for enslaved blacks in eighteenth-century Virginia more often than did their rural counterparts. Randolph's enslaved men, women, and children probably saw families broken apart during estate sales on the steps of the city's taverns. Watt and Johnny might have seen the sales of recently arrived Africans in Yorktown. Enslaved and free blacks witnessed the physical punishment—whippings and hangings—administered to slaves who were found guilty of capital crimes.

However, there were some benefits of urban life for slaves in Williamsburg. The small size of the city made it possible for enslaved persons to develop ties to other slaves in the city. The location of the Randolph house enabled Randolph's slaves to become part of an African American community in the city and a community that also extended past Williamsburg. They visited with enslaved men, women, and children and free people of color who lived and worked in nearby households. Perhaps Randolph's domestic slaves had conversations with slaves who traveled to Virginia's colonial capital from time to time with their owners and with the enslaved persons who were in town on business for their masters.

In the early 1770s, it is probable that Randolph's slaves heard their owner, other Williamsburg residents, or men from across Virginia discuss the possibility of declaring independence from Great Britain. Johnny, Billy, and Eve would have had the greatest opportunity to hear these discussions since their daily work required them to spend time in the dwelling house. In August 1774, it is possible that several Randolph slaves heard Virginia's colonial leaders read and then discuss Thomas Jefferson's *A Summary View of the Rights of British America.* Jefferson was not able to attend the First Virginia Convention, which met in Williamsburg in August 1774. He sent a copy of the resolutions that he had prepared to his cousin, Peyton Randolph. Among other things, Jefferson criticized King George III for refusing to accept the Virginia legislature's attempt to limit the overseas slave trade by adopting a prohibitive tariff on imports. Jefferson also accused Parliament of trying to reduce the colonists to slavery.

Peyton Randolph died less than a month before Governor Dunmore, Virginia's last royal governor, issued a proclamation in which he promised freedom to all slaves and indentured servants who took up arms against their "rebel" masters. Betty Randolph managed her deceased husband's estate in addition to her daily work of managing the household and the work of the urban slaves. If Betty Randolph worried that some or all of her slaves would declare their independence, she left no record of these concerns. However, 14 Randolph slaves claimed their independence. Johnny, Peyton Randolph's personal slave, ran away in late 1777. Sometime between July 1776, when Randolph's inventories were recorded in the record book stored at the York County Courthouse, and the Revolution's final battle at Yorktown, 13 Randolph slaves decided to claim their freedom and to join the British. One day, Betty Randolph sat at her desk and took out the inventories of her husband's personal property in Williamsburg and on the James City County plantations. She added the phrase "gone to the enemy" by the names of eight Williamsburg slaves: Billy, Henry, Sam, Eve and her son George, Aggy, Lucy and her son Peter; and five James City County slaves: Denbo, Roger, Dick, Jimmy, and Nanny.[20] It is likely that the exact date that the Randolph slaves decided to join the British will never be known. What is known is that Betty Randolph's note—"gone to the enemy"—indicates that these enslaved men, women, and children decided to run to the British, and acknowledges their ability to make a decision that affected their lives.

CONCLUSION

Upon careful examination, the different pieces of the material culture puzzle—architectural details, artifacts from archaeological excavations, the many personal possessions listed in (and omitted from) Peyton Randolph's inventory, and written records—go together to create a picture of daily life in a Williamsburg household on the eve of the American Revolution. Each day, Peyton and Betty Randolph used their home to live their public lives as part of Virginia's gentry and to reserve space for their private, family activities. The Randolphs depended on the labor of their slaves for money to buy new, elegant possessions and to do the daily work in their household. Material possessions including furniture, kitchen utensils, carpets, and agricultural tools defined the work that slaves did each day. Slaves cooked, cleaned, made candles and soap, tended a vegetable and herb garden, greeted visitors to the household, straightened beds, washed clothes, groomed horses, and ran errands. Information about daily life at the Randolph house indicates that this was an interconnected household even though Randolph tried to place different parts of his life—public and private, white and black—into specific areas on his property. There was certainly a white and a black presence in the dwelling house on a daily basis.

The material culture pieces that provide information about daily life in Peyton Randolph's Williamsburg household can be found in many different places and different time periods. Examinations of goods, food, clothing, eating utensils, cooking pots, and buildings reveal details about daily life across the North American continent from the time people arrived to present day. In some cases, these objects provide the only information historians have about people who did not leave written records; in other cases, an examination of personal possessions adds details to the record about a well-known individual, particularly where daily life is concerned.

Material culture provides crucial insights into the lives of people such as Native Americans. Over two hundred years before Peyton Randolph's birth, the arrival of European colonists changed the daily lives of Native Americans who lived in the American Southwest, along the shores of the Great Lakes and the St. Lawrence River, and near the Atlantic coast.[21] Native Americans traded furs and food to explorers, missionaries, and settlers for beads, metal objects, and mirrors—items that had symbolic meaning in their cultures. Tribes across the continent also wanted guns and ammunition as well as blankets, cloth, and kettles. Over time, these trade goods became necessities in the lives of many Native Americans because some tribes forgot how to make traditional items such as weapons, knives, and blankets, which they got from European traders.

Native Americans also saw European traders, missionaries, and settlers change the North American landscape. Spanish settlers, soldiers, and missionaries built missions and presidios in present-day Florida, New Mexico, Texas, Arizona, and California. Spaniards cleared fields to grow food to feed themselves and the Indians who settled at their missions. French fur traders established trading posts along the St. Lawrence River and on the shores of the Great Lakes. French colonists built homes in Quebec and Montreal in New France and along the lower Mississippi River in Louisiana. English settlers cut down trees and established towns, farms, and plantations from Massachusetts to Georgia. The farms and plantations had both fields and agricultural buildings such as barns, dairies, storehouses, smokehouses, and stables. Deprived of much of their land for planting and hunting, Native Americans found it nearly impossible to maintain their daily lives and cultures.

In contrast, many Europeans benefited from the colonization of North America. Men, women, and children who remained in Great Britain and Europe ate a wider range of food after ships carried corn, potatoes, pumpkins, pineapples, and turkeys across the Atlantic Ocean.[22] In British North America, farmers and planters sold their crops—including wheat, rice, indigo, and tobacco—and used their profits to buy fashionable clothing, dishes, eating utensils, and bedding. Urban residents also prospered, while many poor colonists moved to cities along the East Coast in the hopes of finding a job. Ornate public buildings in Boston, New York City, Philadelphia, and Charleston reflected the prosperity of the British colonies, as did the refined homes of the wealthy. By the late eighteenth century, many elegant dwellings contained dolls, doll furniture and dishes, dominoes, balls, wagons, sleds, toy horses, and toy soldiers—items not common in households in earlier generations. The presence of toys reveals that parents began to see childhood as a separate, distinct phase of life and that play was an acceptable part of childhood. Here again, material culture offers information about a group—children—otherwise inarticulate, as well as about adult attitudes toward childhood.

Material culture also reveals economic and social differences that existed in the past. Colonial cities and smaller urban areas also had buildings that provided working and living space for artisans and craftsmen as well as small, crowded tenements for the laboring poor. Men, women, and children at the bottom of the economic ladder could not afford to participate in the Consumer Revolution. They used what little money they had for food, shelter, and clothing; the poor did not have enough money to buy anything that was a luxury. They had a material culture, though a limited one, and we can use its evidence to get some sense of the constraints and outlets of daily life.

In the nineteenth century, the poor became the labor force that worked in factories during the Industrial Revolution. In Lowell, Massachusetts; Lawrence, Massachusetts; and Manchester, New Hampshire, young women produced textiles made out of the cotton grown by slaves on plantations along the Gulf Coast. The cost of fabric dropped because factory owners paid low wages to the women who worked in the factories. Factories also manufactured shoes, hats, paper, woolen fabric, and other items Americans used each day.

Today, the proliferation of material objects continues to shape the daily lives of Americans. Like Peyton and Betty Randolph, we can select clothes, furniture, wall decorations, and carpets to create an identity and to make our lives comfortable. Kitchen gadgets from microwaves to food processors and toaster ovens help us to prepare meals for our families each day. It is difficult to avoid material objects in our consumer culture. Newspapers contain advertisements for sales, and television commercials tempt us to buy objects. Internet advertisements remind us of new objects and make it easier than ever to make a purchase. Today, people can sit at a desk and buy books, clothes, dishes, cooking utensils, and even a new house. Instant access to material goods makes it possible for men, women, and children of the twenty-first century to change their material world and daily lives at a pace few could have imagined even a generation ago. In the future, there will be a multitude of objects for historians to study in order to learn about daily life in the early twenty-first century.

Studies of material culture in various periods and places continue to add greatly to our knowledge about how people lived in the past. Once the subject of largely antiquarian concern, with descriptive catalogues of clothing or furniture styles, research on material culture now emphasizes how objects fit into actual patterns of life, including, of course, the divisions of various social groups. Even beyond this, the research seeks to determine what key objects meant to the people who used them, and when they had symbolic or emotional values that went beyond utility. Here, too, is a crucial window into the essential features of daily life.

NOTES

1. The original copies of the Randolph inventories can be found in the Estate Papers of Peyton Randolph, Library of Congress, Washington, D.C. See also Inventory of the Estate of Peyton Randolph in York County, dated 5 January 1776 and recorded 15 July 1776, *York County Wills and Inventories Book* 22 (1771–1783), 337–341; Inventory of the Estate of Peyton Randolph in Charlotte County, dated 20 November 1775 and recorded 15 July 1776, York County Wills and Inventories Book 22 (1771–1783), 341–344; and Inventory of the Estate of Peyton Randolph in James City County, dated 20 December 1775 and recorded 15 July 1776, York County Wills and Inventories Book 22 (1771–1783), 344–346.

2. Inventories are a valuable source for the study of material items owned by men and women who lived in the colonial era. It is important, however, to know that inventories are not perfect and do not always include all of a decedent's personal possessions. In addition, Virginia's colonial inventories did not include details about an individual's real property: the land, the house, and the outbuildings that stood on the property. For information about the use of inventories to learn about daily life, see Judith A. McGaw, "'So Much Depends upon a Red Wheelbarrow': Agricultural Tool Ownership in the Eighteenth-Century Mid-Atlantic," in *Early American Technology: Making and Doing Things from the Colonial Era to 1850*, ed. Judith A. McGaw (Chapel Hill and London: The University of North Carolina Press for the Institute of Early American History and Culture, 1994), 328–357, and "Forum: Towards a History of the Standard of Living in British North America," *William and Mary Quarterly*, 3rd. ser. 45 (1988): 116–170.

3. A cornice is a horizontal molding that crowns the ceiling, roof, or wall of a building. Carl Lounsbury notes that "beginning in the late 17th century, classically inspired cornices, enclosing the juncture of the wall and roof framing at the eaves, generally consisted of a bed molding, soffit, fascia, and crown molding." Carl R. Lounsbury, with editorial assistance from Vanessa E. Patrick, *An Illustrated Glossary of Early Southern Architecture and Landscape* (New York and Oxford: Oxford University Press, 1994), 96.

4. Baseboards are decorative moldings that run along the floor at the base of a plastered or wainscoted wall.

5. Chair boards are horizontal boards attached to a wall at the level of the back of a chair.

6. Sir John Randolph, will and codicil dated 23 December 1735 and 17 February 1736[/7] and recorded 28 April 1737, *Virginia Magazine of History and Biography* 36 (1928): 376–380.

7. Wainscoting is wood paneling used to cover the walls of buildings.

8. Inventory of the Estate of Peyton Randolph in York County, dated 5 January 1776 and recorded 15 July 1776, *York County Wills and Inventories* 22 (1771–1783).

9. Ibid.

10. Ibid.

11. Ibid.

12. A tailor needed three yards of material to make a suit of livery for a man and two and three-quarters yards to make a suit of livery for a boy. Each suit of livery usually had two colors.

13. Inventory of the Estate of Peyton Randolph in York County, dated 5 January 1776 and recorded 15 July 1776, *York County Wills and Inventories* 22 (1771–1783).

14. Ibid.

15. Ibid.

16. Ibid.

17. Peyton Randolph, will dated 18 August 1774 and recorded 20 November 1775, *York County Wills and Inventories* 22 (1771–1783), 308–310.

18. Betty Randolph, will and codicil dated 23 October 1780 and 20 July 1782, and recorded 17 February 1783, *York County Wills and Inventories* 23 (1783–1811), 4–5.

19. Ibid.

20. Estate papers of Peyton Randolph, Library of Congress, Washington, D.C.

21. The European traders and colonists also carried many deadly germs and diseases, including smallpox, malaria, whooping cough, and measles, to North America. These diseases took a heavy toll on the Native American population across the continent because most tribes lacked immunity to the germs.

22. Jacqueline Jones, Peter H. Wood, Thomas Borstelmann, Elaine Tyler May, and Vicki L. Ruiz, *Created Equal: A Social and Political History of the United States*, vol. 1 to 1877 (New York: Longman, 2003), 24–25.

FURTHER READING

On material culture, see Dell Upton, "White and Black Landscapes of Eighteenth-Century Virginia," *Places 2*, no. 2 (1985): 59–72; Robert Blair St. George, ed., *Material Life in America, 1600–1860* (Boston: Northeastern University Press, 1988); Ann Smart Martin, "Material Things and Cultural Meanings: Notes on the Study of Early American Material Culture," *William and Mary Quarterly*, 3rd ser., 53 (1996): 5–12; Patricia Samford, "The Archaeology of African-American Slavery and Material Culture," *William and Mary Quarterly*, 3rd ser., 53 (1996): 87–114; Ann Smart Martin and J. Ritchie Garrison, "Shaping the Field: The Multidisciplinary Perspectives of Material Culture," in *American Material Culture: The Shape of the Field*, ed. Ann Smart Martin and J. Ritchie Garrison (Knoxville: University of Tennessee Press for the Henry Francis du Pont Winterthur Museum, 1997), 1–20; Cary Carson, "Material Culture History: The Scholarship Nobody Knows," in *American Material Culture: The Shape of the Field*, ed. Ann Smart Martin and J. Ritchie Garrison (Knoxville: University of Tennessee Press for the Henry Francis du Pont Winterthur Museum, 1997), 401–428; Linda Baumgarten, "Plains, Plaid and Cotton: Woolens for Slave Clothing," *Ars Textrina* 15 (July 1991): 203–221; Linda Baumgarten, "'Clothes for the People': Slave Clothing in Early Virginia," *Journal of Early Southern Decorative Arts* 14 (1988): 27–70; Carl R. Lounsbury, with editorial assistance from Vanessa E. Patrick, *An Illustrated Glossary of Early Southern Architecture and Landscape* (New York and Oxford: Oxford University Press, 1994).

On the Consumer Revolution, see Richard L. Bushman, *The Refinement of America: Persons, Houses, Cities* (New York: Alfred A. Knopf, 1992); Stephanie Grauman Wolf, *As Various as Their Land: The Everyday Lives of Eighteenth-Century Americans* (New York: HarperCollins Publishers, 1993); Cary Carson, Ronald Hoffman, and Peter J. Albert, eds., *Of Consuming Interests: The Style of Life in the Eighteenth Century* (Charlottesville: University of Virginia Press for the United States Capital Historical Society, 1994); and T. H. Breen, *The Marketplace of Revolution: How Consumer Politics Shaped American Independence* (New York and Oxford: Oxford University Press, 2004).

On eighteenth-century Virginia, slavery in eighteenth-century Virginia, and the gentry lifestyle, see T. H. Breen, "Horses and Gentlemen: The Cultural Significance of Gambling among the Gentry of Virginia," *William and Mary Quarterly,* 3rd. ser., 34 (1977): 239–257; A. G. Roeber, "Authority, Law, and Custom: The Rituals of Court Day in Tidewater Virginia, 1720 to 1750," *William and Mary Quarterly,* 3rd. ser., 37 (1980): 29–52; Mark R. Wenger, "The Central Passage in Virginia: Evolution of an Eighteenth-Century Living Space," in *Perspectives in Vernacular Architecture,* vol. 2, ed. Camille Wells (Columbia: University of Missouri Press, 1986), 137–149; Mark R. Wenger, "The Dining Room in Early Virginia," *Perspectives in Vernacular Architecture,* vol. 3, ed. Thomas Carter and Bernard L. Herman (Columbia: University of Missouri Press, 1989), 149–159; Rhys Isaac, *The Transformation of Virginia, 1740–1790* (Chapel Hill and London: The University of North Carolina Press for the Institute of Early American History and Culture, 1982); Philip D. Morgan, *Slave Counterpoint: Black Culture in the Eighteenth-Century Chesapeake and Lowcountry* (Chapel Hill and London: The University of North Carolina Press for the Omohundro Institute of Early American History and Culture, 1998); and Ira Berlin, *Many Thousands Gone: The First Two Centuries of Slavery in North America* (Cambridge, MA, and London: The Belknap Press of Harvard University Press, 1998).

On eighteenth-century Williamsburg, the Peyton Randolph House, and Peyton Randolph, see John W. Reps, *Tidewater Towns: City Planning in Colonial Virginia and Maryland* (Charlottesville: University of Virginia Press for the Colonial Williamsburg Foundation, 1972); Andrew C. Edwards, Linda K. Derry, and Roy A. Jackson, *A View from the Top: Archaeological Investigations of Peyton Randolph's Urban Plantation* (Williamsburg, VA: Colonial Williamsburg Foundation, 1988); Jan Kirsten Gilliam and Betty Crowe Leviner, *Furnishing Williamsburg's Historic Buildings* (Williamsburg, VA: Colonial Williamsburg Foundation, 1991); Camille Wells, "Interior Designs: Room Furnishings and Historical Interpretations at Colonial Williamsburg," *Southern Quarterly* 31, no. 3 (Spring 1993): 89–111; "The Peyton Randolph House," *Colonial Williamsburg Interpreter* 20, no. 3 (Special Edition, 1999); Carl R. Lounsbury, "Ornaments of Civic Aspiration: The Public Buildings of Williamsburg," in *Williamsburg, Virginia, A City before the State:*

An Illustrated History, ed. Robert P. Maccubbin and Martha Hamilton-Phillips (Charlottesville and London: University of Virginia Press for the City of Williamsburg, 2000), 25–38; Mark R. Wenger, "Boomtown: Williamsburg in the Eighteenth Century," in *Williamsburg, Virginia, A City before the State: An Illustrated History,* ed. Robert P. Maccubbin and Martha Hamilton-Phillips (Charlottesville and London: University of Virginia Press for the City of Williamsburg, 2000), 39–48; Estate Papers of Peyton Randolph, Library of Congress, Washington, D.C.; and York County Court Records, Yorktown, Virginia.

On the use of inventories to study daily life, see Judith A. McGaw, "'So Much Depends upon a Red Wheelbarrow': Agricultural Tool Ownership in the Eighteenth-Century Mid-Atlantic," in *Early American Technology: Making and Doing Things from the Colonial Era to 1850,* ed. Judith A. McGaw (Chapel Hill and London: The University of North Carolina Press for the Institute of Early American History and Culture, 1994), 328–357; "Forum: Towards a History of the Standard of Living in British North America," *William and Mary Quarterly,* 3rd. ser., 45 (1988): 116–170 (especially the articles by Lorena S. Walsh, Gloria Main, and Lois Green Carr and Lorena S. Walsh); and Bernard L. Herman, "The *Bricoleur* Revisited," in *American Material Culture: The Shape of the Field,* ed. Ann Smart Martin and J. Ritchie Garrison (Knoxville: University of Tennessee Press for the Henry Francis du Pont Winterthur Museum, 1997), 37–63.

6

Politics, the State, Crime, and Deviancy

Marilynn S. Johnson

In the years leading up to the Mexican Revolution, a bandit named Santana Rodriguez terrorized the countryside around Veracruz. Known as Santanón, the bandit was a young mestizo (mixed race) who had grown up in slavery-like conditions on a local sugar plantation. He ran away at a young age and was recaptured, but he remained defiant toward his employers. He was later consigned to the army but deserted and joined forces with local bandits. Before long, Santanón was leading attacks against foreign sugar planters and mill owners in the region, recruiting local Indians and mestizos into his band. By 1910, they had murdered one American mill manager and attacked and robbed at least seven others.

Around the same time, a group of radical Liberals who supported the overthrow of the dictatorship of President Porfirio Diaz tried to recruit Santanón to join their cause. Whether he accepted their invitation is unclear, but President Diaz quickly dispatched army troops and federal police to try and apprehend him. For more than a year, Santanón and his followers eluded the authorities as local peasants cheered them on. Like Santanón, many peasants resented the harsh labor regime of the foreign plantations, and they marveled at his narrow escapes from the federal police, who protected foreign capitalists. In October 1910, the authorities finally captured Santanón's band, killing him and seven of his followers. But the bandit's defeat did not reduce his status as a folk hero, which continued to grow after his death. In 1932, in fact, his admirers in Veracruz renamed a local village in his honor, enshrining him as a forerunner of the Mexican Revolution.

The story of Santana Rodriguez nicely illustrates the convergence of politics and crime and its impact on society. Like other "social bandits," as historian Eric Hobsbawm called them, Santanón enjoyed popular support because his exploits reflected more widespread peasant resentments of oppressive landholding and labor practices by foreign sugar growers. To radical Liberals in Veracruz, President Diaz's vilification of Santanón and the latter's success at evading police capture made him a local hero of the emerging revolutionary movement. Santanón and other bandits associated with the revolution became the subject of numerous *corridos* (folk ballads) that reflected popular revolutionary sentiment on the local level.

But Santanón's story can also be read in a different way. Historians who have studied Mexican law-enforcement records have argued that Santanón was in fact a common criminal who terrorized foreign capitalists and local peasants alike. Indians in Veracruz complained that he forcibly recruited their young men and used them as cannon fodder in his attacks. After Santanón's death, some local peasants who were still sufficiently hostile to him joined the authorities in tracking down the remnants of his band. There is not much evidence that Santanón ever embraced the Liberal cause or the movement to oust Diaz. With his attacks on foreign sugar interests, Santanón stirred violent emotions, but his actions never meaningfully challenged the Diaz government. The common people's adulation of the bandit, these historians conclude, was more a diversion from political action than a foundation for it.

These two conflicting interpretations of Santanón—as peasant rebel or common criminal—illustrate some of the difficulties in studying topics like politics and crime in everyday life. First, how do we determine what constitutes politics, especially when examining actions and movements outside the organized mainstream? Likewise, how do we distinguish criminal behavior from political or social resistance? As the state defines and redefines what constitutes crime, how should historians go about measuring or interpreting such behavior? Sources are an important consideration here. Those scholars who rely heavily on popular sources like newspapers and *corridos* have found abundant evidence to support the social bandit thesis. On the other hand, those who rely mainly on official government sources have tended to see bandits as common criminals with little political or social import. For historians of everyday life, however, the phenomenon of banditry cannot be ignored, though exactly how we interpret individual cases depends on a close examination of the historical context using a wide variety of sources. Such an approach has been used in recent years to study a range of daily life topics, from politics and state building to crime and deviancy. This approach has offered a new, bottom-up perspective on the conventional historical narrative of the nation-state, and in the process, changed our understanding of this history by showing how ordinary people helped shape the larger workings of politics, law, and government.

EVERYDAY POLITICS AND THE STATE

Prior to the consolidation of the nation-state, locally based political activity took many forms and was a primary means through which the peasantry challenged elite power. European historians have documented how peasants withheld payments to the nobility and the church, renegotiated rents and taxes, joined dissident religious movements, and staged violent riots and rebellions. Traditionally, peasant rebellions were viewed as irrational outbreaks of murder and mayhem, lead by messianic figures. Since the 1960s, however, historians have traced the social and economic roots of such revolts, arguing that peasant violence was a rational, if tragic, response to hardship and repression. During the fourteenth century, for example, widespread famine, plague, war, and depopulation led to economic and political instability that proved to be fertile ground for peasant uprisings. In both England and France, the imposition of new taxes sparked an outpouring of violence in which crowds murdered nobles, burned their castles, slaughtered their livestock, and raped their wives and daughters. Religious ideology sometimes fed these rebellions as well. In the English peasant revolt of 1381, followers of the Christian dissident John Wycliffe used scriptural references to sanction their revolt. In France and the Holy Roman Empire, religious and secular leaders channeled popular unrest into anti-Semitic persecution, combining longstanding religious animosity toward Jews with more acute economic resentments. In urban areas, crowds also had a political sense, even when they did not attack the state directly. Bread riots in Europe, over high prices and scarcity, expressed a belief that the authorities should prevent starvation and should curb greedy merchants.

After the rise of the nation-state, local politics continued to play an important role in everyday life, particularly in decentralized societies like the United States. In nineteenth-century America, a rich assortment of voluntary associations and parties forged a popular political culture in which large numbers participated. As the French writer Alexis de Tocqueville first observed, antebellum Americans were fervent participants in voluntary societies that ranged from small church groups to large municipal organizations. It was here that they learned the principles of self-government and moral discipline, but as historians have noted, these societies were also sites of social hierarchy and exclusion, particularly for women, African Americans, and the poor. Socially marginalized and politically disenfranchised, these groups founded their own voluntary associations where they organized around issues such as labor reform, temperance, antislavery, education, and suffrage. Their activities would ultimately affect the larger arena of national politics.

Historians of women, for instance, have demonstrated that women played important roles in challenging state power and reforming political life. Beginning in revolutionary times, American women circulated petitions, participated in boycotts of British goods, and supported patriotic campaigns to produce home manufactures. Similarly, in France, thousands of armed Parisian women angered over food shortages stormed the palace at Versailles and abducted the king and his family in 1789. Soon after, sansculotte women organized revolutionary organizations that marched on the National Convention and demanded that legislators recognize the rights of women citizens. The male revolutionaries, however, proved unwilling to grant women equal rights and moved to suppress women's political organizations and public access. The same was true in the new American republic, where the founding fathers did not "remember the women," as Abigail Addams had implored, but limited citizenship rights to white males.

Over the next several decades, however, American women used the rhetoric of the Revolution to increase their access to education. Insisting that they were the "mothers of the new republic" responsible for educating future male citizens, women pressed for greater access to formal education. Their efforts resulted in the opening of female academies, the training of women teachers, and the beginning of female educational and reform networks that would promote abolition, temperance, and women's rights. By the late nineteenth century, women's voluntary organizations had proliferated to address poverty, child welfare, sanitation, and a spate of other urban social problems in both the United States and western Europe. Defining their work as an extension of female domesticity, women reformers brought social concerns into local and national politics and created the foundation for the welfare state. Their efforts resulted in what historian Paula Baker has called "the domestication of politics."[1] But they also fed women's desire for suffrage and economic independence. Attention to local politics, then, can tell us a great deal about important but less visible political activities of women and other subordinate groups.

Even when considering the dominant white male society, local politics offers a window into the dynamics of political life in earlier periods. In the nineteenth-century United States, for example, historians have shown how the national dominance of the Democratic and Republican parties depended on an elaborate grassroots political culture. In an effort to attract voters, local branches of the major parties sponsored an array of community rituals and spectacles that included parades, marching bands, fireworks, and street celebrations. Combining politics with sociability and entertainment, partisan organizations

In the early 1960s, Bob Moses and other volunteers with the Student Nonviolent Coordinating Committee walked the back roads of Mississippi to try and convince local black residents to register to vote. Their grassroots efforts gave rise to a national civil rights campaign that secured the black franchise and ended legal segregation. Danny Lyons/Magnum Photos.

succeeded in turning out 70–80 percent of voters on election day. Individual candidates were relatively unimportant in these campaigns, which sought to inspire loyalty to local political clubs and organizations. In urban areas, political machines organized by neighborhood and ethnicity touched many aspects of daily life. For poorer constituents, they provided patronage jobs and legal assistance, while the wealthy enjoyed lucrative government contracts and a pro-business legal climate. Around the turn of the century, however, this community-based political culture gave way to a more centralized party system that used media and advertising campaigns to promote individual candidates and issues. As voters became more passive spectators, historians argue, electoral participation dropped accordingly.

But this does not mean that politics became the sole terrain of national political leaders. Grassroots political activism, in fact, has been a driving force behind the major social reform efforts of the twentieth century. In the 1930s, local union organizing drives under the Congress of Industrial Organizations put pressure on the Roosevelt administration to pass the Wagner Act, guaranteeing labor's right to organize. This militancy was a product of the unemployment and hardship of the Depression years, but it also grew out of the raised expectations of the 1920s, when corporations introduced employee welfare and benefit programs that promised workers a more humane workplace but failed to deliver it. Organizing among the elderly also had an impact on the New Deal. In the mid-thirties, a burgeoning network of Townsend Clubs, which supported government pensions for the elderly, laid the groundwork for passage of the Social Security Act in 1935.

Focusing on the postwar period, social historians have moved away from a national-level analysis of the civil rights movement to explore its local roots in southern communities. Their work has highlighted the importance of local veterans, women, and college students who built on black community networks and religious traditions to mobilize a larger movement. Historians have shown, for example, that Christian faith and black gospel music were incorporated into daily meetings and political events and became powerful vehicles for movement building. Likewise, black educators used literacy programs to teach people about citizenship rights, a process that fueled local activism and mobilization. It was these grassroots networks that Martin Luther King, Jr., and other national leaders later built on for their national campaigns in the 1960s.

The conservative Right has been equally adept at local political organizing, particularly since the 1960s. Historians have traced the origins of the New Right back to grassroots anti-Communist campaigns of the early sixties in places like Orange County, California, and Dallas, Texas. In these areas, a booming postwar economy fueled rapid suburban development and a deepening commitment to free-market values and property rights. Anti-Communist groups like the John Birch Society organized on the neighborhood level around coffee klatches or backyard barbeques. Local evangelical churches also helped mobilize the conservative movement, especially as social issues such as crime, school prayer, abortion, and gay rights came to the fore in the late sixties and seventies. Working through church networks, Christian conservatives launched prayer groups, petition campaigns, and voter registration drives to help elect Republican candidates and pass local ballot measures. While the election of President Ronald Reagan marks the rise of the New Right in national politics, historical study of local politics shows that this movement had much deeper roots in postwar America.

In cases of totalitarian rule or pervasive social repression, dissident political voices have been more muted. In recent years, however, historians and anthropologists have identified alternate forms of resistance known as "infrapolitics": unorganized and spontaneous types of political discontent expressed privately or in disguised forms. In nineteenth-century India, for example, peasants quietly resisted British rule through a dissident culture expressed in songs, folklore, jokes, and other daily interactions. This "hidden transcript" inspired more overt forms of resistance that might include foot-dragging, sabotage, or theft. Historians of the American South have documented similar cultures of resistance among African slaves. The trickster tales of Brer Rabbit, for example, were used by parents to instruct their children on how to outfox the master and hence survive the harsh regime of slavery. Such stories were openly told and shared with white children, but only those slaves steeped in an opposition culture could understand their significance. Occasionally, infrapolitics would develop into more direct forms of political opposition. In the segregated South of the 1940s, for example, little-known daily conflicts over public space on city buses heightened black impatience with segregation in Alabama. These conflicts paved the way for the successful bus boycott in Montgomery in 1955, when a determined Rosa Parks demanded her right to equal treatment.

Infrapolitics could also take more playful forms. In the Soviet Union, some disaffected workers expressed their hostility toward the Stalinist state by supporting Spartak, a Moscow-based professional soccer club. Sponsored by a retail trades union, Spartak attracted rowdy working-class fans whose drinking and carousing stood in stark contrast to state-sponsored notions of manhood and sportsmanship. Fans were particularly vocal in their animus for Spartak's rival Dinamo, a team sponsored by the secret police. Matches between the two teams thus became forms of political theater in which Spartak's fans, concentrated in the cheaper seats, acted out their resentments against the white-collar bureaucrats below. In the chaotic and anonymous setting of the sports stadium, antistate sentiments could be aired forcefully and openly. The threat that Spartak and its fans posed to the regime became evident in 1942, when the Soviet authorities arrested and exiled the team's managers. As this case suggests, the relationship between politics and sports is a fruitful field for future research.

The study of infrapolitics implies a broad definition of politics—one that includes everyday forms of resistance expressed through work, leisure, religion, and culture. This recasting of politics has invited criticism from some quarters. Practitioners of infrapolitics, the critics argue, tend to romanticize the experiences of subordinate groups, misconstruing daily discontent as meaningful resistance. This critique has been especially prevalent in the case of the *Alltagsgeschichte* (everyday life) school of German history. Focusing on daily life in the Nazi era, some *Alltagsgeschichte* historians emphasized the ways in which ordinary Germans quietly resisted Nazi policies. Other scholars vehemently disagreed, arguing that such cases of resistance have been overemphasized and that most Germans cooperated with Hitler's regime. More recently, some *Alltagsgeschichte* historians have concurred with this view and have instead focused on how and why many ordinary Germans were complicit in Nazism. The heated nature of this debate highlights some of the methodological difficulties in studying inchoate forms of politics. Uncovering forms of everyday resistance can tell us a lot about historical consciousness, but such practices did not always result in larger political change. In many cases, nation-states continued to consolidate power and implement policies that profoundly affected everyday life.

In the modern era, the state has shaped daily life in myriad ways, from promoting health and welfare to regulating social behavior, migration, and population growth. Government initiatives, for example, have had a major impact on public health. In western European and American cities, mortality rates have declined since the nineteenth century due to improved sanitation practices (such as public sewer systems) and cleaner water that was piped and filtered through publicly owned systems. In the mid-twentieth century, mandatory government-subsidized vaccination programs significantly reduced diseases like polio and rubella, especially among children. And since the 1960s, environmental regulations have reduced air and water pollution in the United States and forced cleanup of toxic waste sites that posed serious health hazards to nearby residents.

Social insurance and other public welfare programs have also relieved some of the hardships of unemployment and old age. In the United States, the Social Security Act was the centerpiece of New Deal social welfare reform, providing old-age pensions and unemployment benefits for millions of Americans for the first time. Over the years, provisions of the 1935 act were gradually expanded to a greater percentage of the workforce, while further legislation offered disability and survivor benefits, cost-of-living increases, and coverage of medical expenses under Medicare. Seniors have thus had greater access to doctors and health care, which has contributed to longer life expectancies. Poverty rates among the elderly have fallen from 35 percent in 1960 to around 10 percent today, with especially great improvement evident among elderly women. Without Social Security, economists estimate, almost half of the elders today would be living in poverty. Social Security has also enabled many elders to live independently of their adult children, thus fueling the development of elderly housing and retirement communities throughout the United States in the last 40 years. Here is an obvious case in which state programs significantly impact private life, sometimes with effects that were not anticipated when the measures were proposed.

Western nations have also promoted labor reform by legalizing unions and passing legislation regulating the workplace. In the United States, labor laws have established minimum wage levels while reducing child labor, hours of work, and certain types of hazardous working conditions. Compared to many European countries, however, these gains have been minimal. Since World War II, most workers in western Europe and Canada have enjoyed shorter hours than Americans, as well as national health insurance, paid maternity leave, subsidized child care, and other government-mandated benefits that conservative political interests in the United States have consistently opposed.

Communist states such as the former Soviet Union and the People's Republic of China also instituted labor and welfare policies that raised the standard of living for their poorest citizens. But intense state control also brought new forms of repression and hardship. In both the Soviet Union and China, the collectivization of the economy brought tight restrictions on internal migration and a virtual ban on emigration until the 1980s. In both countries, urban food supplies were subject to rationing, and consumer goods were scarce. Soviet citizens learned to stand in long lines to purchase goods but also circumvented state controls by trading on the black market. In both China and the USSR, one-party rule meant that dissident political and religious groups were outlawed. Those who persisted with such activities had to do so clandestinely and were subject to imprisonment or execution, particularly during Stalin's purges in the 1920s and 1930s and China's Cultural Revolution in the 1960s.

Both Communist and capitalist states have periodically tried to either encourage or discourage population growth to keep pace with food supplies or production needs. In China, the state took strong measures to limit population, which had grown from roughly 540 million in 1949 to more than 800 million by 1980. China's one-child rule, instituted in the late 1970s, helped to slow population growth through penalties that included loss of employment, steep fines, or even forced abortion or sterilization. But this program also had unintended consequences such as female infanticide and abandonment, as well as a burgeoning overseas adoption market for Chinese babies and young girls. Recent changes in government economic policies, however, have led to a loosening of the system. Some well-paid employees in the growing private sector have willingly paid fines to have a second child, while revenue-starved local officials have eagerly accepted these fines and encouraged others to do the same. While China's population policies have been the most extreme, laws governing abortion, birth control, sterilization, and other practices have had a significant impact on women's autonomy and family life around the world.

Education is another vital area where modern states shape daily life, often—along with their regulation of child labor—transforming the nature of childhood in the process. Historians study what officials try to accomplish through school systems, including creation of a loyal citizenry. School programs often force unfamiliar values on some groups, creating resentments. Schools push not only literacy but also values like a modern sense of time or new habits of hygiene.

Modern states do not, however, simply bend ordinary people to their will. Historians study how people sometimes ignore or sidestep government goals, or apply them to other purposes. Most government efforts to promote higher birthrates in the twentieth century—for example, offering bonuses to large families—have had little effect, as most people found it essential to protect themselves against having too many children.

WAR AND SOCIETY

Undoubtedly, the greatest impact of the state on everyday life has come during times of war. Military service and war have had direct and profound effects on society, as recruitment, warfare, occupation, and refugee crises have transformed daily life in myriad ways. On the home front, government and civilian support for war-related activities, as well as citizen opposition to state-led programs, has likewise shaped everyday life and social relations. Historians of daily life have studied both aspects of wartime, showing how these conflicts affected people's lives at the time but also how wars have sometimes permanently changed the societies that waged them.

Although military service has been an enduring feature of most societies, the forms of recruitment have changed over the centuries. In antiquity and feudal times, military service was a requirement of citizenship or land tenure and was usually performed locally and for short intervals. During major wars, slaves, sailors, and boys as young as eight might be pressed into service. With the rise of the nation-state, professional armies staffed by mercenaries or volunteers became more common. In times of war, however, these armies usually proved insufficient. Many large nations thus combined a professional army with a conscription system that compelled service from a broad swath of society, including the lower classes. Prior to World War II, much of this recruiting was done locally, producing geographically and ethnically homogenous combat units whose solidarity was considered good for morale. But when such units engaged in major battles, the resulting casualties could devastate whole communities.

The wartime expansion of the military was often accompanied by rigidly stratified and segregated military units that reproduced larger social inequalities—the racially segregated U.S. Army (prior to 1948) being a prime example. On the other hand, though, military historians have discovered how acute shortages of military personnel sometimes resulted in new social and economic opportunities for subordinate groups. In the major European armies of World War I, for example, the desperate need for experienced commanders resulted in a democratization of the officer corps, as middle-class and working-class men joined the ranks of the once-aristocratic commanders. At the same time, the U.S. government offered immediate naturalization to some Native American and immigrant recruits in exchange for their service. More recently, the all-volunteer U.S. Army has offered cash bonuses and education benefits that have been valuable assets to working-class and minority youth. Such social and economic benefits, however, have come with significant risks.

With the onset of hostilities, troops faced a good likelihood of illness, injury, or death. American historians have shown that prior to World War I, disease and accidents usually accounted for more deaths than combat. In the American Civil War, for example, roughly 110,000 Union troops died from combat, but more than double that number perished from disease. Improved medical and sanitation practices subsequently reduced the threat of disease. As weaponry became more powerful and lethal, both the military and civilian casualty rates increased, peaking at more than 50 million deaths in World War II. Widespread use of airpower and carpet bombing, combined with the unprecedented deployment of atomic weapons in Hiroshima and Nagasaki, produced the highest civilian casualty rates in history. More recently in the United States, combat casualty rates have fallen as a result of improved targeting and body armor, but the percentage of those who survive with severe injuries has increased. Psychological trauma has also taken a toll. First identified as "shell shock" in World War I, post-traumatic stress disorder has resulted in increased substance abuse, suicide, and family discord among veterans. The widespread disabilities and deaths associated with modern wars have had a devastating emotional impact on families and communities, as well as temporarily skewing the sex ratio, lowering marriage rates and birthrates, and increasing the number of widows and orphans.

The brutality and carnage of battle has frequently led to retaliation and escalation, but historians have also identified instances of mutual restraint. In the face of the horrors of trench warfare during World War I, some historians have argued, both Allied and German forces placed limits on combat to spare their own troops. To allow the men time to eat and use latrines, for example, commanders generally avoided shelling in the early morning and evening hours. The heaviest firefights typically occurred at agreed-upon times following lunch and dinner. On Christmas holidays, opposing armies sometimes called a more formal truce, allowing both sides to remove their dead, conduct funerals, and even trade food supplies or play soccer. Restraint was also practiced on an individual level. During the Civil War, both Union and Confederate troops sometimes allowed themselves to be captured in order to be paroled back to their home communities. The widespread abuse of parole, in fact, prompted both sides to discontinue the practice in favor of incarceration in military prisons. In Vietnam, some U.S. soldiers sought to survive their tours of duty by limiting their offensive tactics or by incurring "million-dollar wounds": serious but nonfatal wounds that would require removal from the battlefield. While such behavior was frowned upon by military commanders, it was viewed more sympathetically by enlisted men unwillingly drafted and involved in dangerous and protracted conflicts.

Modern warfare has also critically affected civilians living in combat areas. Residents of communities under siege or occupation could become victims of violence, theft, rape, or homelessness. Cities subject to bombing raids in the twentieth century also saw major damage to local infrastructure, such as railroads, bridges, schools, and hospitals. Rural areas also suffered, as hungry armies fanned out in search of food, crops, and livestock or took over the homes of local farm families. In anticipation of such hardships, many civilians fled in advance of invading armies.

Although refugees were common in premodern wars, the increasingly lethal and mobile nature of modern warfare has produced staggering refugee crises in the twentieth century. During World War I, the German invasion of Belgium resulted in a mass exodus of Belgians to France and England, while the Russian Revolution spurred another wave of out-migration from that country in 1917. For many of these refugees, foreign resettlement was difficult, if not impossible, due partly to the hostile attitudes of native residents. War-related fears of enemy aliens and refugees resulted in a hardening of national boundaries in the 1920s. The relatively open climate of prewar Europe, where citizens moved freely across national borders, soon gave way to a bureaucratic system of passports, visas, and immigration restrictions that limited the movement of individuals and families.

These restrictions, combined with massive warfare and persecution during World War II, produced an even greater refugee crisis in the 1940s. The five-year conflict produced an estimated thirty million refugees, including thousands of Jews fleeing the Holocaust, many of whom found themselves barred from the United States and other Allied countries. As late as the 1950s, there were still millions of officially designated "displaced persons" seeking a permanent home. Subsequent wars, from Vietnam to the Middle East, have produced their own refugee crises and government efforts to resolve them through relief and immigration. Indeed, historians have shown how war refugees played an important role in shaping immigration patterns in the United States, Britain, France, and other countries.

Historians of wartime life have focused much of their attention on the home front. In modern wars, nation-states have used broad powers to mobilize the citizenry. The greatest challenge has been the organization of defense industries and supply operations. In the two world wars, belligerent nations fully mobilized their industries and agriculture, requiring a vast expansion of the workforce. As historians have shown, these developments had a paradoxical influence on social and economic life. On the one hand, a growing number of civilians found economic and social opportunities not available during peacetime, some of which continued into the postwar era.

During World War I, President Woodrow Wilson called on women to serve their country by becoming nurses and relief workers for the Red Cross. In 1919, Wilson honored women's wartime commitment by supporting the Nineteenth Amendment, granting women the right to vote. American Red Cross recruitment poster, 1918. Courtesy of the Library of Congress.

On the other hand, the wartime advancement of subordinate groups also inspired resentments among their neighbors and coworkers, fueling a social backlash both during and after the war. American historians have explored this paradox most extensively in the case of women and African Americans on the home front.

During both world wars, many American women experienced rapid and exhilarating change. In the workforce, women's employment increased and expanded into traditionally male occupations such as shipbuilding, munitions manufacturing, and railroad and streetcar operations. Women also moved into military service in significant numbers, both as civilian clerks and as army nurses. Such opportunities led to increased wages and social autonomy for women, as well as access to new social services, such as child care and health care, available in some defense industries. At the end of World War I, the United

States and several western European nations acknowledged women's support for the war effort by extending the vote to women, a goal long sought by feminist groups.

Nevertheless, women still encountered numerous obstacles to equality. Occupational segregation by sex continued in most industries, and women's family responsibilities (especially if their husbands were in the service) created conflicts with defense jobs that demanded long hours. Absenteeism and turn-over were thus common, leading to charges of female malingering. Likewise, young women's participation in wartime leisure activities produced widespread concern about female promiscuity and restrictions on women's social behavior. Concerns about rising war deaths and falling birthrates also fueled a greater emphasis on pro-natalism by the European powers. During World War I, France and Britain instituted propaganda campaigns encouraging couples to procreate as a patriotic duty. Germany went a step further by reducing access to contra-ceptives and offering maternity allowances to all pregnant women, a program that was renewed with increased vigor under the Third Reich. Historians have shown how these pro-natalist programs reinforced women's domestic roles and discouraged their continued employment. In any case, many women workers were laid off at the end of both wars, losing most of the occupational ground they had gained.

African Americans had a similarly mixed experience in wartime. As U.S. defense industries expanded, they attracted thousands of black migrants from the South, who relocated to northern and western defense centers. This mass movement offered black Southerners new economic opportunities, access to the franchise, and an escape from lynching and legalized segregation. But on the job and in their new communities, African Americans continued to encounter racial discrimination. Resentful whites, facing wartime inflation and shortages, sometimes lashed out with violence and segregation measures. Racial tensions continued in the wake of both wars as veterans returned and employment con-tracted. In particular, 1919 and 1943 stand out as two of the peak years of racial violence in the twentieth century. Mexican Americans and Native Americans encountered a similar mix of opportunity and racial backlash during World War II. The racially contentious climate of those years, which both raised and dashed minority expectations, proved to be the crucible of the modern civil rights move-ment.

Wars have created a conducive climate for other types of social unrest as well. The military draft, rapid inflation, structural changes in the workplace, food shortages, and other problems often sparked unrest among labor and consum-ers. Anger over the inequities of the draft, in which the poor were compelled to serve but the rich could purchase substitutes, sparked draft riots in New York and several other cities during the Civil War. During World War I, when inflation and food shortages became critical, there were widespread strikes and food riots in both Europe and the United States. The most dramatic uprisings occurred in Russia in 1917, where revolutionary workers turned against the war, overthrew the tsarist government, and established a Soviet state.

In an effort to ease hardships, avoid social unrest, and sustain the war effort, modern states implemented a variety of social and economic programs. Many of these efforts began during World War I but were more fully developed and implemented during World War II. Food shortages, inflation, and a burgeoning black market during World War I, for example, lead to government efforts at rationing and price controls in France, England, Germany, and the United States. Initially, these programs were locally run and not very effective; they were later taken over by the national governments. In World War II, these same countries ran national programs that issued ration books for goods such as sugar, meat, gasoline, clothes, and rubber. Citizens learned to adjust their consumption habits and swapped coupons with neighbors and family members as needed. They also learned to make do with ersatz foodstuffs such as turnip jam and barley coffee. In several countries, rationing and price controls lasted well after the end of hostilities. In Britain, for example, the rationing of meat continued until 1954.

National governments also facilitated the migration and resettlement of thousands of civilian residents. During World War II especially, expanded defense industries absorbed local labor supplies and required new workers from other areas. While Germany met this need largely through the forced labor of prisoners of war and concentration camp victims, the United States offered temporary employment to migrants from the South and the Midwest. Concentrated in cities along the coasts, defense contractors recruited hundreds of thousands of migrant workers and used government funds to build large-scale war-housing projects and to provide services to accommodate the workers. On the West Coast especially, these migrant settlements became parallel communities that ultimately transformed local society and culture. As historians have documented, many of these migrants settled there permanently, bringing Southern-style churches, music, and foodways to the urban West.

While civilians gravitated toward urban America, the British government launched a mass evacuation of children from London to the countryside. Hoping to spare them from German bombing raids, British authorities relocated nearly three million schoolchildren in 1939 and fielded them out to rural households. An exciting adventure for some, others were traumatized by the separation from their parents or were abused by their new guardians. Historians have chronicled the human drama of the evacuation through oral histories, letters, and government reports.

But perhaps the most traumatic relocation experience was that of so-called enemy aliens. The relocation and internment of immigrants from enemy nations is a relatively recent phenomenon, arising in the wake of the mass global migrations of the late nineteenth and early twentieth centuries. In an effort to stem espionage and other treasonous activity, governments began requiring the registration and detention of enemy aliens within their territorial borders. These practices were fueled by the emergence of government propaganda agencies that disseminated xenophobic and racist images of the enemy that enflamed antiforeign sentiments. In the United States during World War I, for example, the Committee for Public Information produced films and posters that depicted Germans as bestial Huns who raped and pillaged the Belgian population. The European governments ran similar campaigns on both sides, and internment camps were established for the first time on a mass scale in Britain and Germany. Canada (then part of the British Dominion) also interned some 8,000 enemy aliens, mainly Ukrainian nationals from the Austro-Hungarian Empire. In these

During World War II, more than 100,000 Japanese and Japanese-Americans were interned as "enemy aliens" in remote camps like this one at Heart Mountain, Wyoming. Tom Parker/War Relocation Authority, Courtesy of the National Archives.

cases and others, government authorities claimed that internment was a "protective" measure against anti-immigrant violence, sentiments that government propaganda efforts had served to promote.

The United States resorted to internment during World War II when it evacuated more than 100,000 Japanese immigrants and their children from the West Coast and shipped them to internment camps in the interior. Historians have documented the wrenching losses and dislocations that accompanied internment, as many Japanese lost their homes and livelihoods and saw their family ties eroded. Debates about whether internment was justified were put to rest by one historian's startling discovery in 1981: long-lost government documents that asserted that the Roosevelt administration was well aware that Japanese Americans posed no threat of treason during the war. Such historical findings helped win congressional passage of the Japanese American Redress Act of 1988, which provided former internees with an official apology and cash reparations.

Internment was practiced on a much larger and more horrific scale in Nazi Germany, where millions of Jews and other minority groups were confined and often exterminated. Survival during the Holocaust has been a rich field of study, documenting the daily experiences of Jews from the terror of Kristallnacht to the "final solution." Holocaust historians have chronicled the devastating impact of Nazi rule on people's lives as well as the heroism of the resistance. Moreover, they have examined how ordinary aspects of living—obtaining food, educating children, and practicing religion—took on new significance during the Holocaust and constituted forms of resistance in their own right. Their documentation and findings have become the basis for numerous Holocaust exhibits and museums around the world.

Finally, historians of the home front have also examined how some wartime problems and government programs stimulated long-term social change. American Civil War historians, for example, have shown how the military pension system and homes for disabled soldiers established after the war laid the foundation for the present-day Veterans' Administration. This agency provided vital services for veterans and set a precedent for the later expansion of the welfare state. The Servicemen's Readjustment Act, commonly known as the GI Bill, was even more important. Passed in 1944, the bill provided housing loans, tuition assistance, medical care, and job training for millions of World War II veterans. Although historians debate how equitably these benefits were distributed, they agree that these measures helped promote postwar suburbanization and the expansion of higher education to a greater number of Americans. In Britain, wartime events also stimulated the development of the welfare state. Historians argue that the exposure of urban poverty and health problems, particularly evident during the children's evacuation, helped shape social policy embodied in the Beveridge Plan of 1942, a blueprint for the postwar welfare state.

Assessing the impact of war on long-term social and political transformation, however, is a tricky business. Those who study the social history of war sometimes assume that shifts evident during the war were *caused* by the war itself, rather than merely accelerated by it. In many cases, in fact, wartime social trends, such as women's workforce participation or racial prejudice, were already evident before the war and thus had deeper historical roots. In order to properly assess the degree of change or continuity, historians must research their topic before, during, and after the war years to get a better long-term view. Indeed, many of the early books published on wartime life exaggerated the degree of change, viewing the war as a major social watershed. Subsequent works have been more careful to delineate short-term versus long-term change and to identify the prewar roots and precedents for wartime transformations.

The kinds of sources historians rely on in their research can also shape their findings. Because modern wars have been highly organized and promoted by state authorities, government records contain a wealth of information about both military and civilian war activities. These documents have been a terrific starting point for research, but they also generally reflect the state's interest in promoting the war effort. Glowing accounts of military prowess in battle and social harmony and productivity on the home front are recurring themes in these archives. To get beneath the surface, however, historians need to seek out the voices of ordinary people on the local level to get their views from the ground up. Discussions of social tensions, antiwar dissent, military insubordination, and other problematic aspects of war are most evident in personal reminiscences, in the press accounts, and through court records. As historians have mined such sources, they have tended to take a less rosy view of wartime society. Government-projected images of social unity and shared sacrifice have thus given way to more critical portrayals of social conflict and inequality.

CRIME AND DEVIANCY

Because crime is such a critical issue today, the historical study of crime and criminal justice has been a fruitful field of research. Studying the history of crime not only tells us about past crime patterns and causes but also how crime was defined in different historical contexts and who got to define it. As such, studying crime helps us learn about the norms of earlier societies and the power relations between different classes, races, and gender groups in those societies.

The methodological problems involved in studying the history of crime, however, are formidable. For starters, the availability of historical data on crime varies widely by location and time period. In early modern England, for example, there is a treasure trove of court records, ranging from local manorial and ecclesiastical courts to the King's Bench. With such a wealth of documents, historians are often forced to limit their studies to particular regions, time periods, or types of crimes. But in other countries and time periods, the opposite is true: crime records are nonexistent or fragmentary at best, making sustained analysis impossible. Even when good data exist, they are most useful when correlated with population figures (modern crime statistics are usually calculated per 100,000 people). Such demographic information is not always available (particularly in the premodern period), thus thwarting comparative analysis over time. More importantly, even the best data sets do not reflect unreported or nonprosecuted crimes and thus reveal only the tip of the iceberg. Moreover, the rate of unreported crime varies historically depending on the political and social climate, the economic resources required to pursue prosecution (in many premodern societies, crimes were prosecuted privately), and other factors. The actual levels of criminal behavior at any given time are thus ultimately unknowable.

An even more fundamental concern for historians is how crime comes to be defined in the first place. Because state authorities represent specific social groups and cultural values, their views of what constitutes crime will also vary. In colonial America, where stern child rearing was considered a Christian duty, parents commonly whipped or used other forms of corporal punishment to discipline children. By the twentieth century, however, such harsh beatings were classified as child abuse and might result in the arrest of parents and the termination of custody. Likewise, many customary forms of economic subsistence, such as hunting, fishing, distilling alcohol, or rounding up stray livestock, were systematically restricted or outlawed as elites consolidated control of land and commerce. At the same time, however, governments often ignored pilfering and other corrupt practices by elites. In the past, as in the present, law enforcement has focused disproportionately on the street crimes of the poor and the working class while tolerating many forms of elite or white-collar crime.

While such problems of definition complicate our efforts to identify criminal behavior in the past, they can also tell us a great deal about the history of criminal justice and the power relations behind it. Indeed, crime was not simply a result of poverty or social dysfunction but was also *created* by authorities or states that decided what kinds of behavior were appropriate. With the rise of industrial capitalism in the nineteenth century, for example, governments in western Europe and the United States passed a battery of laws to control vagrancy, public drunkenness, and prostitution. Such measures were designed to uphold middle-class standards of order and respectability, but also to help instill the discipline and self-control necessary for a successful industrial regime. The mass of arrests for such offenses was less a reflection of new forms of behavior than it was of new forms of social control. Examining such public order campaigns thus sheds light on nineteenth-century class and ethnic relations and the social impact of industrial capitalism.

A crucial case of changing definitions involves vandalism against property. Before the late nineteenth century, European and American authorities tolerated minor property destruction by young men on occasions such as Halloween, believing that youth needed some outlets for high spirits. New ideas about juvenile delinquency around 1900 converted such actions into crimes, even while punishing youth separately from adult criminals. Arrest rates of working-class young men shot up in consequence of the redefinition, convincing some adults that crime rates were getting out of hand.

While offenses like vagrancy, vandalism, and public drunkenness might or might not be defined as crimes, most forms of murder have been universally condemned and outlawed. In nearly all societies, the taking of human life outside of warfare is grounds for severe punishment and is usually recorded in death records and legal proceedings (infanticide being the main exception). For this reason, historians interested in the history of interpersonal violence have focused much attention on homicide. They have sought to answer a number of important questions: Has modern life become more or less violent than in the past? Have some countries and regions been historically more violent than others? And what conditions gave rise to greater and lesser levels of violence?

Studies of homicide rates in western Europe indicate that high levels of lethal violence in the medieval and early modern period gradually decreased beginning in the seventeenth century, particularly in urban areas. Contrary to social scientists' earlier theories that industrialization led to a more disciplined and less violent populace, the European studies indicate that the decline predated the industrial revolution. The reduction of lethal violence, these historians argue, occurred as the state expanded its power over the population, particularly in urban areas. This monopolization of violence by the state (in the form of police and military forces) was part of a larger "civilizing process" that accompanied the shift to a modern state and market economy. Rural areas, which remained less affected by state power, continued to experience higher per capita levels of violence than the urban centers. Many colonial territories (including the American West) also experienced high levels of lethal violence, but historians disagree as to why this was so and to what extent.

The overall downward trend in lethal violence continued through the first half of the twentieth century, but then shot upward after World War II. This was particularly true in the United States, which experienced a tidal wave of homicidal crime from the 1960s to the 1980s, but the surge was also evident throughout the Western world. Historians and criminologists suspect that demographic shifts in the postwar population along with global economic restructuring fueled this sharp rise in crime and violence. Whether this upward surge has peaked (the U.S. homicide rate declined in the 1990s) or will resume remains to be seen. In any case, historians have described the homicide rate as a U-shaped curve, thus dashing any hopes that the pacification of violence would continue indefinitely.

Beyond the issue of homicide, there has been little consensus among historians on other forms of crime. In the 1960s, a group of French historians suggested that with the rise of capitalism, violent crime rates fell while property crime increased (as wealth accumulation and economic inequalities became more conspicuous). Local historical studies of property crime, however, do not support this view—property crime seems to have gone both up and down in response to a wide variety of factors. Economic crises were one obvious stimulant to property crime. Depressions, plagues, and famines often caused such offenses to increase, as was the case in the years following the Black Death in the fourteenth century. But the relationship between economic variables and crime is by no means automatic. During the Great Depression, for example, the overall crime rate fell precipitously in the United States, with only a modest rise in property offenses. Clearly, other factors such as demographics, the role of the welfare state, and the effectiveness of law enforcement and social controls have augmented or mitigated the likelihood of theft.

Demographic factors, particularly age and gender, seem to be good indicators of past and present crime trends. As is true today, young men in their teens and twenties have been responsible for a disproportionate amount of crime (especially violent offenses), a trend dating back to medieval times. Most scholars agree, in fact, that the coming of age of young male baby boomers beginning in the 1960s has been one of the key causes of the recent upsurge in homicide and other crimes. American historians also explain the high rates of homicide on the western frontier as partly a result of the high percentage of single young males in western boomtowns. By the same token, the withdrawal of large numbers of young men out of the civilian population and into the military has generally led to lower rates of crime during foreign wars. Indeed, some historians maintain that the interpersonal violence that was pacified in "civilizing" Western societies was in fact rechannelled into military conflicts with other states and the violent subjugation of colonial lands and peoples.

By contrast, historians have found that women have been consistently underrepresented as crime perpetrators, as they still are today. European and American historians have discovered somewhat higher rates of female criminality (particularly theft and prostitution) in urban areas where women were more likely to be living alone or as heads of families. A handful of offenses (witchcraft, infanticide, prostitution, and abortion) have been female dominated, but the degree to which such behavior was criminalized varied according to dominant gender relations and society's need to control female sexuality. Infanticide, for example, was not a crime prior to the sixteenth and seventeenth centuries, when most European states passed harsh infanticide laws (often prescribing the death penalty). Such laws and subsequent prosecutions were apparently a response to the growing number of illegitimate births among young female servants who sometimes killed their newborns to avoid social stigma and the loss of their jobs. A similar process of criminalization occurred around abortion in the nineteenth century, targeting poor and working-class women who, without access to the birth control devices available to middle-class women, desperately tried to limit the size of their families. Although women's historical involvement in crime has been limited, studying it can tell us a great deal about changing gender and class relations over time.

Historians have also sought to test the findings of social scientists that argue that guns and alcohol use fuel violent crime. Historical homicide and assault records from a variety of places and time periods indicate that alcohol use frequently accompanies violent behavior. On the other hand, society's attempts to restrict alcohol use have had paradoxical effects. As part of the civilizing process, campaigns for temperance likely helped reduce lethal violence in the eighteenth and nineteenth centuries. In the 1920s, however, government-mandated Prohibition in the United States unleashed a short-term explosion of bootlegging, racketeering, and organized crime that boosted homicide and other violent crime rates sharply. The criminalization of narcotics has had a similar effect more recently. Moreover, most historians agree that widespread gun ownership and a pervasive gun culture helped make the United States the most violent country in the Western world. They disagree, however, as to when this arming of America took hold or whether it dates back to colonial times and the revolutionary legacy of the right to bear arms.

POLICING AND PUNISHMENT

Research on crime and on the impact of the state must involve attention to police action. Governments established courts to deal with crime very early on; they existed, for example, in ancient Mesopotamia. But police forces came later, developing fully only in the nineteenth century in places like Britain and the United States. Even this modern policing, however, has a history. Technologies have changed, with the arrival of techniques like fingerprinting and the switch from beat walking to patrol cars. Functions have changed as well. Police in the mid-nineteenth century spent half their time trying to regulate popular leisure habits, to prevent gambling or animal contests like cockfights. By 1900, with popular leisure now somewhat more respectable, police turned more toward crime fighting. At some points, at least, police efforts did have a positive impact on crime rates. Relationships between police and society also include questions of targeting. At many points in American history, police were far more likely to arrest and jail members of minority racial groups than was true for the population at large.

Histories of the states' response to crime must also deal with punishment. Traditional states usually levied fairly drastic punishments for many crimes, with public executions, whippings, or maimings, to set wide examples. Shame was also used for some offenses, like adultery, with people placed in stocks to be jeered at by passers-by. Around 1800 in the West, however, opinion began to shift. Capital punishments were cut back and made private, to avoid inflaming passions. Imprisonment for many crimes now became the preferred form of punishment, involving huge investments for societies that were becoming wealthier. Ideas about punishment continued to change in the twentieth century, with human rights campaigns against torture, for example, or the European Union's requirement that member nations abolish the death penalty outright. Comparative issues persisted: the United States and Japan differed with Europe over the death penalty, though in 2005 the United States did abolish capital punishment for minors. High rates of imprisonment in the United States contrasted with moves in Europe to find alternative punishments for lesser crimes. Explaining modern developments and differences, and their consequences for crime and for state-society relations, provides ample room for further historical analysis.

Politics, wars, and state building have traditionally been at the center of historical inquiry because they chronicle the power relations of elite leaders. In recent years, however, historians of everyday life have expanded our knowledge of how ordinary people contribute to these public endeavors as well as how they have been affected by them. By expanding our notion of politics, historians of social activism and popular culture have explored the nature and impact of a wide variety of political activity, often recasting our understanding of national political developments. In the modern era, historians have also looked in the opposite direction, examining how the welfare and warfare states have transformed society in both positive and negative ways. Those who do not conform to the dictates of the state are labeled deviant or criminal, and these groups have also earned considerable historical attention as scholars have analyzed trends in both behavior and enforcement. There are, however, areas that remain relatively unexplored. We know surprisingly little, for example, about the environmental impact of state policies and how such changes, in turn, affect society. Although we have learned a great deal about the militarization of society in wartime, we need more research on the long-term social impact of military development both at home and abroad since 1945. In the areas of crime and law enforcement, broader quantitative studies should be supplemented with more fine-grained research that explores how criminal behavior comes to be defined and how enforcement varies for different groups at different times. Such research will continue to enhance the study of history by making connections between the daily lives of ordinary people and the seemingly distant worlds of political elites and nation-states.

NOTE

1. Paula Baker, "The Domestication of Politics: Women and American Political Society, 1780–1920," *American Historical Review* 89 (June 1984).

FURTHER READING

The banditry of Santana Rodriguez is discussed in Paul J. Vanderwood, *Disorder and Progress: Bandits, Police, and Mexican Development* (Lincoln, NE, 1981), 100–103. On social banditry generally, see Gilbert Joseph, "On the Trail of Latin American Bandits: A Reexamination of Peasant Resistance," *Latin American Research Review* 25, no. 3 (1990): 7–53; and E. J. Hobsbawm, *Primitive Rebels: Studies in Archaic Forms of Social Movements in the Nineteenth and Twentieth Centuries* (Manchester, UK, 1971).

Early European peasant uprisings are covered in Rodney Hilton, *Bond Men Made Free: Medieval Peasant Movements and the English Rising of 1381* (London, 2003); and Barbara W. Tuchman, *A Distant Mirror: The Calamitous Fourteenth Century* (New York, 1978). On popular political culture in the United States, see Michael McGerr, *The Decline of Popular Politics: The American North, 1865–1928* (New York, 1989); Mary Ryan, *Civic Wars: Democracy and Public Life in the American City during the Nineteenth Century* (Berkeley, CA, 1997); and Meg Jacobs, William Novak, and Julian Zelizer, eds., *The Democratic Experiment: New Directions in American Political History* (Princeton, NJ, 2003). Women's role in revolution is examined by Mary Beth Norton, *Liberty's Daughters: The Revolutionary Experience of American Women, 1750–1800* (Boston, 1980); and by Dominique Godineau,

The Women of Paris and Their French Revolution (Berkeley, CA, 1998). Paula Baker analyzes women's political culture in "The Domestication of Politics: Women and American Political Society, 1780–1920," *American Historical Review* 89 (June 1984): 620–47.

Grassroots political activism in the twentieth century is covered in Lizabeth Cohen, *Making a New Deal: Industrial Workers in Chicago, 1919–1939* (New York, 1990); Charles Hayden, *I've Got the Light of Freedom: The Organizing Tradition and the Mississippi Freedom Struggle* (Berkeley, CA, 1995); and Lisa McGirr, *Suburban Warriors: The Origins of the New American Right* (Princeton, NJ, 2001). Infrapolitics was first introduced by Ranajit Guha, *Elementary Aspects of Peasant Insurgency in Colonial India* (Delhi, India, 1983), and further developed by James C. Scott, *Weapons of the Weak: Everyday Forms of Peasant Resistance* (New Haven, CT, 1986). Robin Kelley, *Race Rebels: Culture, Politics, and the Black Working Class* (New York, 1994) analyzes African American infrapolitics in the United States. Robert Edelman uses a similar approach in "A Small Way of Saying No: Moscow Working Men, Spartak Soccer, and the Communist Party, 1900–1945," *American Historical Review* 107 (December 2000): 1441–74. On German *Alltagsgeschichte,* see Alf Ludtke, ed., *The History of Everyday Life: Reconstructing Historical Experiences and Ways of Life,* trans. W. Templer (Princeton, NJ, 1995); and Geoff Eley, "Labor History, Social History, Alltagsgeschichte," *Journal of Modern History* 61 (1989): 297–343.

On the state's impact on public health and welfare, see Robert V. Wells, *Uncle Sam's Family: Issues in and Perspectives on American Demographic History* (Albany, NY, 1985); Barbara G. Rosenkrantz, *Public Health and the State: Changing Views in Massachusetts, 1842–1936* (Cambridge, MA, 1972); James T. Patterson, *America's Struggle against Poverty in the Twentieth Century* (Cambridge, MA, 2000); Michael Katz, *In the Shadow of the Poorhouse: A Social History of Welfare in America* (New York, 1986); and Howard Glennerster, *British Social Policy since 1945* (Malden, MA, 2000). On the state's impact on the environment, see Carolyn Merchant, *The Columbia Guide to American Environmental History* (New York, 2002). The impact of Communist state policies is examined in Sheila Fitzpatrick, *Everyday Stalinism: Ordinary Life in Extraordinary Times: Soviet Russia in the 1930s* (New York, 1999); Linda Benson, *China since 1949* (Harlow, UK, 2002); and Maria Antonietta Macciocchi, *Daily Life in Revolutionary China* (New York, 1972).

Life during wartime is the subject of several books in the Daily Life Series published by Greenwood Press. Works focusing on early American wars include Ray Raphael, *A People's History of the American Revolution* (New York, 1991); and James McPherson, *Battle Cry of Freedom* (New York, 1988) on the Civil War. Historians examining World War I include Byron Farwell, *Over There: The United States in the Great War, 1917–1918* (New York, 1999); David Kennedy, *Over Here: The First World War and American Society* (New York, 1982); Jurgen Kocka, *Facing Total War: German Society, 1914–1918* (Cambridge, MA, 1984); John Williams, *The Other Battleground: The Home Fronts: Britain, France, and Germany, 1914–1918* (Chicago, 1972); John Ellis, *Eye-Deep in Hell: Trench Warfare in World War I* (New York, 1976); Tony Ashworth, *Trench Warfare, 1914–1918: The Live and Let Live System* (London, 1980).

World War II is covered in David Kennedy, *Freedom from Fear: The American People in Depression and War* (New York, 1999); Marilynn S. Johnson, *The Second*

Gold Rush: Oakland and the East Bay in World War II (Berkeley, CA, 1993); Angus Calder, *The People's War: Britain 1939–1945* (London, 1969); Julian Jackson, *France: The Dark Years, 1940–1944* (New York, 2001); Daniel J. Goldhagen, *Hitler's Willing Executioners: Ordinary Germans and the Holocaust* (New York, 1997); Omer Bartov, *Hitler's Army: Soldiers, Nazis, and War in the Third Reich* (New York, 1991). The Vietnam experience is covered by Christian Appy, *Working-Class War: American Combat Soldiers in Vietnam* (Chapel Hill, 1993).

More-specialized studies of women in wartime include Maurine Greenwald, *Women, War, and Work: The Impact of World War I on Women Workers in the United States* (Westport, CT, 1980); Susan Grayzel, *Women's Identities at War: Gender, Identity, and Politics in Britain and France during the First World War* (Chapel Hill, NC, 1999); Karen Anderson, *Wartime Women: Sex Roles, Family Relations, and the Status of Women during World War II* (Westport, CT, 1981); and Claudia Koontz, *Mothers in the Fatherland: Women, the Family, and Nazi Politics* (New York, 1986). On race and ethnic relations during World War II, see Ronald Takaki, *Double Victory: A Multicultural History of America in World War II* (Boston, 2000); Roger Daniels, *Concentration Camps USA: Japanese Americans and World War II* (Malabar, FL, 1993); and David Wyman, *The Abandonment of the Jews: America and the Holocaust* (New York, 1998). On American veterans, see Richard Severo, *The Wages of War: When America's Soldiers Came Home—from Valley Forge to Vietnam* (New York, 1989).

A good overview of crime patterns from medieval times to the present can be found in Eric Monkkonen and Eric Johnson, eds., *The Civilization of Crime: Violence in Town and Country since the Middle Ages* (Urbana, IL, 1996). Important earlier essays can also be found in V.A.C. Gatrell, Bruce Lenman, and Geoffrey Parker, eds., *Crime and the Law: The Social History of Crime in Western Europe since 1500* (London, 1980). Two excellent overviews of English crime are J.A. Sharpe, *Crime in Early Modern England, 1550–1750* (Harlow, UK, 1999); and Clive Emsley, *Crime and Society in England, 1750–1900* (Harlow, UK, 1996). Studies of American homicide include Roger Lane, *Murder in America* (Columbus, OH, 1997) and *Violent Death in the City* (Cambridge, MA, 1979); and Eric Monkkonen, *Murder in New York* (Berkeley, CA, 2001). On the western frontier, see Clare McKanna, *Homicide, Race, and Justice in the American West, 1880–1920* (Tucson, AZ, 1997).

7

Economic Life as Daily Life: Work, Living Standards, and Consumerism

Peter N. Stearns

In the early nineteenth century, when the industrial revolution was just taking shape in western Europe, many employers faced a puzzle with their workers. When they wanted to induce a worker to accept more responsibility or a higher skill level, they were sometimes willing to offer higher pay. To them, with their definition of economic life and work rewards, this was a logical combination, and they tended to feel that hard work was a good thing in any event. But most workers involved used the higher pay to take more time off, rather than working harder. Greater control over their energy, not greater purchasing power, made more sense to them, particularly since they were being monitored and pressed in new ways on the job. To employers, this economic culture was a sign of laziness and irresponsibility.

For several decades, scholars have debated the meaning of retirement in modern life. There is no question that mass retirement is a modern phenom- enon. In agricultural societies, older people might retire if they were unusually wealthy, or they might just cut back on their activities, but they rarely could drop out of the workforce altogether. For some observers, forcing modern workers to retire at a certain age is a sign of rejection of the elderly in a work-oriented society, a condemnation to uselessness and marginality. And doubtless, some older workers experience retirement this way. But many people, for example in the United States, retire earlier than required to, when they think they can afford it. Blue-collar workers are particularly prone, but white-collar employees are not far behind. Where does retirement fit in the modern history of work and economic life? What does it say about contemporary work that so many older people want nothing more than to escape it—or is this a standard human impulse simply made more possible by modern prosperity?

In many premodern societies, urban craftsmen enjoyed a work progression that was both clear and meaningful, at least in principle, and often enforced by guild organizations. One started as a teenage apprentice—a period that could last around seven years and ensured possession of a real skill, whether in masonry or metal forging. Then came the journeyman years, when the worker was employed by a master artisan while also often living in his home (and sometimes marrying his daughter); some journeymen spent a few years wandering around from job to job, which could provide rich experience as well. Then, in mature adulthood, the journeyman gained a shop of his own, as a master artisan, and continued to work the craft but with clearer prestige and decision-making power. The system sounds great, and it could work well. But many apprentices were exploited and mistreated by journeymen and masters. Many journeymen could never rise beyond their subordinate stations, and bitter resentments could result. This was a system different from characteristic, modern patterns, and historians have tried to penetrate the surface to understand how it functioned.

Rural work is not easy to interpret, particularly in past times. This is especially true for rural laborers, who were employed by small (or large) farmers and had no real hope of owning land of their own. Ill paid and often required to do backbreaking work at harvest time, rural workers only rarely organized and protested. What (if any) pleasure could they derive from their jobs? Was the opportunity to work with growing things a satisfaction? When all of one's family members joined in, as is still true for many migrant agricultural workers, was this a reward, or was it frustrating not to be able to envisage greater opportunities for one's children?

Around 1905, printers in Paris went on strike against new, automatic typesetting machines. They claimed the machines debased their skills and prevented them from reading what they printed (a blow to their intellectual identity); the machines even allowed women to be employed in the craft. The printers finally agreed to accept the machines, though not female colleagues, in return for higher pay, which would allow a better economic life. This trade-off, where less meaningful work is accepted as a means to a higher standard of living, is called instrumentalism. Many scholars believe that instrumentalism is both new and widespread, the most common reaction to modern work. Some of them also believe that it constitutes a bad choice, as opposed to continuing to press for job dignity and intrinsic satisfaction.

During the past several decades, formal leisure has increased very little in the United States. In contrast, western European and Japanese workers have experienced an expansion of vacation time, in some European cases up to five or six weeks per year. Why do contemporary Americans work so much? Is it a voluntary choice? How does it relate to other aspects of economic life?

In seventeenth-century Holland, tulip buying became a consumer passion. People just had to have the latest bulbs. When they lacked the actual flowers, they bought paintings of them, which became a big business in its own right. This is an early example of modern consumerism: a deep though often faddish delight in goods that are not necessary to life. Tracing consumer patterns is not too hard. Figuring out what they mean to the individuals and the societies involved is another matter. Why seventeenth-century Holland? Why tulips?

Historians have been imaginative in the sources they have uncovered to understand the early phases of modern consumerism. For eighteenth-century England, for example, they look not only at what shopkeepers were doing, but also at theft records. Here they find that thefts of stylish clothing began to accelerate after about 1730, suggesting a new kind of consumer demand that was outstripping abilities to pay. They look at wills, finding that women, by the 1780s, were often leaving consumer items (jewels, furniture) to specific heirs, with loving phrases both about the items themselves and about the heirs that would enjoy them—again, a sign of a new attitude toward things and their relationship to family emotions.

Around 1900, American parents increasingly surrounded babies with consumer items, including the new teddy bear (named after an American president). A few traditionalists worried about this, but most authorities assured that having things to love was important for children. It would also, of course, prepare them for a consumer childhood. By the 1920s parents were being told to buy additional toys for children to help them overcome emotional problems like fear or jealousy. Here was a reflection of a new stage of consumerism and an encouragement to further adult commitments as well.

Historian Ruth Cowan has studied the impact of new household devices in the United States from the late nineteenth to the mid-twentieth century—the

Machines and men at work mining bituminous coal around 1900. Reprinted by permission of Carnegie Library of Pittsburgh.

period in which more and more Americans acquired sewing machines, vacuum cleaners, refrigerators, and the like. These "labor-saving" devices did not, in fact, reduce housewives' work efforts, for standards of cleanliness and food preparation were intensified to erase any new ease. Why would women accept this domestic treadmill?

In the late-twentieth-century United States, household chores for children declined steadily. Girls continued to do more work than boys, while 10-year-olds on the average did more than 16-year-olds. Children with a stepparent were particularly unlikely to do chores. What is, and what should be, the relationship of modern children to work?

Occupational diseases offer insight into the history of work and economic life. Coal miners have long suffered from accumulation of coal dust in the lungs. In early textile factories, managers kept windows closed because they believed that fresh air would damage threads and fabrics; so textile dust accumulated, making many workers sick. (Workers were clearly seen as more expendable than cloth.) Handloom weavers often pushed their looms forward with their chests, and developed chest diseases and spinal defects as a result; many people could identify a professional weaver by looking at his or her body. Many workers on computer keyboards encountered a new disease: carpal tunnel syndrome, the latest in a long line of human-tool interactions for the sake of work and output.

Americans, though intensely diet conscious, gained a bit of weight on average during the period 1950–1980. (Revealingly, newspaper advertisements for weight-reduction programs had proliferated early in the twentieth century, increasingly replacing ads for programs that would help underweight people gain weight.) Then in the 1980s, weight problems exploded: by 2002 the surgeon general contended that 62 percent of the population was overweight or obese, up from 48 percent in 1980. Childhood obesity rates tripled. By 2004 obesity problems were surfacing in western Europe and in urban populations in India and China, particularly among children. What was going on? Here is a fascinating and important contemporary twist on the history of living standards and consumerism.

The job of foreman is one of the most interesting and significant in modern work history. In early industrial factories, owners believed they could not depend on workers to organize their own work appropriately, but they lacked the time to provide direct supervision themselves. This predicament led to the creation of foremen, who were usually former workers but were now directed to represent management—a tough job. For workers, much of the quality of work life depended on the personality of the foreman, and some of the bitterest disputes involved foremen viewed as harsh or unfair. In the 1920s, the job of foreman was reevaluated in many factories. His initiative was scaled back in favor of more systematic work regulations devised by efficiency experts. But he was required to become more diplomatic—"Never show anger" was one new slogan—and, possibly, manipulative, particularly in order to reduce worker grievances. One tactic was to get a worker to repeat a grievance three times, by the end of which, hopefully, he'd become embarrassed and back off the grievance. Many foremen found this new emphasis on personnel expertise more challenging than the earlier system had been.

Economic life forms a vital aspect of daily life more generally, and it is no surprise, therefore, that it has attracted great attention from historians during the past 30 years. As Freud once suggested, people judge their lives mainly by how they play, how they love—and how they work. And for many people in many times and places, work has taken up the greatest amount of daily time within that trinity. Work is not, of course, the only facet of economic life. Living standards play a crucial role as well, and in many modern societies (with hints earlier) the importance of consumerism—beyond basic living standards—looms large as well.

Furthermore, economic life has greatly changed during the past two centuries, and in many parts of the world it is still changing. Large numbers of people have shifted from rural to urban living standards. They have replaced agricultural work and attendant occupations with factory and white-collar labor. They have often added consumerism to the list of material criteria by which they evaluate their lives.

Studying economic life relates closely to other aspects of daily life. Standards of living and even work deeply affect health conditions. Indeed, many historians working on living standards have used disease and mortality rates to try to determine whether living standards were getting better or worse. Work relates closely to leisure. The kind of leisure people seek or need depends to a great extent on what kinds of work they do. In agricultural societies, many people mixed what we would call leisure with work on a regular basis. That is, they would take breaks from work to chat or wander around or snooze. They would sometimes drink on the job (a habit that persists, though it is disapproved of in modern work settings). European construction workers often had a shot before work in the morning, in order (as a French phrase put it) to "kill the worm." Many rural societies organized special work sessions in a setting of sociability: women often sewed or made clothing in evening gatherings where they could gossip and enjoy some special foods; in the United States, barn raisings by a community mixed important work with feasting and family gatherings. There were distinct leisure opportunities in premodern society as well, but on a daily basis, work and recreation intertwined. In contrast, most modern work settings strive to get people to concentrate more strictly on work alone; rules in early factories always tried to ban snoozing, socializing, even singing on the job. By the same token, these same modern work settings push people to define a period of daily leisure off the job, to compensate for the intensity and concentration of work itself.

Finally, economic life relates closely to material life. Discussions of standards of living, most directly, involve evaluations of housing, available foods, and so on, though not usually with the detail or the same kinds of evidence that historians of material life employ. Consumerism, by definition, changes the nature of material life, with clothing an early and continuing example. The point is obvious: economic life must be evaluated within the context of daily life more generally.

Historians have tried, however, to focus on economic life directly, and to talk about conditions of work and basic living standards and the kinds of changes and continuities involved in these aspects of the human experience. They have used this focus to try to get a handle on the human side of more general historical categories like slavery or industrialization. We know what slavery means in a legal sense; but while legal servitude, being owned, was an important fact in its own right, the actual lives slaves led often had more to do with the work they did than with their formal legal conditions. In American slavery, the distinction between field hands, put to work on sugar or cotton plantations, and house slaves was very great. Field hands had much harder physical labor and were supervised more relentlessly than house slaves. Some slaves did artisanal work—blacksmithing, for example—and sometimes even ran their own operations; this was a third work category in what might otherwise seem to be an undifferentiated human experience.

Industrialization gains human meaning when evaluated through work patterns. Initially, historians tended to approach industrialization in terms of inventions, government policies, or the obvious shift in occupational categories from rural to urban, craft to factory. These categories, while important, are too abstract: the actual experience of industrialization, for large numbers of people, was a work experience above all. It involved heightened specialization, a new interaction with power-driven machinery in contrast to the use of hand tools, and a related change in the pace of work—toward greater intensity—and new methods of supervision, compared to the typical work settings of a farm or a craft shop. As many historians have become more interested in what life was really like in the past, and how it changed, they have sought new insights into economic life, and they have produced important new data and analysis in the process.

Dealing with the history of economic daily life involves three characteristic tensions, in terms of historical methods and sources. The first tension involves differences in the kinds of evidence necessary to provide the fullest possible picture of economic life. The second tension involves the importance of social categories in economic life, from premodern times to the present; it is dangerous to offer sweeping generalizations about economic life without attending to social class, gender, and age. The third tension highlights the importance of protest in the study of economic life, but also the potentially misleading implications of protest activity. Exploring all three tensions illustrates characteristic challenges in this aspect of the history of daily life, but also some of the achievements in the field as well.

The first tension focuses on types of materials. Economic life challenges historians to seek objective, sometimes quantifiable data. What tools and machines were actually used on the job (another connection with the history of material life)? Museums like Sturbridge Village (Massachusetts), Williamsburg (Virginia), and Lowell (Massachusetts—on early factories) have increasingly sought to illustrate the kinds of equipment used in the past, and without question, these demonstrations help us figure out what work used to be like in the past. Health and accident data constitute another objective, potentially quantifiable source. Work safety was often appallingly neglected in early industrialization (and this is still true in some rapidly industrializing countries). Screens to protect workers, even child laborers, from the moving parts of machines were not considered, if only because they added to expense. Employers enjoyed blaming workers' carelessness for most of the accidents that did occur. Gradually, in part through pressure from workers themselves and from governments, safety conditions became more regulated, and it is possible to trace this process statistically (while noting that many arguably avoidable accidents still occur). It is, admittedly, much harder to get relevant statistical data on premodern work, though we have some vivid impressions about accidents and occupational illnesses. Still, historians can find manuals that describe work processes—how-to books on work spread widely in western Europe during the seventeenth and eighteenth centuries, for example—and this, along with recovered or reconstructed equipment, can help describe objective work processes in the past.

Standards-of-living questions involve quantifiable data as well, though again more obviously for modern societies than for premodern ones. Historians have spent a great deal of time reconstructing living costs, the availability of bread and other basic foodstuffs, the size of housing units, and so on, for various times and places in the past. This is not as popular a topic today as it was 20 years ago, but it is still available. Health data and, more recently, data on the human body have also contributed to assessments of living standards. Rates of child mortality can tell us a lot about living standards. Changes in the size of the body, on average, can reveal improvements or deteriorations in diets and housing.

On the other hand—and this is where the tension comes in—quantifiable data (quite apart from inevitable gaps and inadequacies) do not necessarily tell us much about how people *experienced* work or living standards. So historians also use qualitative sources. Worker autobiographies and letters often focus very heavily on work and sometimes offer asides on living standards as well, and historians have been very inventive in uncovering these materials during the past three decades. Inevitably, as worker literacy improved, these sources become more available for modern than for premodern periods, but there is diary evidence from premodern European artisans and from Japanese farmers as well. Travelers and, in the modern period, self-appointed investigators also try to describe the experience of work, along with trying to portray equipment and other aspects of objective conditions. In late-eighteenth-century Russia, a socially conscious nobleman, Alexander Radischev, talked with peasants about how they experienced work; a traveling Englishman, Arthur Young, did the same in France. Industrialization drew many people, as well as government agencies, to inquire about work. Parliamentary commissions in England in the 1830s asked workers about the experience of child labor. Doctors like René Villermé in France went from city to city both to paint statistical pictures of work and living standards and to ask workers how they lived their economic lives. And of course, employers, slave owners, and others from the top provided their comments as well, and while their biases could be obvious, including a frequent tendency to evaluate workers as lazy, they can provide important material about the nature of the work experience.

The same effort to tap qualitative sources can apply to living standards. It's useful to try to calculate how much bread or meat was available to a given family in an early industrial city. But how did families experience this supply? When we know, from the comments of workers themselves or social observers, that many working-class families carefully provided available meat to the adult males—because they needed the energy for the work that would support the family—with wives and children receiving much less, we may know more about actual life than raw statistics can convey.

Ideally, then, historians of economic life try to figure out characteristic work experiences and living standards through reasonably objective materials, while also trying to figure out how the people involved evaluated their economic circumstances.

And one final point on the qualitative angle: dealing with the evaluation aspect may involve some confrontation with belief systems, whether implicit or explicit. Groups imbued with the idea that material conditions should improve in a well-run society will obviously interpret a particular aspect of living standards differently from groups that feel that living standards are unlikely to change or, sometimes, actually should not change. (In the 1990s some Russians expressed dismay that certain groups were gaining ground in terms of living standards; an older peasant value system, which communism had to some extent reinforced, argued for immobility—everybody should share the suffering.) Evaluations of work, finally, depend greatly on group or individual positions concerning the modern middle-class work ethic (which tended to measure in terms of the more work, the better), as opposed to equally valid but less sanctioned alternatives. One of the contributions offered by historians of work life, in fact, is to highlight the extent to which different societies, groups, and places bring quite different perspectives to bear on the work experience.

A similar tension between context and experience applies to consumerism. Many historians of early consumerism have focused on changes in shops, in advertising, and in the nature of goods available. It says a lot about consumerism in eighteenth-century England, for example, that the pottery maker Josiah Wedgewood deliberately sought market data from his chain of shops to determine what styles were working and what styles were falling flat, so that he could adjust his production accordingly. Or that shop owners, again in eighteenth-century England, began to experiment with "loss leaders," goods that could be offered on sale and cheap in order to get people to come to the shops, where, in theory and often in fact, they would buy a lot of regularly priced stuff as well. But consumerism is more than an inquiry into sales, production methods, and advertising. It also involves an attempt to figure out what consumers themselves thought about their activities and their acquisitions. In this crucial respect, a wider variety of materials is required: diaries, wills that bequeathed consumer goods to heirs (sometimes with comments about the meaning of a cabinet or a fancy dress), social commentary by observers who thought they knew why a given group of people was engaging in new forms of consumerism, and so on.

Here, too, there is finally a question of value systems. Dealing with consumerism historically involves a recognition that patterns of evaluation will range, depending on time and place, from eager embrace to genuine disgust at consumerist behaviors. In between, and perhaps most interesting, are groups that say they accept consumerism but then express vigorous dislike of groups whose participation in consumerism is seen as inappropriate, such as minority races or women. This practice suggests not only racism, anti-Semitism, or misogyny, but some real ambivalence about consumerism itself.

Tension number one, then—getting at economic life, whether work or living standards or consumerism—involves a combination of materials about objective context (types of machines, health conditions, sales strategies) with more diffuse, subjective materials. These subjective materials help historians explore how people actually experienced the context, what they thought about the economic life in which they found themselves, and what value systems they used in their thinking.

Tension number two involves differentiation among social groups. This is a factor in any inquiry into any aspect of daily life, but it may apply to economic life particularly strongly.

Indeed, economic life—both work and standards of living, including access to consumerism—forms the most crucial measurement of social class, though historians and sociologists also debate the role of self-conscious awareness. In premodern societies, groups differentiated themselves characteristically by the work they did. Urban guilds in both Europe and Asia proudly identified each major craft, from butchers to goldsmiths, with distinctive uniforms (at least for public occasions), rituals, and imagery. Craft guilds formed in many traditional societies—they have been identified in ancient Egypt and Mesopotomia—because they provide group protection in matters like training standards, but also because they offer collective identity. Other groups, though less tightly organized than artisanal guilds, can also express distinctive work values, as when they display public pride in their freedom from manual labor. In the Balkans, clerks often let the fingernails of their little fingers grow, as an open demonstration of the fact that, though they might be poor, at least their work was nonmanual. Work also provided one of the great distinctions between rural and urban, even when material living standards varied only slightly.

Premodern societies also saw significant differences in standards of living. Most obvious was the huge gap between the wealthy few and the masses, both urban and rural. Only the rich in premodern Europe or China had any real access to consumerism, though even they might be constrained by social norms hostile to display. Differences in living standards showed in physical size as well as health: the upper classes were much taller, on average, than their lower-class counterparts because of greater access to protein in their diets from childhood onward.

Increasingly, however, historians have also realized that there were some significant distinctions within the masses in premodern societies, in terms of living standards. Too often, the peasantry has been characterized by references to a subsistence economy, as if there was no variety in their material standards. Despite a common reliance on agriculture, however, and certainly a common subjection to periodic crop failures and subsistence crises, some peasants did better than others. This would show not only through the possession of larger amounts of land, but also in more substantial housing; also (by the sixteenth century in Europe) in some extra furnishings, such as formal bedding rather than straw pallets, or a glass-paned window or two; and doubtless in richer diets as well. Even more obviously, regional differences reflected different soil fertility and weather. As late as the early nineteenth century there were peasant areas in central France where bread baking occurred only twice a year, yielding obviously meager and hideously stale diets as the months wore on; in contrast, in the wheat-growing belt of Normandy and Picardy, diets were far more abundant, and more sophisticated food preparation could be routinely afforded.

Modern societies reflect some of the same class distinctions as those of their premodern counterparts. There is often still a bias against manual as opposed to nonmanual labor. Variations in living standards reflect huge class differences. Of course, in the most prosperous, industrialized modern societies, the terms of measurement change. Many groups, even among the fairly poor, have some access to consumerism, so their class position will show in less frequent or less ambitious vacations than those of their wealthier counterparts, or a need to rely on used cars rather than the newest models. Differences in body size between the middle class and the working class continued into the mid-twentieth century; British workers in the 1930s were several inches shorter than their middle-class counterparts. But by the twenty-first century, body differences in industrial societies more commonly showed a greater tendency for lower-class (and rural) populations to be obese, compared with middle-class counterparts. Social class continues to reflect differences in economic life, but the nature of the measurements change in significant ways.

Social class is not, of course, the only marker for economic life. In recent decades, historians have paid great attention to gender, where again, differences in work life can be a crucial reflection of social distinctions while in turn causing further distinctions. European historians have shown how, from the late Middle Ages to the eighteenth century, urban women tended to be driven out of most of the skilled urban crafts, where they had maintained some access earlier, and confined to a few demanding, low-paying sectors like lace making. Colonial Americanists have examined what farm women did, showing that certain tasks tended to be gender-segregated even though in a pinch (when men were away at war or when husbands died) women could and did perform the full range of agricultural chores. As noted above, there have been increasing and successful efforts to study the history of housework against an earlier stereotype that middle-class women in modern societies, at least until recently, were idle and pedestaled. On the standards of living side, women have often been confined to lower standards than men in the same social groups because of an inferior power position and/or the felt need to provide men, as principal breadwinners, with a more abundant diet. In contrast, women have often been particularly associated with consumerism; the modern opportunities to shop and to enjoy new clothing and other products have provided outlets for women that may have different meanings than do consumer experiences for men. But historians have also noted that critics of women and consumerism have often underplayed the extent to which men, too, consume and frequently have more consumer opportunities than women. Here, too, gender plays important but complex roles in economic life.

Age groups constitute a final social category relevant to economic life. Children routinely work in agricultural societies, and family economies in all but the wealthiest classes depend on this labor. However, while children's work provides opportunities for training, it also provides opportunities for abuse, which differentiates it from the work of many adults. Many children have been subject to harsh discipline, including physical abuse or sexual exploitation, as part of their work lives. Benjamin Franklin was apprenticed as a printer to his brother in Massachusetts, but finally fled to Philadelphia because he was being beaten so often. Continued attention to child labor and to abuses preoccupies many international agencies today; while the percentage of children at work steadily declines on a global basis, there are many exceptions, and rates of child labor are actually increasing in South and Southeast Asia.

The big historical story about child labor, however, does involve its decline in modern societies, sometime after a period of intensified exploitation during early industrialization. (Both Britain in the early nineteenth century and Japan around 1900 depended heavily on low-wage child labor; in Japan, many girls were essentially sold by their families to provide workers for the sweated silk industry, on which the nation depended for export earnings.) Attacks on child labor began to develop in western Europe and the United States from the early nineteenth century onward; younger children and then adolescents were gradually withdrawn from the labor force, greatly changing both the history of work and the history of childhood.

Older workers have received less attention, but here too they form an important category in economic life. In premodern societies, older workers, as they became more infirm, frequently faced deterioration in their standards of living. Poorhouses and other institutions designed to provide some assistance to the most destitute always dealt with a disproportionately large number of older people (and also of women). In western Europe, older workers, including peasants and farmers, frequently made deals with their adult children, turning over part of their land or shops in return for promises of regular food supplies; but this arrangement frequently involved great tension and did not ensure an adequate living standard. Economic life, in other words, figures prominently in the premodern history of older age. In modern societies, the big topic at the later end of the age spectrum involves the origins and impact of retirement. Older workers were clearly found less fit for industrial work than their younger counterparts, but at the same time, retirement funding, where adequate, could help older workers deal with problems of living standards and work capacity that were not entirely new to industrial life. By the twenty-first century, with the growth of the older population in Western and Japanese societies, questions about putting the elderly back to work suggested the possibility of yet another period in the history of age categories and economic life.

The importance of social categories in economic life applies to all aspects of the subject. It has been explored with particular subtlety in two cases. The lower-middle class—emerging as an important social group by the 1870s in western Europe and the United States, and later in other industrial societies—offers an intriguing puzzle. On the one hand, many lower-middle-class workers—secretaries, cashiers, file clerks, telephone operators—have relatively menial jobs, no more intrinsically interesting (sometimes less so) than those of factory workers. They are subjected to similar kinds of work supervision and discipline, pressures to increase output, and the like. In one respect they are even more strongly manipulated than factory workers are: they are often required to adjust their emotional demeanor in order to present a smiling and uncomplaining face to customers; elaborate training programs toward this end were being instituted in industrial societies by 1900. Finally, white-collar workers do not necessarily earn more than factory workers do, and again, sometimes less.

But because of a combination of distinctive work—beginning with the fact that the jobs were nonmanual and depended on some degree of formal education including literacy and numeracy, and extending to the consciousness of the workers themselves—white-collar workers have characteristically regarded themselves as a different social class from blue-collar workers. They have been, among other things, less likely to unionize and more eager to be seen as part of the larger middle class. These distinctive attitudes about work, which Marxist leaders bitterly denounced as false consciousness, spilled over into other aspects of economic life. Although white-collar workers earned about the same wages as other urban workers—despite the fact that their pay was usually carefully called a salary, to highlight the distinctiveness of the group—they usually spent more on clothing (which had to approximate middle-class standards) and entertainment than blue-collar workers did, and less on food. And as already noted, they were slightly less eager to retire than their blue-collar counterparts did, again maintaining a somewhat distinctive evaluation of their work life.

Women, whose economic lives involve some special subtleties (as already noted), constitute a second category. Two aspects deserve particular attention, amid a rich array of topics. First, as against some earlier impressions, industrialization tended to reduce women's participation in the formal labor force. This was true not only in western Europe and the United States, despite the involvement of women in early factories. It also applied to places like India and Latin America, where European factory items displaced traditional skills. The fact was that industrial products, particularly textiles, reduced work opportunities for women in manual manufacturing, driving hundreds of thousands out of the labor force during the nineteenth century and beyond.

This, in turn, means that women in many modern societies have had to pursue distinctive work opportunities, including, of course, housework and production in the home. In many urban societies, including western Europe and

This silk factory, based on imported technology and designed mainly for the burgeoning export trade to the West, is representative of early Japanese industrialization and its workers.

the United States in the nineteenth century, domestic service long constituted the largest female job category in modern times. Long ignored, the history of domestic service offers some revealing insights into some of the special transitions involved in women's work between premodern and fully contemporary periods. Domestics performed family and household jobs, thus adhering to then-current definitions of women's work. They could also learn some new habits of hygiene and literacy, but at the same time were subjected to often annoying levels of supervision from the mistress of the house. Ultimately, women workers themselves largely decided to seek other work alternatives, and domestic service declined in industrial societies.

This leads to the second aspect. Women ultimately began to fill large numbers of white-collar jobs, as well as jobs in certain professional categories such as nursing. Then, in Western society in the 1950s, as these jobs expanded, women took an increasingly large role in the formal labor force. Historians grapple with some of the questions that this great transformation involved: why did women want more formal work? Included here are issues about standards of living and consumer goals. As they became almost half of the labor force (by the 1970s in western Europe and the United States), did their work patterns and expectations converge with those of men, or did women retain a distinctive work ethic along with some of the gender barriers they continued to face in the job market? The history of women's economic life in recent decades provides a dynamic background to some of the issues with which women and their families continue to grapple.

Tension number three goes back to historical materials and evidence again, but with a special twist that can often relate as well to issues of social class and other differentiating categories like gender.

Many social historians developed an interest in work or standard of living initially because of their desire to grasp the nature of social protest, which in turn was often based on economic life. For premodern protest, aside from major peasant risings that often had to do with access to land more than work life per se, this encouraged research on standards of living. Many urban and peasant protests (usually separately, sometimes in combination) had to do with bitter resentment against food shortages (particularly grain) or rising bread prices or both. Bread and grain riots were probably the most common single form of collective protest in western Europe between the Middle Ages and 1789. People had certain expectations about the staple foods that should be available to them, and about reasonable prices. When conditions fell short, for example as a result of a crop failure, they characteristically looked for one of two targets, or both. The first target involved merchants who transported grain or sold bread; it was often assumed that they were excessively greedy, shipping grain out to better-paying markets and so causing local shortages, or manipulating bread prices in the cities. Riots, in turn, frequently seized grain convoys or attacked bakeries, sometimes assaulting merchants in the process. Target number two was the government itself, assumed, at least by the late seventeenth century, to have some responsibility for maintaining a basic subsistence standard that would allow people enough food to survive.

Bread riots offer a number of additional facets. They could involve both men and women in active, even violent protest; as the family cooks, women frequently had a better idea about food adequacy than men did. When additional ingredients were present, bread riots could occasionally build into full-scale revolutions. Bread riots played a role in the unfolding of the great French Revolution of 1789. Another intriguing twist was that the very poorest groups were rarely prominent in the bread riots because they lacked the physical energy or community structure that was required. The most common spur to a bread riot involved deterioration in supply or an increase in price that affected mainstream peasants or artisans; the traditional supply or price could be used as the measurement that could justify an uprising.

Finally, bread riots ultimately declined as a protest form, though they still surfaced in western Europe as late as the early twentieth century, with women prominently involved. In their stead, popular protest increasingly focused on work and pay grievances, and in the same process strikes began to replace riots as the most common form of protest expression. A few strikes had occurred in premodern times, mainly involving journeymen artisans protesting conditions set by the shop owners, but they were atypical. When they focused on pay (or, by the twentieth century, pay and benefits), modern strikes obviously still reflected concerns about living standards, though they could also pick up a desire to compensate for unattractive work through pay in the instrumentalist fashion described earlier. Many strikes, however, also sought to accommodate work grievances directly. Efforts to reduce hours of work reflected new desires for leisure, but also a need to alleviate the increased intensity of industrial work. Many strikes were directed against abusive supervisors, while demands for recognition of unions as bargaining agents constituted a more systematic desire to modify the power of foremen and employers to boss workers unilaterally.

Both premodern and modern protest forms highlight cases in which many people found fault with the conditions of their daily economic lives. They are dramatic; they produce special kinds of sources in proclamations of grievances and in police reports about agitation. In addition, economic protests sometimes triggered major developments, from revolutions to labor union movements, which is another reason to pay attention.

There are limitations, however, in using protests to measure economic life. Most people do not protest, if only because they lack the resources or community backing. Women, for example, have been much less likely to strike than men, though there are some vivid exceptions. They were less welcome in trade unions; they often saw their work as supplemental, rather than fundamental, to their lives as wives and mothers; and their jobs were often more insecure in any event. Does this mean that women are more contented with their modern work roles? Does it mean we should pay less attention to women as workers?—for one of the effects of protest-based research is to downplay groups who loom less large, which was one reason why women as workers were long neglected in favor of men. Even for groups that do protest, there are often problems of balance and interpretation. Protest leaders might make ringing statements about the horrors of factory work, but does that mean that ordinary strikers agreed, particularly once an incident that had sparked their anger faded in memory or was actually corrected?

Increasingly, research on economic life has moved away from a primary attention to protest situations. This has allowed historians to pay attention to groups not usually prominent in protest, like women or white-collar workers, and to a phenomenon like body size, which capture standard-of-living issues quite apart from bread riots. It has also allowed historians to look for expressions of discontent separate from formal, collective protest. Domestic servants almost never protested collectively; but imaginative historians have uncovered evidence that, among other things, when displeased, the servants would sometimes urinate in the soup before they brought it to the mistress's table from the kitchen. Working more slowly than desired, stealing work materials, and changing jobs often (a characteristic of early industrial societies) were other ways to express dissatisfaction without resorting to formal protest. Even songs could help workers let off steam—from the slave song "Jimmy Crack Corn," which implies successful violence against an abusive master, to more recent popular productions like "Take This Job and Shove It."

In sum, historians have become increasingly interested in groups that had revealing work histories that did not show up in protest, and in a wider range of adjustments and expressions of discontent. In the process, protest history has somewhat receded, though this may also reflect the fact that work-based protest itself had declined in Western society since the 1950s, with a brief revival at the end of the 1960s. Studies of consumerism, finally, rarely involve much attention to protest materials, save in popular criticisms of consumerism or efforts to rouse consumer boycotts. Consumerism, with its material distractions, often seems an antidote to protest, though this may create its own set of problems.

In final analysis, much of the most serious historical assessment of economic factors in daily life boils down to an attempt to figure out meanings. It's important to get at descriptive characteristics: What was the balance among skilled, semiskilled, and unskilled workers, and what defined each category? How many women and children worked? How much bread or meat did ordinary people consume in a given day, and how much clothing could they afford? What were the most important tools or machines, and how did they function? And, of course, what changes in conditions or in expectations could generate collective protest concerning economic life? But understanding meaning is even more revealing. Work, even in modern, instrumental societies, is an important facet of identity to many people, and they can often find some purpose even in jobs that might seem absolutely dismal, taking pride in reliability or a bit of special skill even if the rest of the world takes their performance for granted. There are, at least in modern societies, some absolutely alienated workers who find their conditions appalling, their employers rank exploiters, their work lives without any merit, and their colleagues dumb clods. Far more workers probably mix some sense of alienation and discontent with a certain satisfaction at bringing home a paycheck, with some pleasure at social contacts on the job, and with some pride in personal input. A somewhat similar complexity may apply to consumerism: a degree of herdlike conformism to the latest fad, and some recognition of superficiality, but also some ability to use consumerism to express one's own sense of identity and connection to wider excitement. At the risk of oversimplification, it's clear that many historians dealing with economic life seek to capture this mixture of reactions, while noting changes in objective conditions and in the balance of motivations.

Many historians of work or living standards deal with particular periods in either premodern or modern societies. But there is no question that in this area, the transition from agricultural to industrial societies, in its implications for economic life, has commanded particular attention.

Work changed, quite obviously. While early factories were small and, by contemporary standards, technologically unsophisticated, the trends of modern work were quickly present and contrasted dramatically with conditions of craft or peasant labor. The pace quickened; workers concentrated on more limited phases of production, which on average reduced skill and, perhaps, the sense of creativity on the job; foremen and shop rules restricted independence; and work was separated from home and, increasingly, family. These trends would soon spill over, though in modified fashion, to craft shops, offices, and other work sites.

Historians have explored all of these changes. They have paid particular attention to the new dominance of power-driven equipment—what one historian has summed up as "mechanization takes command."[1] A revealing symbol was found in France in the mid-1830s when one factory owner began putting a bouquet of flowers on the machine that had been the most productive during the previous week—not for the workers directly, but for the mechanical loom. Many workers felt increasingly driven by machines, which were the main source of the growing pace of work. By the early twentieth century, headed by industrial engineers in the United States and then by business leaders like Henry Ford, new efforts were devoted to making workers as machinelike as possible—operating along an automatic assembly line, their every motion charted and discretionary action eliminated as fully as possible. Small wonder that again by 1900, workers in various fields began to report that nervousness and stress were mounting, replacing physical dangers as the chief downsides of work.

A new subordination to the clock was another measurement of modern work. English workers began buying watches in the eighteenth century, even for craft jobs. The notion of fixed hours of work and timing of jobs introduced new elements into human labor—indeed, into human lives more generally. One of the functions of modern schooling, though rarely explicitly acknowledged, is to drive home to children the necessary sense of clock time. Early factories had to enforce the new time sense quite rigorously: many locked their doors 15 minutes after the workday was to begin, forcing tardy workers to miss a half day (at least), with loss of pay and an equivalent fine as punishment. Later, the time clock became a ubiquitous symbol of modern work. In early industry, workdays were also long, though not necessarily longer than agricultural tasks required during the summer (the introduction of gas, then electric lighting obviously created new options for indoor work). But the new timing and the related rigorous pace did generate a new experience that could involve real stress even when, as industry matured, the workday began to shrink.

Changes in the social context of work constituted a final area of attention, vital to the lived experience of work. In preindustrial societies, most work occurred in and around the home. Non–family members might be involved, but as in most craft operations, they usually lived with employer families. This was not necessarily a plus: real tensions and abuse could occur within familial settings, and some workers were openly delighted with the more impersonal work context that factories or offices provided, where, among other things, one could meet more new people. Others, however, found modern work, with its encounters

In the Soviet Union in the 1920s and 1930s, "socialist realist" art glorified workers and their labor. Reprinted by permission of Sovfoto/Eastfoto.

with an array of strangers, challenging, and they also worried about their ties to family, now largely separate from the workplace itself. A few modern workers developed the habit of stopping in a bar between work and home, partly to nurture new social ties but also partly to allow some transition between work moods and domestic requirements. Again, the implications of innovation were neither simple nor uniform, but the innovation itself was considerable.

Needless to say, many workers suffered during the transition to modern work conditions. Almost every industrial society saw direct attacks on new machinery—called Luddism after the mythical leader Ned Ludd, who was said to inspire British antimachine riots between 1810 and 1820. For a time, at least, many workers simply wished that modern work would go away, but it never did.

Over time, even as modern work trends in most ways intensified, workers have found other ways to protest or to accommodate, and the history of work traces this process as well, right up to the present day.

There is a danger, of course, in the premodern-modern work formulation. Change may be exaggerated or overgeneralized. Modern conditions never applied as starkly to crafts like construction work as they did to factories.

Housework changed but certainly less than work outside the home. A related danger is undue nostalgia about premodern work conditions. Many traditional jobs involved intense subordination to master artisans or landowners, even aside from outright slavery. Physical strain could be considerable. Women and other groups could face severe limitations in work opportunities. On the other hand, though historians debate the subject still, it is important not to paint modern work with too harsh a brush, quite apart from greater rewards in the form of higher wages and shorter hours. Here, too, different individuals and different categories of workers had diverse reactions and experiences, and historians of work have become increasingly skillful in dealing with distinctions and nuances without losing a basic definition of modern work.

A similar attention to the shift between premodern and modern life has colored analysis of standards of living. The most intense historical discussion of living standards, now a generation old, debates whether material life improved or deteriorated for British workers in the first decades of the industrial revolution. Tremendous effort went into assessing housing, food, budgets, and health, with strong points scored by both sides in the debate and no conclusive winner. The whole controversy advanced historians' understanding of the sources, methods, and issues involved in assessing living standards in the past. The debate itself waned for several reasons: exhaustion and inconclusiveness; the fading of cold war polarizations between Marxist partisans (who argued for deterioration) and capitalist partisans (who wanted to find benefits in industrial capitalism); and the increasingly obvious fact that, whatever the situation in early industry, sheer material conditions ultimately did improve, not only in Britain but in all successful industrial societies.

Since the great debate, and with growing attention given to cultural rather than material issues in social history, research on the history of living standards has been less prominent. An interest in changes and variations in rural societies is a significant gain, as was suggested earlier. Growing precision about the history of the physical human body, as a reflection of shifts and differences in living standards, offers exciting results. These results range from attempts to explain average height differences in premodern Europe (why were northern Europeans taller?) to the dramatic recent finding that, whereas western Europeans have grown several inches in average height since the 1950s, average American height has changed almost not at all (a challenging comment on American living standards and nutritional habits). Related attention to food history and, in a few pioneering works, the history of obesity probe living conditions from yet another angle.

It can be suggested, however, that more systematic, renewed attention to the history of living standards would be welcome as part of a more balanced understanding of changes and continuities in daily life. A historian of India made the point precisely: at a time in the early twenty-first century, when inequality of living standards and, for some groups, outright misery have been increasing, historians have turned away from an interest in tracing the evolution of material poverty, including changing definitions and causes around the world.[2]

Part of the historical energy available for research on material conditions has unquestionably been transferred to the exciting field of consumerism, now a major historical subject after long neglect. We increasingly understand that modern consumerism is not simply a natural result of growing prosperity: many societies in the past, and some still, have actively opposed consumerism in favor of restraint (including religious restraint), traditional styles over shifting fads, or more community-oriented investments. Periodically, for example, both premodern China and premodern Europe displayed active hostility to people who seemed to indulge individual consumer tastes, burning luxury products or even executing particularly ostentatious individuals. What caused modern consumerism and its intensification, and what consumerism means to the people involved become legitimate, indeed truly significant historical questions.

And major discoveries have followed this basic insight. We know of course, thanks to research that began in the 1980s, that modern mass consumerism began in seventeenth- and eighteenth-century western Europe, before industrialization rather than as its result—a major reversal of historical thinking. Changes in value systems and a blurring of traditional social class lines, as well as growing prosperity for many groups, underwrote this shift, though discussion of basic causation continues. We know that consumerism, as it advanced, redefined beliefs even further: in the United States, for example, envy was criticized as a fault until about 1900, when it shifted, in advice to children, to being a virtue. We know that extremes of consumerism generated a brand new disease, kleptomania, first noted in western Europe and the United States in the 1870s. We know that one of the reasons Americans avoided major gains in leisure time by 2000 involved an unusually great commitment not to work per se, but to earnings that would sustain consumerism. We are beginning to trace the emergence of Japan, also by 2000, as a world leader in consumer styles as the nation's sales of "cool" fashions and equipment became its leading export category.

Much more knowledge is now available about the economic lives of ordinary people in various societies than was true 20 years ago, thanks to a real flowering of historical research. Exploration of fundamental changes in work, as a result of industrialization but then from further developments such as the rise of white-collar categories and new activities by women, moved constructively from an initial interest in protest to a broader set of inquiries including unrest. Consumerism has become a major research category, appropriately enough given its importance in modern life around the world. Sources and methods for understanding the human experience of work and living standards have become more sophisticated, though challenges remain. At the same time, there is both opportunity and need for additional study. Somewhat oddly, for example, though we now realize that modern consumerism was not an American invention, we know less about transitions toward consumerism in the United States during the first half of the nineteenth century than would be desirable. Fuller historical perspectives on global issues of poverty should be high on the research agenda. The need to relate the growing understanding of changes and continuities in economic life to other aspects of daily life offers fascinating opportunities as well. Have expressive leisure outlets, to take an obvious example, kept pace with changes and, many would argue, constrictions in the capacity to find meaning in work? Topics like this invite an interaction with history that at the same time explores the nature of our own lives and of the societies around us.

NOTES

1. Sigfried Gideon, *Mechanization Takes Command: A Contribution to Anonymous History* (New York, 1948).

2. Prasannan Parthasarathi, "The State of Indian Social History," *Journal of Social History* 37 (2003): 47–54.

FURTHER READING

On the great standard of living debate, see Arthur J. Taylor, ed., *The Standard of Living in Britain in the Industrial Revolution* (London, 1975), particularly the articles by Eric Hobsbawm and R.M. Hartwell. See also Eric Hobsbawm and R.M. Hartwell, "The Standard of Living during the Industrial Revolution: A Discussion," *Economic History Review,* 2d ser., 16 (1963–64): 119–146. See also Paul Johnson, *Saving and Spending: The Working Class Economy in Britain, 1870–1939* (New York, 1985).

For the recent work on living standards and the human body, John Komlos, ed., *Stature, Living Standards, and Economic Development: Essays in Anthropometric History* (Chicago, 1994) and the special issue of *Social Science History* 28 (2004), guest edited by Komlos and Joerg Baten.

For work on the related topic of poverty, Michael Katz, *In the Shadow of the Poorhouse: A Social History of Welfare in America* (New York, 1986) and *Undeserving Poor: From the War on Poverty to the War on Welfare* (New York, 1989). On European poverty, Catharina Lis, *Social Change and the Labouring Poor: Antwerp, 1770–1860* (New Haven, CT, 1986); James Treble, *Urban Poverty in Britain, 1830–1914* (New York, 1979); Mary Lindemann, *Patriots and Paupers: Hamburg, 1712–1930* (New York, 1990). As noted, recent historical work is rarer, but see John Iliffe, *The African Poor: A History* (Cambridge, UK, 1990) and David Green, *From Artisans to Paupers: Economic Change and Poverty in London, 1790–1870* (Hants, UK, 1995).

On work and related protest, a classic is E.P. Thompson, *The Making of the English Working Class* (New York, 1964). See also Eric Hobsbawm, *Labouring Men: Studies in the History of Labour* (New York, 1964); Neil J. Smelser, *Social Change in the Industrial Revolution* (London, 1971); Lenard Berlanstein, *The Working People of Paris, 1871–1914* (Baltimore, 1984); Reginald Zelnik, *Labor and Society in Tsarist Russia: The Factory Workers of St. Petersburg, 1855–1870* (Stanford, CA, 1971); Patrick Joyce, *Work, Society, and Politics: The Culture of the Factory in Later Victorian England* (New Brunswick, NJ, 1980) and his edited work, *The Historical Meanings of Work* (New York, 1987); Peter N. Stearns, *Lives of Labor: Work in a Maturing Industrial Society* (New York, 1975). On a special group of modern workers, Stephen Castles, *Migrant Workers and the Transformation of Western Societies* (Ithaca, NY, 1989). On Japan, Andrew Gordon, *The Evolution of Labor Relations in Japan: Heavy Industry, 1853–1955* (Cambridge, MA, 1985) and W. Dean Kinzley, *Industrial Harmony in Modern Japan: The Invention of a Tradition* (London, 1991).

On the American side, Alan Dawley, *Class and Community: The Industrial Revolution in Lynn* (Cambridge, MA, 1976); Jonathan Prude, *The Coming of Industrial Order: Town and Factory Life in Rural Massachusetts, 1810–1860* (Cambridge, MA, 1983); Joe Trotter, *Black Milwaukee: The Making of an Urban Proletariat, 1915–45* (Urbana, IL, 1988); Jacqueline Jones, *American Work: Four Centuries of Black and White Labor* (New York, 1998); Walter Licht, *Industrializing*

America: The Nineteenth Century (Baltimore, 1995); Eugene D. Genovese, Roll, Jordan, Roll (New York, 1974). An immensely interesting set of interviews about work is Studs Terkel, *Working: People Talk about What They Do All Day and How They Feel about What They Do* (New York, 1985).

On women's work, Deborah Simonton, *A History of European Women's Work 1700 to the Present* (London, 1998); Leonore Davidoff and Ruth Hawthorn, *A Day in the Life of a Victorian Domestic Servant* (New York, 1976); Jacqueline Jones, *Labor of Love, Labor of Sorrow: Black Women, Work, and the Family from Slavery to the Present* (New York, 1985); Tim Meldrum, *Domestic Service and Gender, 1660–1750: Life and Work in the London Household* (London, 2000); Alice Kessler-Harris, *Out to Work: A History of Wage-Earning Women in the United States* (New York, 2003); Ruth Schwartz Cowan, *More Work for Mother: The Ironies of Household Technology from the Open Hearth to the Microwave* (New York, 1983); Joan Wallach Scott and Louise Tilly, *Women, Work, and Family* (New York, 1978); Rose L. Glickman, *Russian Factory Women: Workplace and Society, 1880–1914* (New York, 1984); Lee Holcombe, *Victorian Ladies at Work: Middle-Class Working Women in England and Wales, 1850–1914* (Hamden, CT, 1973); Gay L. Gullickson, *Spinners and Weavers of Auffay: Rural Industry and Sexual Division of Labor in a French Village, 1750–1850* (Cambridge, UK, 1986); Daniel E. Sutherland, *Americans and Their Servants: Domestic Service in the United States from 1800–1920* (Baton Rouge, LA, 1981). A classic on early national America is Laurel Ulrich, *A Midwife's Tale: The Life of Martha Ballard, Based on her Diary, 1785–1812* (New York, 1991).

On children, Viviana A Rotman Zelizer, *Pricing the Priceless Child: The Changing Social Value of Children* (New York, 1993); Peter N. Stearns, *Anxious Parents: A History of Modern Childrearing in America* (New York, 2003); Colin Heywood, *Childhood in Nineteenth-Century France: Work, Health, and Education among the Classes Populaires* (Cambridge, UK, 1988).

On white-collar work, Susan Porter Benson, *Counter Cultures: Saleswomen, Managers, and Customers in American Department Stores, 1890–1940* (Urbana, IL, 1986); Michael Barry Miller, *The Bon Marché: Bourgeois Culture and the Department Store, 1869–1920* (Princeton, NJ, 1981); David Lockwood, *The Blackcoated Worker: A Study in Class Consciousness* (New York, 1989); Jürgen Kocka, *White Collar Workers in America, 1890–1940: A Social-Political History in International Perspective* (Beverly Hills, CA, 1980).

On work-related social protest, Charles Tilly and Edward Shorter, *Strikes in France, 1830–1968* (Cambridge, UK, 1974); Malcolm Thomis, *The Luddites: Machine-Breaking in Regency England* (Newton Abbot, UK, 1970); David Grimsted, *American Mobbing, 1828–1861: Toward Civil War* (New York, 1998).

On consumerism, John Brewer and Roy Porter, eds., *Consumption and the World of Goods* (New York, 1993); Neil McKendrick, Colin Brewer, and J.H. Plumb, *The Birth of a Consumer Society: The Commercialization of Eighteenth-Century England* (Bloomington, IN, 1982), a pioneering work; Carole Shammas, *The Pre-Industrial Consumer in England and America* (Oxford, 1990); Peter N. Stearns, *Consumerism in World History* (London, 2001); Susan Matt, *Keeping Up with the Joneses: Envy in American Consumer Society, 1890–1930* (Philadelphia, 2003); Lisa Jacobson, *Raising Consumers: Children and Consumer Society in the Early 20th Century* (New York, 2005); Lawrence Glickman, ed., *Consumer Society in American History: A Reader* (Ithaca, NY, 1999); Elaine Abelson, *When Ladies Go A-thieving: Middle-Class*

Shoplifters in the Victorian Department Store (New York, 1989); David Horowitz, *The Morality of Spending; Attitudes toward Consumer Society in the United States* (Chicago, 1993); Peter N. Stearns, *Fat History: Bodies and Beauty in the Modern West*, rev. ed. (New York, 2000); Timothy Burke, *Lifebuoy Men, Lux Women: Commodification, Consumption, and Cleanliness in Modern Zimbabwe* (London, 1996); Karen Hansen, *Salaula: The World of Secondhand Clothing in Zambia* (Chicago, 2000); James Watson, ed., *Golden Arches East: McDonald's in East Asia* (Stanford, CA, 1998); Joseph Tobin, *Re-made in Japan: Everyday Life and Consumer Taste in a Changing Society* (New Haven, 1992). Lawrence Glickman, *A Living Wage: American Workers and the Making of Consumer Society* (Ithaca, NY, 1997) deals with connections in the history of economic life.

8

Leisure and Recreation

Gary Cross

For most people the desire for leisure and recreation is almost reflexive, often the very purpose of work and wealth. Yet, until recently, this longing has not won the attention of many social scientists or humanists. Leisure activities—all those things that people do when they are not obliged to work or take care of others and themselves—run the gambit of human needs and aspirations. Sports and other physical activities, games, crafts, artistic expression and appreciation, holidaymaking, and so many other pleasure-seeking pursuits have always been what people would "rather do." By exploring these preferences in all their divergence and change in American and modern European (especially British) history, we can learn much about the meaning of daily life.

Despite the fact that many congratulate technology and enterprise for having freed humanity from the drudgery of endless hours of work, many also think the study of that freedom unimportant. Even when scholars concede that the history of theater or even hiking is worthy of study, elitist bias makes the history of bar brawling, penny arcades, or sewing bees seem unworthy. Leisure is often treated as a by-product of prevailing economic and cultural standards and systems that should be studied only as derivatives. From this perspective, play and entertainment are seen merely as means for elite social control or a factor in the construction of gender and class roles. Leisure activities, however, also were expressions of freedom from work and social obligation. In order to understand the varieties of leisure, it is necessary to study why specific people *enjoyed* leisure activities. Moreover, leisure not only was shaped by broader social and cultural trends but also impacted those trends.

Until recently, few historians have studied leisure. For many years, Foster Rhea Dulles's *American Learns to Play,* first published in 1940, was the only serious survey of the topic and it was largely descriptive. With the "new" social history in the 1960s and 1970s, we see the beginning of new appreciations of leisure and other forms of daily life in the past. This scholarly movement insisted that history could be fully understood only by exploring the aspirations, attitudes, and behaviors of nonelite people in their daily lives, often from the perspectives of class, ethnicity, region and race, gender, and generation. While at first much of the research focused on work, migration, and dissident social movements, by the end of the 1970s historians began to look seriously at the social meanings of leisure (especially class and gender). Others studied sites of leisure like seaside resorts to understand broad changes in culture.

In general terms, leisure history research may be broken down into studies of activities, places, and times. The variety of activities has increased with the reduction of work time, rise in affluence, and increase in social and economic contacts across communities. Musical activities were obviously transformed by the advent of mass-produced pianos and even more by the phonograph, radio, tape player, and MP-3 technology. Leisure activities have also become more organized and governed by rules over time. In medieval Europe, ball games were played mostly during intermittent festivals and differed remarkably from village to village by rules and equipment. Only in 1863 did Association Football (or soccer) emerge in England to set the standards of a game that may be played weekly in long seasons and that through global communications became the world's most favored sport.

Leisure can also be approached by reference to place. This too includes a wide range, from natural sites like seasides and hot springs to economic centers like commercial entertainment districts. A leisure place may be a home, a site separate from the crowd, or a setting that creates crowds, like a city square or an amusement park. These places catered to different kinds of playful crowds, some mixing entertainment with more-serious activities. Leisure places have changed in interesting ways. Mountains and seashores were not naturally sites of leisure; they only became so with changes in sensibilities. And the notion of traveling to a leisure site (tourism) has its own fascinating history. Some sites of leisure were fixed, but many, such as circuses, fairs, and minstrel shows, were migratory or temporary.

The most obvious leisure times are holidays and festivals. Most preindustrial leisure (at least for which we have records) certainly took place during seasonal respites from work. For many reasons, modern peoples have invented more-regular and frequent holidays (for example, the two-day weekend) and longer evenings free from work. They have abandoned many of the special practices of traditional (especially) religious holidays, even though holidays remain central to the annual cycle of life in modern societies.

Leisure can best be framed within the broader history of modern societies. Most agree that the industrialization of Western economies is the critical factor in the transformation of work, community, class, technology, and politics. Commonly, modern social history is divided into preindustrial (ca. 1500–1800), industrializing (roughly the nineteenth century), and consumer phases (twentieth century).

DOING PREINDUSTRIAL LEISURE HISTORY

Historians usually root the leisure practices of preindustrial societies in production and communication technology. Although workdays were long, the pace of farm and shop work was often episodic and production could not easily be regularized or made more intense. Even hardworking merchants experienced unavoidable lulls in business due to the infrequent delivery of goods by slow and unreliable ships or carts. Most of these work-free days, though often religious holidays, were spaced during lulls in production, especially the winter (e.g., Christmas and Mardi Gras).

The Saturnalian practices of festivals are perhaps the most interesting topic of preindustrial popular leisure. Used in reference to the ancient Roman custom of a week of drinking in early December, Saturnalia was firstly a binge, common in many poor societies. Saturnalia, especially during Carnival, also meant a variety of games, plays, and songs. How these activities expressed social tensions, especially protest against the rich and powerful, is a common way of understanding

The Cock-pit.
from Hogarth's Engraving.

An eighteenth-century English view of the sport of cockfighting, with the battling birds surrounded by excited spectators and gamblers. Source "The Cock Pit," by William Hogarth. Austin Dobson, *William Hogarth* (London, 1893).

the festival. A British variant was holiday mumming, where groups of youth went door to door in costume and demanded food and drink. This custom, like so many, survives among children in the relatively placid form of American trick-or-treating on Halloween and deserves more research. Saturnalian outbursts could be violent, but elite response to them varied and was often tolerant because holiday disorders were confined in time and place, and authorities felt that these festivals released otherwise dangerous tensions. Sites of religious devotion (especially of pilgrimage) doubled as places of play—drinking, gambling, theatrics, and parades. These principles were displayed in many variations and survived in subtle ways into the modern period, offering ample opportunities for new research.

All this did not mean that nothing changed in the centuries before industrialization: a favored topic has been the rise of elite urban societies in northern Italy in the early sixteenth century that led to more individualistic forms of leisure, especially the cultivation of nonmilitary skills and the arts and elite obsession with change or fashion. By the seventeenth century, royal capitals were becoming centers of pleasure as well as power with the emergence of the secular theater, concert hall, and even tennis court. Urban aristocrats greatly refined the private dwelling, dividing space into areas for receiving guests and private chambers for residents, and creating specialized rooms for dining and entertaining. All this was the beginning of new kinds of domestic leisure that are still in need of more study today. In the larger towns, new venues for socializing appeared: coffeehouses and pleasure gardens, for example—some becoming centers of lively conversation, others featuring gambling or newspaper reading. Aristocratic pleasure gardens—commercialized expanses of green space, fountains, alcoves, and walkways—were prominent in eighteenth-century London and imitated elsewhere. They also introduced innovations like mechanical amusement rides and fireworks spectacles—the beginning of new ideas about pleasure that would culminate in the modern theme parks. Other new sites were the inland springs like Bath, where a daily routine of morning bathing and drinking of waters was combined with rounds of socializing, which set the stage for the modern seaside resort of the nineteenth century. Both of these links need more study. Although these were European inventions, rich American colonists emulated and adapted them to their religious and physical environment (including the fashionable promenades around Hanover Square in New York and the visits of Southern gentry to Annapolis, Williamsburg, or Charleston for balls or plays). Diaries of Southern planters reveal details of private plantation parties featuring bowling, boat and horse racing, dancing, concerts, and even cockfights and fox hunts.

Another theme of study is the physical pastimes of this predominantly rural and hierarchical society, especially rough team and blood sports. Often noted is the contrast with modern sports. Until banned in the 1830s, a free-for-all ball game took place in Derby, England, on Shrove Tuesday afternoon, in which hundreds of males crowded around a ball, fighting to drive the ball toward "goals" on either side of town. Historians have argued that these annual contests were remembrances or sublimated forms of war between closely knit rivals. Similar patterns of rough and nearly ruleless sport are seen in cudgeling and boxing matches. Rural men competed in contests of physical skill and endurance: foot racing, hammer throwing, and other natural extensions of everyday work lives.

A very common pleasure was what many moderns would call cruelty to animals. Examples are cock throwing (hurling stones at a rooster until it was dead), ratting (a dog trained to kill rodents in a special pit), and especially cockfighting (a fight to the death between trained roosters). The social and cultural meaning of this behavior still needs to be better understood.

A much more elite activity was hunting. Long associated with ownership of land and possession of weapons, it was usually the privilege of the European aristocracy—a point of much tension between the classes. In the American colonies where land and game were plentiful, hunting was practiced by most men as much for utilitarian reasons as for sport and with far less concern for conservation. This is a topic of great importance because of its lasting impact on American society and is still in need of more detailed and comparative regional research. While fishing was a more democratic sport in Europe, it was even more common in the American colonies. In the seventeenth and eighteenth centuries, horse racing was likewise an aristocratic pursuit in Europe (leading to the development of the thoroughbred), but far more widespread and democratic in America. Why this was so needs more study.

Integral to most sports (and much social life) was gambling. It was essential to the development of aristocratic racetracks and coffeehouse card playing in late-seventeenth-century England. As John Findlay has shown, gambling was also at the heart of colonization and the western migration in America (including lotteries to fund the settlement of Jamestown and to support public improvements of many colonial towns). Historians have focused on how gambling has affirmed masculine and upper-class identity, but have neglected its wider appeal.

Many historians have shown how alcohol played probably even a greater role in preindustrial society than it does today. Economic and other practical matters encouraged the use of intoxicants: beer, wine, and spirits were ageless means of conserving fruit and grain in a world without modern food preservation. Alcoholic beverages were often safer to drink than ordinary water and milk and were integral to the workday in many trades and on farms. Why alcohol was so much more commonly accepted by all social classes (and even in moderation by Puritans) is a common theme of research.

Social historians have long emphasized how leisure was likely to be intermixed with work in preindustrial societies. Male sports and contests were often welcomed breaks in a long workday. But for women especially, socializing and entertainment often took place during special group-work projects. The sewing bee is an obvious example, but "frolics" for candle dipping and other essential projects also involved a feast, wine, and dancing to the music of amateur fiddlers. Even the serious event of childbirth often included partying by female friends of the mother on the birthing stool. In frontier America, crowds of revelers were attracted to the fringes of religious revivals in the periodic camp meetings, sometimes taunting the pious with their dancing and drinking. These mixes, so strange to us moderns who segment activities to an extreme degree, are key to understanding preindustrial leisure and the societies from which they came.

Another common theme is the role of religion in shaping leisure. While many have addressed how English and colonial Puritans tried to destroy the old festival calendar (replacing it with the Sabbath devoted to worship), Catholic reformers also attempted to eliminate the most extreme Saturnalia practices from Carnival and other festivals. While Puritans in England and in the northern American colonies had a well-deserved reputation for attempting to eliminate gambling, theater, and drunkenness, they did recognize "improving" leisure like physical exercise, and their passion of hymn singing and Bible reading later translated into new forms of leisure (choral singing and modern literature, for example). The fascinating connections between religious beliefs and acceptable leisure practices need more research, especially on a comparative level.

Preindustrial leisure is obviously not just a Western topic. There are great opportunities for studying leisure traditions in other societies and developing serious comparative analysis. We know, for example, of quite violent games in Central America, before the arrival of Europeans. Pilgrimages to Mecca in Islam, or Shinto pilgrimages in Japan, offered opportunities for travel (to women as well as men) and some vacation-like experiences along with their serious religious purpose. Chinese leisure included the introduction of various board games, some of which would spread to other societies. Differences in leisure focus could involve differences in the meaning of leisure to participants, though common elements, including community formation and opportunities for children's play, need to be considered as well.

DOING THE LEISURE HISTORY OF INDUSTRIALIZING SOCIETIES

After about 1770, mechanized labor and disciplined factories and offices created a more intense work regimen, but also, over time, new wealth and more time free from work. All this led to new attitudes toward leisure and its place in society. A major theme of social history is how industrialization separated work time (for income) from "free" private time (eventually, in part, for leisure). This occurred when jobs were removed from the household and centralized in the workshop or office and made possible the creation of a family-oriented leisure culture. English historians have stressed how industrialization also disrupted traditional village or community culture, forcing rural workers into new industrial towns. Robert Malcolmson shows how old paternalistic ties between elites and the common people were torn when the wealthy withdrew support from festivals and when the powerful attempted to create new leisure standards and persuade a sometimes-reluctant population to participate. In this way, the history of leisure, especially in the nineteenth century, has often been about class identity and conflict. Finally, industrialization produced a new affluence, first primarily among elites and then trickling down to wage earners. More specifically, the technologies of rail and steamboat transportation, cheap printing, and early films dramatically impacted leisure opportunities in still unexplored ways.

A persistent question has been just when and where mechanization actually changed work and leisure. It first affected textiles, mining, metalworking, and, beginning in 1825, the railroad. Factory managers intensified work by introducing machines, and because they controlled the centralized work environment, they also purged play from the workday. The play of children was obviously affected by industrialization, as revealed in many reports on early factories and mines in Britain especially. Long hours of work in factories were no longer eased by periodic bouts of play or distraction, common in preindustrial societies. But historians also note that many artisans saw little mechanization before 1850, and especially in skilled trades, workers were able to retain old leisure traditions (like in-work play, drinking breaks, and the custom of St. Monday).

Controversy still reigns over the impact of economic change of work and leisure time. A recent study by Hans-Joachim Voth shows that in northern England, yearly working hours rose from 2,860 to 3,366 between 1759 and 1830, due mostly to the loss of holidays. What made workers "give up" their vaunted leisure? Voth and others stress the rise in population and, with it, downward pressure on wages and job opportunities. But he also makes a more controversial point that increased access to consumer (and especially leisure) goods may have increased the pressure to work more hours (perhaps reversing an older preference of free time).

How did this increase in work impact leisure? One common theme is that it led to more drinking. Historians confirm that consumption increased in both America and Britain, especially in the 1820s and 1830s. William Rorabaugh stresses how "solo-drinking" in America increased in this period of mass mobility and social breakdown. But historians of bars note also that industrial-age taverns were social and cultural institutions of the working man (seldom of women). The owner often replaced the church and gentry in patronizing traditional sports (e.g., bullbaiting) or serving as the impresario of musical entertainment.

After about 1850, industrialization (and much political and organized effort) began to bring a reduction of worktime (declining from about 3,000–3,600 to about 1,600–2,000 today in Europe and the United States). Simultaneously, the work life of the average individual has also sharply decreased at both ends—as the entry into the full-time workforce was eventually delayed until adulthood or beyond, and retirement before death has become a common experience. The study of the origins of retirement and the rise of childhood play have yet to be fully explored. Industrialization drove play from labor and eliminated the seasonal ebbs in the flow of work so characteristic of artisan and agricultural life. Yet it also made possible new forms of leisure time, including the modern notions of free evenings, the weekend, and paid summer vacations. Short hours meant a more regular, predictable, and compressed workday, which freed relatively long blocks of time for autonomous family and leisure activity.

The gradual removal of work from the home with the expansion of factories, offices, and other specialized workplaces had an even more profound impact on leisure. Women and family historians have explored how the home became a place of leisure for many in the nineteenth century—a haven from impersonal labor and economic competition. The industrial system encouraged women either to withdrawal from the economy (especially if their husbands had high incomes) or to work outside the home until marriage and childbirth obliged them to remain at home. As a result, women became the organizers of the privatized realm of leisure. The home remained for the industrial-era housewife a place of both work and leisure, while husbands tended to see the domestic realm as a place exclusively for relaxation and where they compensated for their perceived loss of control and creativity on the job. The implications of this gender divide have yet to be fully explored. Historians of domestic architecture and culture (e.g., Clifford Clark) show how the home increasingly became a retreat from the market for a small circle of family members. Middle-class women—increasingly freed from arduous work with the hiring of servants and later with domestic appliances, and liberated from lifelong child care with small families—were at the center of this "domestication" of leisure. Historians of women have shown how reformers from the churches, temperance organizations, and elsewhere called on women at home to refine the recreational lives of husbands and children.

The history of modern suburbanization is another way of exploring this topic. It began in the 1790s, when merchant families first abandoned their townhouses of London for more-spacious neighborhoods far from business, factories, the rowdy poor, and the self-indulgent aristocracy. The object, in part, was to create a new leisure culture that was private, familial, and ultimately uplifting. These suburban homes set many precedents: situated on large private lots, the homes allowed enough room for gardens (and, as a later American variant, extensive front and back lawns), providing opportunities for the cultivation of plant life and a parklike setting for family games. The suburban Victorian home was designed to separate space: formal front parlors vs. private family sitting rooms, male "libraries" vs. female boudoirs, adult bedrooms vs. children's nurseries. The British historian Leonore Davidoff describes the social "season" that women of affluence organized in Victorian Britain. New, elaborate rites of passage emerged, especially the "white weddings" documented by Elizabeth Pleck. Women's magazines and the works of early advocates of home economics, like the American Catherine Beecher, are excellent sources on these trends. Even the "respectable" working class devoted a large share of scarce living space to a dining room and a parlor, often never used except for the formal visit of guests. These are difficult topics to tap, but advertising and magazines concerned with domestic arts along with memoirs reveal much.

Another theme is the nineteenth century's reorganization of holidays. Particularly fruitful are studies of the transformation of Christmas from an often rowdy holiday of public drinking, feasting, and theater to a private celebration of family, focused especially on young children. New rites and customs are particularly well documented in popular magazines, advertising, and memoirs. Americans, who in the early nineteenth century had celebrated July 4th with the bacchanalian abandon of a village Mardi Gras, turned to family picnics by the 1850s. And, after the Civil War, the American Thanksgiving became a tradition of family reunion.

At the heart of this domestic ideal, but still scarcely explored, was a new attitude toward children's play. Older practices, including children's participation in adult activities, were abandoned for a more protected environment of playgrounds and nursery rooms that fostered child-appropriate play. New manufacturing techniques and greater affluence in the middle class meant that children's games and toys became increasingly available. In the home progressively devoid of productive tasks, toys served to simulate adult roles. Moreover, though hardly explored, training children to play musical instruments and to sing and dance became major improving activities in middle-class households.

Tracing children's play involves some of the classic issues in the history of leisure, made more difficult because available sources limit what we can learn about how children thought about their leisure in the past. One approach is purely descriptive: what were the toys and games available, and how did they change? A good bit of the history of leisure, particularly in earlier generations, started and ended at this level. But there are also deeper questions: how did the state and other agencies try to shape children's play, through schools for instance, to serve larger goals (including disciplining teenagers or trying to prevent delinquency)? Deeper still are the kinds of issues posed by some analysts who have argued that the play element began to be diminished for children as adult controls and spectator activities limited spontaneity and the true benefits play should provide for children.

Industrialization also tended to break up older rural leisure traditions built around church and village when the propertyless wage earners migrated to urban and industrial centers. As we have seen, elites also withdrew patronage from popular leisure. There was a growing revulsion against the violence of traditional leisure, but fear of the "dangerous classes" of the urban working poor prompted most of this response. Some, especially Marxist, historians have dismissed the efforts of British and American evangelicals to "Christianize" the new urban working class as exercises in social control, designed to pacify and discipline labor (with Sabbath restrictions and Sunday school indoctrination of middle-class morality). But other historians show how Sunday gradually became a day of family recreation, and Sunday schools, especially in Britain, offered musical training, formal teas, excursions, and amateur football (soccer) to attract pupils. Further research in this area will provide more subtle understandings.

Perhaps even more typical of a seemingly manipulative approach to leisure was temperance or the more extreme prohibitionism that sought to outlaw all alcoholic drink. A persistent historical question is the motivations of movement leaders and why American and British opponents of drink took different approaches. Whereas in Britain prohibitionism was always politically marginal, in the United States by the 1840s it became a political force that led to the banning of drink from 1919 to 1933. In Britain, even voluntary teetotalism never had such success, though early-closing legislation managed to shorten drinking bouts. But in both countries, temperance movements attempted to create bars featuring tea and coffee and wholesome leisure activities. In the United States, the conflict between the bar and temperance cultures was deep and abiding, often separating urban and immigrant groups from small-town native Protestants.

A final restrictionist approach to reforming city pleasures was the campaign against prostitution. "Social purity" movements in America had also been an offshoot of the revivalist activism of the 1820s. While red-light districts in many American cities were cleaned out by 1920, in England, whorehouses were outlawed in 1885, but the private sale of sex was tolerated. Government sources and exposés in magazines and newspapers are good sources in exploring this topic. Comparative explorations of regulating pleasure offer promising prospects.

Historians have explored how reformers tried to reshape working-class leisure to affirm middle-class values of religion, family, and self-development and to counteract the presumed breakdown of traditional rural life and the demoralizing impact of industrialization. In Britain these efforts were called "rational recreation." Some historians (e.g., Donajgrodski) have seen these efforts as simply an extension of the class war fought by the rich against the poor, but others (Cunningham and Bailey) also note that many upwardly mobile workers embraced these activities and values and others used them for their own purposes. The late nineteenth and early twentieth centuries were something of a battleground between middle- and working-class leisure in places like Britain and the United States. Middle-class values gradually reformed worker practices like shouting in theaters. But a tamed working-class leisure culture also attracted middle-class attendance—in the music halls, for example—for it provided greater excitement and titillation.

There were a number of sites of rational recreation. In 1850s Britain, Working Men's Social Clubs became respectable but relaxing alternatives to the gin mill. The Young Men's Christian Association (YMCA) was established in London in 1844 to provide a homelike and respectable setting for young male clerks tempted by drink and ladies of the night. The American Andrew Carnegie's subsidy of public libraries from the 1890s was only one of many similar efforts. Other sites of rational recreation were public walkways and parks for families (Frederick Olmsted's Central Park in New York City). Extensive parks and art and natural history museums were built in the 1890s in many American cities, a topic still barely touched by leisure historians. These facilities claimed to reach out to a broad audience, but elite values and didacticism limited crowds.

Another venue of rational recreation was the Victorian world's fair. London's international exhibition of 1851, along with its imposing Crystal Palace, set the precedent for many world's fairs of the nineteenth and twentieth centuries in Europe and especially in the United States. American cities showed off their growth and wealth, but also tried to instill civic virtue and culture in a long series of exhibitions beginning in Philadelphia in 1876, followed by Chicago (1893), Nashville (1897), Omaha (1898), Buffalo (1901), St. Louis (1904), Chicago (1933), and especially New York (1939–40). The core of all these exhibits was the promise of technological progress and received culture. But crowds were also drawn to more exuberant plebeian amusements like Chicago's midway, which featured the exotic belly dancing of "Little Egypt" and the thrill of the new Ferris wheel. This blending of the respectable and improving ideas of rational recreation with the anarchic sensuous and emotional release of plebeian play marked American commercial leisure culture and could be explored in many settings (e.g., music halls, amusement parks, theaters, and picnic grounds).

Leisure activities also became ways that youth sought identity and autonomy from elders. The industrializing city provided new and sometimes dangerous diversions. Whereas youth leisure had previously been bound to tradition—rituals and rules of their trade or the informal strictures of the festival—the newly urbanized youth of the nineteenth century was largely cut adrift from time-honored codes of behavior. By 1850, youth formed a street-corner society built around social clubs or gangs in most American and British cities. Leisure was at the core of generational conflict and of moralists' fears of working-class independence and precocity. Nineteenth-century youth gangs have not been thoroughly studied, especially in this context.

The Victorian British elite's ideal was to isolate the boy in school until age 16 or 17, where the boy not only obtained a formal education, but found diversion in increasingly formalized sports (e.g., soccer). In America, organized sports emerged from different settings but often served similar goals—community groups like volunteer fire companies (baseball), the YMCA (basketball), and colleges (American football). By 1870, the American "Y" had become a sports and physical fitness center for the urban middle class. Aiming at a younger male was the Boy Scouts, founded in 1908. Historians like David Macleod and Michael Rosenthal stress the conservative, middle-class orientation of the scouts. Reaching out to youth across the class divide was the playground movement, with neighborhood parks in immigrant areas of Chicago and other American cities in the 1890s and the Playground Association (founded in 1906). Begun as an extension of the schools and churches after the Civil War, the summer camp for youth was unique to North America. Recent studies of camps (especially around gender themes) have not made the broader linkages between the camp and the rational recreation movement. The contrast between the youth-oriented camps in America as opposed to the adult and family camps of Europe is worth study.

How successful were efforts to uplift and rationalize youth leisure? Historian Dom Cavallo doubts that more than 10–20 percent of immigrant youth visited urban playgrounds in the period 1900–1920. Middle-class values had limited success in American volunteer fire departments where members from different stations fought between each other for pride and power. Other institutions like choral societies, ethnic fraternal organizations, and brass bands were dominated by ordinary wage earners. And historians have long noted that respectability in middle- and working-class circles differed. While historians have studied the class tensions in these venues of rational recreation, other dynamics (many yet to be explored, including age and ethnic and gender styles) also were acted out in them. The goals of rational recreation were also undermined by the failure of elites to actually practice them. As Thorstein Veblen's *Theory of the Leisure Class* (1899) shows, the American rich used their leisure time to display their status through an elaborate culture of parties, extravagant homes, fashion, and touring. No doubt, these rituals were more complex and are worthy of further study.

Finally, the wealth created by industrialization produced new opportunities for recreation and leisure. While increased income and lower prices certainly raised the demand for popular leisure goods (tobacco, drink, cheap theater, and reading), they also allowed for a trickle down of middle-class leisure activities. For example, when some working-class families purchased excursion tickets for travel or home pianos, members tended to spend less on alcohol. These broad shifts in commercialized pleasure across classes and time need more documentation.

Modern capitalist business practices based on the mass market and unfettered competition created a mass entertainment industry centralized in the hands of relatively few corporations of national and even international influence. For example, impresarios of entertainment like the Americans P. T. Barnum and Tony Pastor succeeded in creating wide audiences by appealing to a variety of social classes, ethnic groups, and ages in their museums, circuses, and vaudeville circuits. Impresarios promoted celebrities like the singer Jenny Lynd and fads like roller skating and cycling. They adapted quickly to new technological innovations like electricity (introduced early in Times Square, the entertainment center of New York, and the English resort town of Blackpool). While major figures like Barnum have been studied, the role of the entertainment entrepreneur has still barely been explored.

The railroad (beginning about 1830) and the electric streetcar (from the late 1880s) had the most dramatic impact on commercial leisure. Railroads made distant travel accessible to the middle class and, with the gradual reduction in prices, to time-starved workers, allowing an escape from the neighborhood and town. How railroads led to the decline of smaller local fairs and the development of larger, more commercialized amusements has yet to be studied. The impact of this transportation revolution, especially on creating cross-national and even cross-Atlantic exchanges of celebrities and entertainment technologies (e.g., amusement park rides), is worth researching.

Reading, of course, was a major leisure activity, especially with the spread of free and compulsory elementary education by the 1870s. Press historians note how technology (steam press and mechanized bookbinding in the 1840s) and the abolition of taxes on newspapers facilitated a huge growth in popular reading. The ways that the popular press, especially magazines like the famous American *Godey's Lady's Book,* shaped leisure activities (domestic refinement, fashion, tourism, and the celebrity culture) needs further study. An adolescent and working-class press also emerged in both countries, especially after 1860 (with Western, detective, and adventure themes in particular). The young and working-class crowds at cheap theaters (e.g., the penny or "gaff" theaters in London, which flourished between 1830 and 1880) and the appeal of crime drama especially are worth exploring. More attention has perhaps been paid to the dime museums in New York City with their sideshow-like exhibitions of freaks and wax works. Still, worthy of note is how the dime museum succeeded in appealing not only to the working-class crowd, but also to a broader middle-class audience with its claims of historical and geographical education (such as in the dioramas: oversized paintings with scenic accessories depicting well-known dramatic events). The origins and development of the tabloid press in the 1880s, especially in England, is well known, but the leisure activity content (especially the travel, gossip, comic strip, and sports news) needs to be fleshed out.

In both Britain and the United States, the demand for indoor music and variety programs grew enormously in the nineteenth century. The music hall, or vaudeville show, had its roots in the informal and often disreputable singing saloons, where drink mixed with singing and rough male fellowship. Charles Morton of London converted this into the more formal music hall in the 1850s, and a decade later New Yorker Tony Pastor enticed a family audience to his "Opera House" with a program of well-publicized music, comedy, and animal and acrobatic acts. By 1900, dance halls were sweeping American and English towns. As Kathy Peiss shows, in New York they attracted respectable working women with cut-price entrance fees. Much was written about these halls, often by moralistic middle-class witnesses, who expressed concern about the charged sexual atmosphere. But a close read of all sources, including diaries, offers a more nuanced understanding of the rituals practiced and needs served.

New technology of the 1880s and 1890s changed the form but not always the content of catch-as-catch-can pleasures. Mechanical games and gramophones, offered in penny arcades, hotel lobbies, and amusement parks, often adapted to the pleasures of the museum or penny theater. The peep show, or kinetoscope, introduced by Thomas Edison in 1894, offered the viewer a short show of acrobatics, cockfights, and mock executions. Although the motion picture would

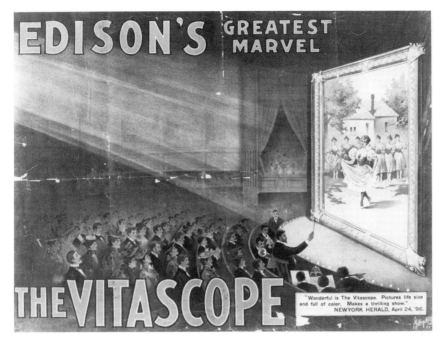

Edison's late 1890s marvel, the Vitascope movie projector, followed European in-novators and turned the peep show film into a theatrical experience. Courtesy of the Library of Congress.

eventually appeal to middle-class audiences, with stories and exhibition halls modeled after the "legitimate theater," until about 1910 it was mostly a work-ing-class and youth entertainment. These commercial leisure sites need further work.

Furthermore, there are always questions about what leisure meant and what values it brought. As leisure increasingly involved spectatorship—watching pro-fessional leisure workers work—and escapism, some historians have argued that real values such as the play element and real community contact deteriorated, even as people had more leisure time. Others, however, contend that if people chose contemporary leisure forms, they must be finding value. And they stress those aspects of contemporary leisure that helped people re-form community—in bars, or stadium crowds—thus serving older purposes in new ways. There's much to debate here, for decisions about the nature of change in leisure force us to think about our own leisure as well.

Continuity and change certainly defined the nineteenth-century circus. Crude traveling menageries of a few caged wagons of animals and acrobatic perfor-mances at local fairs became elaborate displays of animal and human acts fol-lowing a long process of legitimization. Barnum and others vastly improved the size and quality of the circus with the creation of the circus train. A related topic is the birth of the amusement park and traveling carnivals or fairs in the 1890s. Amusement park rides emerged in close parallel with other mechanical innovations (e.g., the electric street car and the roller coaster). As John Kasson notes, these rides were greatly influenced by the amusement sections of the world's fairs (especially the midway of the Chicago fair of 1893). Although there have been many suggestive works, especially on the amusement parks of Coney Island, a serious study of the amusement park's origins and fate has yet to be written. Here would be an excellent case for a comparative approach given the differences in style and content (as well as much borrowing between them).

Similarly, the seaside resort became a site of popular holidaymaking. In ways, this was a case of the trickling down of aristocratic and middle-class leisure practices developed earlier in Britain and the United States. Genteel seaside buildings and entertainment zones like the Blackpool's Tower, with dance hall, zoo, and observation deck, contrasted with its Golden Mile of cheap sideshows, rock candy, and fish and chips shops. There is a persistent interest in Victorian tourism. Similarly, the aristocrat's Grand Tour of Europe was democratized when Thomas Cook offered guided tours to busy middle-class and clerical workers who had neither the time nor the knowledge to plan educational trips. Associations with the ideals of rational recreation were long lasting. Tourism changed uses and meanings of places. By the 1880s, for example, Britons of means began to visit Switzerland in the winter (for skiing) as well as in the summer. In America, sites of natural beauty became part of the American Grand Tour and the See America First movement. The history of tourism is built on published guides. Local histories of tourist sites, however, are still rare.

AGE OF CONSUMER LEISURE

No single or even cluster of processes characterized the consumer age of leisure in the United States and western Europe when it began about 1900. Still, some important changes shaped it: (1) the dramatic increase in personal income facilitated a much-greater commercialization of leisure and, to a degree, a narrowing of the class and regional differences; (2) work time declined significantly, the paid vacation (especially in Europe) became nearly universal, and tourism and hobbies and crafts expanded greatly; (3) the automobile facilitated rapid mobility and dramatically increased the role of private and personal leisure; (4) new media (film, radio, television, and personal computer) created not only passive and isolated audiences but also common national and even global entertainment experiences, reducing interactions in pleasure crowds and recreational groups by creating global culture; (5) a new middle-class leisure culture emerged that both affirmed and modified the genteel and rational recreation ideals of the nineteenth century as it adapted to commercialized leisure; and (6) increased affluence and mobility allowed regional, ethnic, and working-class patterns to persist and new groups built around leisure preferences to emerge. Some of these were age-based (youth and elders); others were defined by lifestyle activities such as hobbies and specialty sports.

The cost of leisure declined with the shift from the relatively expensive music hall to the cinema and radio. The installment plan in the United States, which financed the purchase of most cars, radios, and furniture by 1930, along with gradually rising incomes, made possible a more commercialized leisure, displacing informal and low-cost recreations (like card playing or even visiting with friends). This presumably led to more uniformity across regions and classes in leisure pursuits, but, as Steven Gelber shows, affluence also made possible a radical expansion of individual choice—new opportunities for specialized sports, crafts, and hobbies rather than consumerist conformity. Much of the historiography ignores these trends, and a correction is in order.

The eight-hour workday (48-hour week) became the norm after World War I, reducing the total hours in the workweek by six to twelve hours. In Europe, the paid vacation became a right of most wage earners by the mid-1930s. Even though this trend stalled in the 1930s, continental Europeans won the 40-hour week in the 1960s (reduced to 35 hours in France by 2000) and have extended paid vacations up to six weeks per year. An important question raised by Hunnicutt, Schor, and Cross is why free-time movements have stalled (especially in the United States in regard to vacations).

As a result of the increase in free time in the interwar years, there were a variety of government and political efforts to organize leisure. For example, the Italian Fascists' *dopo lavoro* and the Nazis' *Kraft durch Freude* shared with the leftist French Popular Front the goal of inculcating patriotic and political values in organized tourism, sports, and leisure activities. These efforts seem to have had a short-lived and disappointing impact. Volunteer efforts (like the British Holiday Fellowship) were bested by commercial efforts like the Butlin camps by the end of the 1930s. An important question is why and to what extent public and volunteer leisure organizations failed to develop social practices and dynamics that would have allowed them to compete with commercial efforts.

An ongoing theme is how and why cars played different roles in shaping leisure and daily life in different countries. The fact that the automobile remained a luxury in Europe far longer than in the United States is critical to understanding very different ways that commercialized leisure developed. By 1927, the United States produced 85 percent of the world's cars, and the passenger trains declined sharply after World War II. Despite the emergence of the mass-produced car in western Europe in the 1960s, the train remains a major force, reinforcing an urban culture and preserving central entertainment and shopping districts in most towns and cities.

Most studies on the car culture are American. In the United States, automobiles made possible individualized touring and reinforced the goal of making the family the focus of holidays. By the 1920s, thanks to new highways, car owners could avoid the traditional crowds of seaside resorts and amusement parks reached by the less affluent via public transportation. As a result, for example, New York's Coney Island slipped into decline after 1920. Opened in 1955, Disneyland linked to a sprawling network of Southern California highways and was a culmination of a trend toward the car-based amusement park. Warren Belasco's study of the rise of modern car camping and the motel details how adventuresome early car travel led to a quest for predictability in modern name-brand accommodations and other roadside amenities. The ongoing relationship between the auto tourist and the commercialization of the road after 1950 would make a good study. By the mid-1930s, lodgings had become mobile in the trailer. The car also produced a plethora of privatized pleasures, from the drive-in restaurant of the early 1920s to the drive-in theater of the 1930s. In the mid-1920s, shopping centers providing large parking lots appeared (first in Kansas City), and by the 1950s, the automobile had begun to displace the downtown business district because of insufficient parking and traffic. Case studies of the decline of downtown shopping districts and the traditional rites of Christmas displays and parades would be of value, along with more analyses of the uses and meanings of the car-based suburban malls.

The car also transformed the home and domestic leisure. Studies of suburban domesticity have centered on new, more informal housing types (e.g., the bungalow and ranch home), on the attached garage replacing the front porch, and on the "lawn" culture. There remain many gaps in this history, especially developments after 1960. The suburb originally was to create a spatial segmentation of work and pleasure, the duality of male industry and female domesticity. The quality of life in these car-based suburbs has been found wanting by urban moralists and sociologists since their construction. This view has been challenged by scholars like Barbara Kelly, who finds diversity and self-expression in the leisure habits of suburbanites from the 1950s.

The car set all this in motion, but air travel also transformed leisure. This remains practically virgin territory for the leisure historian. As early as 1914, "flying boats" transported tourists between Florida and Caribbean resorts, and

Pensioners enjoying retirement at a trailer court in Florida, 1941. Courtesy of the Library of Congress.

in 1929 the first transcontinental service combined air and rail travel in a grueling 48-hour trip. But airplanes remained for the adventuresome elite until 1954, when the Boeing Company revolutionized travel with its 707, a plane that could transport 189 people at 600 miles per hour. We still need a scholarly history of how the modern system of cheap, long-distance aerial destination tourism revolutionized travel between the United States and Europe, made possible short winter vacations, and displaced old resorts like Atlantic City and Blackpool.

The mechanized entertainment of film, radio, and television both homogenized and privatized twentieth-century leisure. New entertainment technology offered an enticing alternative to the social pleasures of the bar, theater, home, and neighborhood—a change yet to be fleshed out. While early movies gathered like-minded groups of mostly wage earners with fare appealing to their experiences, the long-term trend by the 1920s was toward corporate concentration and of films that appealed to a broad mass audience (crossing gender and class lines). More subtly, while silent-film exhibitors tolerated crowd interaction, with the coming of sound after 1926, the screen talked while the audience became silent, privately viewing the imposing screen and sound even if in a crowd. The simple fact that millions saw the same featured film in the same week had a profound impact on culture—accelerating the pace of fads and celebrities, for example. Another theme is how and why Americans came to dominate the cinema by 1920. With control over the huge American market and, thus, lower fixed production and distribution costs, the American filmmakers prevailed over the Europeans. Most film historians focus on the content or business of the movies, but just as important were the sites of film viewing, the history of the storefront nickelodeons and the rise of the movie palaces, and the rituals of viewing (for example, the rise of the heterosexual dating system or children's Saturday matinees).

The phonograph, radio, and TV may ultimately have had even a more powerful impact on isolating and homogenizing culture than did the movie. The phonograph (invented in 1876, but marketed only after 1887) created a new, more accessible, passive, and private way of listening as compared to live theater concerts or home piano playing. Nuances of this change have hardly been explored. More work has been done on the impact of the radio. Only accessible for domestic use from about 1910, it remained a hobbyist tool (or toy) until the 1920s, when it became an entertainment appliance in the home, into which three networks of centralized programs were broadcast (after 1926). The transformation of early radio and the changing rituals for using and relating to the radio have attracted interest (especially the contrasts between the mostly male and young amateur radio enthusiasts and the domesticated and increasingly female network radio listeners). This is a topic that cries out for comparisons between the American development of commercial-funded broadcasting of popular entertainment and the European tendency to use the radio for political propaganda and cultural "uplift." How radio adapted to private household activities (and driving) and relieved the isolation of homemakers and other increasingly isolated people with a form of companionship has yet to be developed. The radio allowed listeners to avoid the crowd while enjoying a national, even global entertainment in private. As Susan Douglas notes, the radio and radio's social uses changed dramatically after 1950, when network TV supplanted most of its earlier functions and radio began to serve more diverse and dispersed social groups (teens, traveling salesmen, political conservatives, and many "taste" communities defined by interest in particular brands of music).

Television, perhaps even more than radio, reinforced the domestication of leisure, even as it produced cultural uniformity through broadcasting. Most historians of television have been American and focused on the 1950s, when American families learned to "adapt" to the box and tried to reconcile their mixed feelings about it. Less work has been done on how television led to the decline of collective leisure (soccer matches in Britain and minor league baseball in America, for example). Only beginning to be explored is the transformation of TV with the emergence of multiple sets and proliferation of channels since the 1970s. As Joseph Turow shows, these trends have led to a multitude of tastes and a reversal of the mass cultural trends of early TV. The advent of the home computer in the 1980s and the Internet in the 1990s has only reinforced the private character of leisure while also extending the entertainment and informational horizons of Web surfers. Children's street games have been replaced with video games, and face-to-face communication has been transformed with e-mails, electronic chat groups, and Web surfing.

More broadly, affluence has reinforced the individualization of leisure since 1960. The growth of multiple-car families (especially in America, where the ratio of people to cars dropped from 3.74 in 1950 to 1.86 by 1980) has led to more personalized recreation. The same process is evident with cheaper and more portable radios and electronic gadgets with transistors from the mid-1950s and electronic chips from the 1980s. Consumerism has made it possible for each family member to have an increasingly large array of personal leisure tools, be they a child's own toy box that is replaced almost yearly, a basement hobby shop full of a father's tools, or a kitchen equipped with exotic cookbooks and appliances. In addition, personal vacations and separate activities on family vacations have appeared, even if they remain mostly restricted to the two-income professional classes. These trends suggest new topics for contemporary historical research.

In many ways these changes affirmed nineteenth-century middle-class values. By the 1950s, homogenized (but isolated) leisure built around mass media, automobility, and the suburb seemed to have obliterated most remaining remnants of local, ethnic, or class traditions in Anglo-American society and confirmed the victory of a middle-class ethos. Yet middle-class leisure culture itself was transformed in the twentieth century in ways that have yet to be fully described and analyzed. To be sure, the genteel values of uplift, character building, and restful reflection survived long after the Victorian Era. Advocates of gentility tried valiantly to maintain cultural distance and uplift—from adult liberal-arts education and ad-free classical music on the radio to the Book-of-the-Month Club. Still, beginning in the 1920s, the broad middle class gradually abandoned the expectation that it was really necessary to embrace genteel values to rise in social status or to fully enjoy life. This can be seen in the content of popular magazines and the embrace of more playful and more tolerant views toward children's play and fantasy. Note, for example, how the middle-class at Disneyland ignored the crush by gathering delighted children around them.

Cultural historian Jackson Lears explains the change in American middle-class leisure about 1910. He identifies an erosion of the religious and moral underpinnings of the ideas of rational recreation and its replacement by a culture of social adjustment and self-fulfillment, which demanded more spend-free attitudes. The excitement of consumption also helped to overcome growing feelings of emptiness resulting from a decline in religion and contact with nature. He also argues that, as more middle-class people worked in bureaucracies, their work satisfaction declined, creating another partial vacuum that leisure might fill. Combined with a revolt against the formality and repressive self-control of the Victorian Era, this sense of vacuum led to the popular embrace of youthful vitality and openness to playful innovations. Shopping and rites of consumption certainly became central to this process. This analysis, however, remains largely theoretical and needs more close study in various social settings.

Homogeneity in leisure was not the inevitable product of twentieth-century technology and affluence; in fact, consumerism facilitated differences. A significant theme of popular cultural studies is the persistence of working-class, ethnic, and regional deviations from the middle-class norm. In part, this is the story of the income lag of these groups and, in part, how they rejected middle-class uses of new technology and affluence to preserve their own identities. In northern England, the annual weeklong holiday at Blackpool remained strong long after Coney Island and other working-class resorts in the United States had fallen into decay. Traditional rites of "treating" or "standing rounds" persisted, where participants would take turns buying drinks for a circle of friends and acquaintances. We shouldn't neglect the persistence of churchgoing and church socials, which reemerged after 1950 in suburban churches. Church attendance, especially for many working-class and black women, remained a counter to male drinking and sports culture.

Youth leisure had long been a problem, but a rapidly changing consumer culture directed toward the young made for greater intergenerational conflicts. This topic is largely unexplored. Soon after 1900, amusement parks, dance halls, neighborhood milk bars, soda fountains, penny arcades, and nickelodeons were sites of youth recreation and spending in cities. Paula Fass shows how American colleges became venues for a new peer-group culture built around dating, parties, and style-setting organizations like fraternities and sororities. Class and ethnic divisions were often reproduced in these youth leisure groups. A great topic would be a study of the peer leisure of a high school over several generations. Increased mobility due to cheap streetcars and, by the 1930s in America, used cars accelerated the liberation of the young. One of the best ways to explore this autonomy of youth leisure is through its media: movies by 1910; radio in the 1930s; new fantasy literature, especially the comic book from 1938; rock radio and records from 1954; and action figures and video games from the 1970s.

This topic inevitably focuses on the moral panics of adults against youth crazes. In part, adults feared youth leisure because it symbolized rapid change and the inability of parents to control the culture of their offspring, which seemed to be dominated by commercial entertainment. Because teenage leisure constantly changed, adults did not see it as similar to their own period of sowing wild oats. And, despite repeated efforts, adults found it difficult to control youth culture. As James Gilbert shows, panics were often caused by middle-class parents' fears that their children were adopting minority or working-class pleasures (as they sometimes were). Many panics were eventually resolved when adults

A video arcade from the late 1970s drew the young into the solitary challenges displayed on the electronic screen. Courtesy of the Library of Congress.

embraced at least part of the innovation (for example, rock music and dancing by the early 1960s).

In the United States and Britain, commercialized youth leisure grew during and after World War II due to wartime disruption of parental control and increased affluence. New technologies like the 45 rpm record and the transistor radio primarily served youth. The breakup of old neighborhoods and increased migration of minorities to cities produced a gang culture. British groups like the Teddy Boys, Mods, and skinheads have been studied by sociologists who stress the role that clothing and other consumer goods played in defining gang identity. While males dominated these deviant cultures and their study, more recent scholarship (Currie) focused on girls' consumer culture, especially around the use of magazines. The counterculture of the 1960s was far more individualistic than the gang culture of the working class of the 1950s, challenging suburban lifestyles, gender roles, and the work ethic. According to Thomas Frank, however, it was less radical than thought at the time, but instead was part of a wider trend toward more personalized consumption.

Equally important are trends in older adult leisure. Lengthy retirement for the masses has become possible only recently with pensions and increased life expectancy. Explaining the migration of healthy, often relatively young elders to resort communities, often far from former work, friends, and family, has been a focus of research: what prompted the apparent abandonment of grandchildren and a desire to live in a peer culture of the aged? Even though the dream of many migrants to these retirement sites was a permanent vacation or unending weekend, many differences based on income and values developed between these elder leisure communities.

The new affluence ultimately created a far more complex variety of identity groups that can hardly be touched on here: historical reenactors, devotees of extreme sports, collectors and restorers of antique cars, and fan clubs, for example. Increased free time and greater disposable income only begin an explanation of these activities. Longing for communities of identity in a world of social mobility and impersonal society certainly explain more. But, because of their particularity, the history of these activities needs to be individually studied or, at least, in clusters. Some are driven by a relatively new emotion—nostalgia, born of rapid cultural change. Some are a response to a sense of loss of contact with nature; others appeal to needs of competition. The age of consumerist leisure produced as much diversity as conformity. Here too, leisure history, placing the present in light of the past, improves our capacity to understand not only leisure forms, but also the functions and meanings involved.

FURTHER READING

General theoretical histories of leisure include Sabastian de Grazia, *Of Time, Work, and Leisure* (New York, 1967); Thorstein Veblen, *The Theory of the Leisure Class* (New York, 1953 [1899]); and Peter Stearns, *Battleground of Desire: The Struggle for Self-Control in Modern America* (New York, 1999). On the relationship between work and leisure and movements for free time, see Gary Cross, *Time and Money: The Making of Consumer Culture* (London, 1993); Benjamin Hunnicutt, *Work without End: Abandoning Shorter Hours for the Right to Work* (Philadelphia, 1988); Juliet Schor, *The Overworked American: The Unexpected Decline of Leisure in America* (New York, 1991); and Hans J. Joachim Voth, *Time and Work in England, 1750–1850* (Oxford, UK, 2000). Surveys include Gary Cross, *A Social History of Leisure since 1600* (State College, PA, 1990); Foster Rhea Dulles, *A History of Recreation: America Learns to Play* (New York, 1940); and John Lowerson and John Myerscough, *Time to Spare in Victorian England* (Brighton, UK, 1977).

Among the topical studies of preindustrial leisure histories are Robert Malcolmson, *Popular Recreations in English Society, 1700–1850* (Cambridge, UK, 1973); Robert Muchembled, *Popular Culture and Elite Culture in France, 1400–1750* (Baton Rouge, LA, 1985); David Underdown, *Revel, Riot, and Rebellion: Popular Politics in England, 1603–1660* (Oxford, UK, 1985); Phyllis Hembry, *The English Spa, 1560–1815* (London, 1991); Peter Burke, *Popular Culture in Early Modern Europe* (New York, 1978).

The impact of industrialization on leisure is documented in Hugh Cunningham, *Leisure in the Industrial Revolution* (New York, 1980); Tom Dublin, *Women at Work: The Transformation of Work and Community in Lowell, Massachusetts, 1826–1860* (New York, 1979); W. J. Rorabaugh, *The Alcoholic Republic: An American Tradition* (New York,1979); and Roy Rosenzweig, *Eight Hours for What We Will: Workers and Leisure in an Industrial City, 1870–1920* (New York, 1983).

The domestication of modern leisure is explored in many works, including Richard Bushman, *The Refinement of America: Persons, Houses, and Cities* (New York, 1992); Clifford Clark, *The American Family Home, 1800–1960* (Chapel Hill, NC, 1986); Leonore Davidoff, *The Best Circles* (London, 1973); Robert Fishman, *Bourgeois Utopias: The Rise and Fall of Suburbia* (New York, 1987); Katherine Grier, *Culture and Comfort: People, Parlors, and Upholstery, 1850–1930* (Washington DC,

1997); Virginia Jenkins, *The Lawn: A History of an American Obsession* (Washington, DC, 1994). Studies focusing on family rituals are Stephan Nissenbaum, *The Battle for Christmas* (New York, 1996); Elizabeth Pleck, *Celebrating the Family: Ethnicity, Consumer Culture, and Family Rituals* (Cambridge, MA, 2000); Leigh Schmidt, *Consumer Rites: The Buying and Selling of American Holidays* (Princeton, NJ, 1996); and for a more theoretical treatment, Mihaly Csikszentmihalyi and Eugene Rochberg-Halton, *The Meaning of Things: Domestic Symbols of the Self* (New York, 1981).

The rise of tourism and the vacation are treated in Cindy Aron, *Working at Play: A History of Vacations in the United States* (New York, 1999); Alain Corbin, *The Lure of the Sea* (Cambridge, 1994); Gary Cross and John Walton, *The Playful Crowd* (New York, 2005); Ellen Furlough and S. Baranowski, eds., *Being Elsewhere: Tourism, Consumer Culture, and Identity in Modern Europe and North America* (Ann Arbor, MI, 2001); Barbara Kirshenblatt-Gimblett, *Destination Culture: Tourism, Museums, and Heritage* (Berkeley, CA, 1998); John A. R. Pimlott, *The Englishman's Holiday, A Social History* (Brighton, UK, 1976, [1947]); Robert Rydell, *World of Fairs: The Century-of-Progress Expositions* (Chicago, 1993); John Sears, *Sacred Places: American Tourist Attractions in the Nineteenth Century* (New York, 1989); Jon Sterngass, *First Resorts: Pursuing Pleasure at Saratoga Springs, Newport, and Coney Island* (Baltimore, 2001); John K. Walton, *The British Seaside: Holidays and Resorts in the Twentieth Century* (Manchester, UK, 2000); and James Weeks, *Gettysburg: Memory, Market, and an American Shrine* (Princeton, NJ, 2003).

How various alternative leisures have been used by elites to exercise social control is studied in Victorian de Grazia, *The Culture of Consent: Mass Organization of Leisure in Fascist Italy* (New York, 1981); A. P. Donajgrodski, ed., *Social Control in Nineteenth Century Britain* (London, 1977); Brian Harrison, *Drink and the Victorians: The Temperance Question in England, 1815–1872* (Pittsburgh, 1971); Thomas Laqueur, *Religion and Respectability: Sunday Schools and Working Class Culture, 1780–1850* (New Haven, CT, 1976); Roy Rosenzweig and Elizabeth Blackmar, *The Park and the People: A History of Central Park* (Ithaca, NY, 1992); Ian Tyrrell, *Sobering Up: From Temperance to Prohibition in Antebellum America, 1800–1860* (Westport, CT, 1979); and for a theoretical treatment, see Norbert Elias, *The Civilizing Process: Sociogenetic and Psychogenetic Investigations*, rev. ed. (Oxford, UK, 2000).

Histories of the popular press and literature that relate to our topic include George Boyce, James Curran, and Pauline Wingate, *Newspaper History: From the Seventeenth Century to the Present Day* (London, 1978); Michael Denning, *Mechanical Accents: Dime Novels and Working-Class Culture in America* (New York, 1989); Erin Smith, *Hard-Boiled: Working-Class Readers and Pulp Magazines* (Philadelphia, 2000); Larry Sullivan and Lydia Schuman, *Pioneers, Passionate Ladies, and Private Eyes: Dime Novels, Series Books, and Paperbacks* (New York, 1996).

The history of sports and camping is vast, though it still focuses on the nineteenth century. Good titles to start with include Eric Dunning and Kenneth Sheard, *Barbarians, Gentlemen, and Players* (Wellington, NZ, 1979); Eric Dunning, ed., *Fighting Fans: Football Hooliganism as a World Phenomenon* (Dublin, 2002); Eleanor Eells, *History of Organized Camping: The First 100 Years* (Martinsville, IN, 1986); Allan Guttmann, *Sports Spectators* (New York, 1986); John Hargreaves,

Sport, Power, and Culture (Cambridge, UK, 1986); J.A. Mangan, *Athleticism in the Victorian and Edwardian Public School* (Cambridge, UK, 1981); Donald Mrozek, *Sport and the American Mentality, 1880–1910* (Knoxville, KT, 1983); Steven Riess, *Touching Base: Professional Baseball and American Culture in the Progressive Era* (Westport, CT, 1979); and Steven Tischler, *Footballers and Businessmen: The Origins of Professional Soccer in England* (New York, 1981).

The broader topic of the commercialization of leisure can be explored through Peter Bailey, *Popular Culture and Performance in the Victorian City* (Cambridge, UK, 1998); Lewis Erenberg, *Steppin' Out: New York Nightlife and the Transformation of American Culture, 1890–1930* (Westport, CT, 1981); John Findlay, *People of Chance: Gambling in American Society from Jamestown to Las Vegas* (New York, 1986); Thomas Frank, *Conquest of Cool* (Chicago, 1997); John Kasson, *Amusing the Million* (New York, 1978); Gary Kyriazi, *The Great American Amusement Parks* (Secaucus, NJ, 1976); Jackson Leurs and Richard Fox, eds. *The Culture of Consumption* (New York: 1983); Karal Ann Marling, ed., *Designing Disney's Theme Parks* (New York, 1997); David Nasaw, *Going Out: The Rise and Fall of Public Amusements* (New York, 1993); Kathy Peiss, *Cheap Amusements: Working Women and Leisure in Turn-of-the-Century New York* (Philadelphia, 1986). Note also Joan Rubin, *The Making of Middle/Brow Culture* (Chapel Hill, NC, 1992) and Lawrence Levine, *Highbrow/Lowbrow: The Emergence of a Cultural Hierarchy in America* (Cambridge, MA, 1988) for the reaction to commercialization.

The impact of transportation and suburbanization on leisure in the twentieth century is considered in Warren Belasco, *Americans on the Road: From Autocamp to Motel, 1910–1945* (Cambridge, MA, 1979); Barbara Kelly, *Expanding the American Dream* (Albany, NY, 1993); David Lewis and Laurence Goldstein, eds., *The Automobile and American Culture* (Ann Arbor, 1983); George Lundberg and Mirra Komarovsky, *Leisure, A Suburban Study* (New York, 1934); Robert Lynd and Helen Lynd, *Middletown* (New York, 1929); David Riesman et al., *The Lonely Crowd* (New Haven, CT, 1950); Carl Solberg, *Conquest of the Skies: The History of Commercial Aviation in America* (Boston, 1979); Roger White, *Home on the Road: The Motor Home in America* (Washington, DC, 2000).

The broad impact of electronic media on leisure is explored in Tino Balio, ed., *Grand Design: Hollywood as a Modern Business Enterprise, 1930–1930* (New York, 1993); Susan Douglass, *Listening In: Radio and the American Imagination* (New York, 1999); David Martin, *Off the Record: The Technology and Culture of Sound Recording in America* (New Brunswick, NJ, 2000); Paddy Scannell and David Cardiff, *A Social History of British Broadcasting* (Oxford, UK, 1991); Robert Sklar, *Movie-Made America: A Cultural History of American Movies* (New York, 1976); Susan Smulyan, *Selling Radio: The Commercialization of American Broadcasting, 1920–1934* (Washington, DC, 1994); Lynn Spigel, *Make Room for TV: Television and the Family Ideal in Postwar America* (Chicago, 1992); and Joseph Turow, *Breaking Up America: Advertisers and the New Media World* (Chicago, 1998).

The importance of youth and child leisure is especially evident in twentieth-century studies including Dom Cavallo, *Muscles and Morals: Organized Playgrounds and Urban Reform, 1880–1920* (Philadelphia, 1981); Gary Cross, *The Cute and the Cool: Wondrous Innocence and Modern American Childhood* (New York, 2004); Dawn Currie, *Girl Talk: Adolescent Magazines and Their Readers* (Toronto, 1999); Paula Fass, *The Damned and the Beautiful, American Youth in the 1920s* (New

York, 1977); Simon Frith, *Sociology of Rock* (London, 1978); James Gilbert, *Cycles of Outrage: America's Reaction to the Juvenile Delinquent in the 1950s* (New York, 1986); Steven Kline, *Out of the Garden: Toys, TV, and Children's Culture in the Age of Marketing* (New York, 1993); David Macleod, *Building Character in the American Boy: The Boy Scouts, YMCA, and Their Forerunners, 1870–1920* (Madison, WI, 1983); Grace Palladino, *Teenagers: An American History* (New York, 1986); Michael Rosenthal, *The Character Factory: Baden-Powell and the Origins of the Boy Scout Movement* (New York, 1984); and Bradford Wright, *Comic Book Nation* (Baltimore, 2001).

Lifestyle leisure as a recent phenomenon is treated in Jeff Bishop and Paul Hoggett, *Organising around Enthusiasms: Mutual Aid in Leisure* (London, 1986); Steven Gelber, *Hobbies: Leisure and the Culture of Work in America* (New York, 1999); and Richard Hoggart, *The Uses of Literacy: Changing Patterns of English Popular Culture* (Boston, 1961).

Bibliography

Each of the chapters in this book has an extensive list of suggested readings. This final bibliography is intended to further an acquaintance with the history of the daily life field as a whole. It consists of suggestions, many drawn from the chapter lists, that have unusual scope, but also of books that are particularly successful in illustrating aspects of daily life in more specific contexts—books that constitute a set of model case studies.

For the field overall: Alf Luedtke, ed., *The History of Everyday Life: Reconstructing Historical Experiences and Ways of Life,* trans. W. Templer (Princeton, NJ, 1995). For an earlier American effort, James Gardner and Rollie Adams, eds., *Ordinary People and Everyday Life; Perspectives on the New Social History* (Nashville, TN, 1983). Two books, among many, do an unusually good job of discussing daily life aspects in notorious situations in recent world history: Sheila Fitzpatrick, *Everyday Stalinism: Ordinary Life in Extraordinary Times: Soviet Russia in the 1930s* (New York, 1998) and William Allen, *The Nazi Seizure of Power: The Experience of a Single German Town* (New York, 1984). For explicit efforts to link daily life history to understanding daily life today, see Peter N. Stearns, ed., *American Behavioral History* (New York, 2005).

On the history of the family and personal life, and related topics: Steven Mintz, *Huck's Raft: A History of American Childhood* (Cambridge, MA, 2004); Beth L. Bailey, *Sex in the Heartland* (Cambridge, MA, 1999); John D'Emilio and Estelle Freedman, *Intimate Matters: A History of Sexuality in America* (New York, 1988). On emotions and the senses, Peter N. Stearns, *American Cool: Constructing a Twentieth-Century Emotional Style* (New York, 1994); C. Dallet Hemphill, *Bowing to Necessities; A History of Manners in America 1620–1860* (New York, 2001); Alain Corbin, *Time, Desire and Horror: Towards a History of the Senses,* trans. Jean Birrell (Cambridge, MA, 1995); Richard Rath, *How Early America Sounded* (Ithaca, NY, 2003).

On health and the body: Thomas Laqueur, *Making Sex: Body and Gender from the Greeks to Freud* (Cambridge, MA, 1992); Peter N. Stearns, *Fat History: Bodies and Beauty in the Modern West* (New York, 1997); Barbara Bates, *Bargaining for Life: A Social History of Tuberculosis* (Philadelphia, 1992); Joan Jacobs Brumberg, *Fasting Girls: The Emergence of Anorexia Nervosa as a Modern Disease* (Cambridge, MA, 1988); Judith Walzer Leavitt, *Brought to Bed: Childbearing in America, 1750 to 1950* (New York, 1986).

On popular culture: Carlo Ginzburg, *The Cheese and the Worms: The Cosmos of a Sixteenth-Century Miller,* trans. Anne and John Tedeschi (Baltimore, 1980); Edward Muir, *Ritual in Early Modern Europe* (Cambridge, UK, 1997); Rhys Isaac, *The Transformation of Virginia, 1740–1790* (Chapel Hill and London, 1982).

On material culture, Ann Martin and J.R. Garrison, eds., *American Material Culture: The Shape of the Field* (Knoxville, 1997); John Brewer and Roy Porter, eds., *Consumption and the World of Goods* (New York, 1993). See also Susan Matt, *Keeping Up with the Joneses: Envy in American Consumer Society* (Philadelphia, 2003). On politics and everyday life, Lizabeth Cohen, *Making a New Deal: Industrial Workers in Chicago 1919–1939* (New York, 1990).

On work and leisure, Lenard Berlanstein, *The Working People of Paris, 1871–1914* (Baltimore, 1984); Patrick Joyce, *Work, Society and Politics: The Culture of the Factory in Later Victorian England* (New Brunswick, NJ, 1980); Joe Trotter, *Black Milwaukee: The Making of an Urban Proletariat* (Urbana, IL, 1988); Ruth Cowen, *More Work for Mother* (New York, 1983); Gary Cross, *A Social History of Leisure since 1600* (State College, PA, 1990); Allan Guttmann, *Sports Spectators* (New York, 1986); Stephan Nissenbaum, *The Battle for Christmas* (New York, 1996); Roy Rosenzweig, *Eight Hours for What We Will: Workers and Leisure in an Industrial City* (New York, 1983).

Index

About the Contributors

GARY CROSS, Distinguished Professor of Modern History at Pennsylvania State University, is author or editor of 11 books of retrospection on contemporary American and European society, popular culture, work, and leisure. His recent books include *The Playful Crowd: Pleasure Places across the Twentieth Century* (with John Walton), *The Cute and the Cool: Wondrous Innocence and Modern American Children's Culture*, and *An All-Consuming Century: Why Commercialism Won in Modern America*.

MARILYNN S. JOHNSON is Professor of History at Boston College. She is the author of *Street Justice: A History of Police Violence in New York City* (2003) and *The Second Gold Rush: Oakland and the East Bay in World War II* (1993) and is currently editing a collection on violence in the American West.

STEVEN MINTZ is the John and Rebecca Moores Professor of History at the University of Houston, where he directs the American Cultures Program. His books include *Domestic Revolutions: A Social History of American Family Life*, *Huck's Raft: A History of American Childhood*, and *A Prison of Expectations: The Family in Victorian Culture*.

LYNN WOOD MOLLENAUER, Assistant Professor of History at the University of North Carolina–Wilmington, is the author of *The Politics of Poison: Courtiers and Criminals in the Affair of the Poisons*, forthcoming from Penn State Press. She is currently editing a translated collection of French criminal trials for use in the college classroom.

JULIE RICHTER, an independent scholar, is a consultant to the Colonial Williamsburg Foundation and the National Institute of American History and Democracy at the College of William and Mary, and a lecturer in the History Department at William and Mary. Richter is the author of several articles in the *Colonial Williamsburg Interpreter* about slaves, free blacks, and the slave community in eighteenth-century Williamsburg and the editor of the *Enslaving Virginia Resource Book* (1998), a resource manual used by Colonial Williamsburg interpreters.

PETER N. STEARNS is Provost and Professor at George Mason University. He has written widely on behavioral history, particularly in areas such as emotion, old age, and dieting/obesity. He is editor of the *Journal of Social History* and past Vice President (teaching division) of the American Historical Association.

JACQUELINE S. WILKIE is Professor of History at Luther College, where she teaches in both history and women's studies programs. She is the author of *The History of Health and Medicine* (1982), a textbook for high school students, and eight articles on the history of health, medicine, and nursing in the United States. She is currently writing a book on how American standards of personal cleanliness carried ideas about racial superiority and social order.